NODDY

THE AUTHORISED BIOGRAPHY OF MICHAEL LYNAGH

To Caroline, Hannah and Tom and the memory of
grandfathers missed, Rex and Cec.

NODDY

THE AUTHORISED BIOGRAPHY OF MICHAEL LYNAGH

ANDREW SLACK

William Heinemann Australia

Published 1995 by William Heinemann Australia
a part of Reed Books Australia
22 Salmon Street, Port Melbourne, Victoria 3207
a division of Reed International Books Australia Pty Limited

Edited by Janet Bunny
Typeset in Janson Text by J&M Typesetting Services
Printed and bound in Australia by Griffin Paperbacks

National Library of Australia
cataloguing-in-publication data:

Slack, Andrew.
    Noddy: the authorised biography of Michael Lynagh.

    Includes index.
    ISBN 0 85561 571 0.

    1. Lynagh, Michael, 1955– . 2. Rugby Union football
    players – Australia – Biography. I. Title.

796.333092

CONTENTS

ACKNOWLEDGEMENTS

My deepest gratitude goes to the many who turned this idea into reality. I thank my family for their patience and my friends who coped with my incessant whingeing about the difficulties of the project. I also thank all those who gave their time and whose thoughts and quotes are the essence of this story. In particular, Marie and Ian Lynagh and Jane Connor for the insights only a family can provide, and the Baudino family who helped when my total lack of computer skills came to the fore.

Editor Jan Bunny has probably never had to deal with such a novice and I appreciate her support and skill in helping sort out the mess I periodically sent to her.

Finally, I thank the subject himself, who put his trust in me and was always open and honest.

The author wishes to acknowledge the use of material from the following persons and organisations:

David Campese with Peter Bills, *On a Wing and a Prayer*, Macdonald Queen Anne Press/Maxwell Macmillan Publishing, London 1991.

Bill Beaumont, *Thanks to Rugby*, Stanley Paul & Co., London 1982.

Mark Ella and Terry Smith, *Path to Victory*, ABC Enterprises, Sydney 1987.

The Australian: excerpts of articles by Greg Campbell 6.9.86, Bob Dwyer 17.5.88, Michael Lynagh 22.7.91, P. Jenkins 30.7.94.

Courier-Mail (Brisbane): excerpts of articles by Frank O'Callaghan 11.4.82, Bob Dwyer 11.7.88, Michael Lynagh 3.6.89 and 12.8.89, Wayne Smith 17.6.89, Bill Campbell 4.7.89.

Sunday Mail (Brisbane): excerpts of articles by Wayne Smith 9.7.89, Alan Langer 24.6.90, Bob Dwyer 3.7.88.

Gold Coast Bulletin: July 1971.

Telegraph (Brisbane): excerpts of articles by John Morton 12.1.82, Wayne Smith 8.3.82.

Daily Sun (Brisbane): excerpts of articles by Jim Tucker March 1984 and 6.5.91, David Codey 14.7.88.

New Zealand Herald: excerpt of article by D.J. Cameron 30.4.84.

Sunday Times (UK): excerpt of article by Stephen Jones 4.11.84.

Scotsman (UK): excerpt of article by Norman Mair 9.12.84.

Sydney Morning Herald: excerpts of articles by Mark Ella 15.6.85, Alan Jones 6.3.88, Greg Growden 3.5.94.

Sunday Sun (Brisbane): excerpt of article by Mark Oberhardt 18.9.88.

Every effort was made to trace copyright ownership and obtain permission where necessary. In some cases this proved impossible. The author apologises for any such omissions.

PREFACE

I first met Michael Lynagh in the late 1970s at Ballymore, after I'd played a match for Queensland. As word travels pretty swiftly within Brisbane sporting circles, I'd already heard about his prowess in rugby and cricket on school playing fields by the time his father Ian introduced us. There was no hint however, of a brash, over-confident youngster. Sporting stardom in the revered Greater Public Schools competition had not bred arrogance. He was respectful, well mannered and quiet. As I spoke with this courteous teenager the thought didn't cross my mind that within a couple of years we would be Queensland and Australian team-mates.

The next time I saw him was when we played against each other during his first-grade rugby debut at the beginning of 1982. I have a vivid memory of the sidestep he used to elude my tackle. He made me, a veteran of seven seasons in the Queensland team, look an absolute novice. In wet conditions he produced a kicking display that left no doubt that he was a cut above the rest.

I enjoyed the privilege of playing in teams with Michael for six years, during which we were together on four Wallaby tours and part of Australia's squad for the inaugural Rugby World Cup in 1987.

Throughout that time and over the ensuing years in which I have followed his career from the sidelines, he has never dropped his standards. Occasionally his form has wavered, but not once through lack of endeavour in his preparation or approach to the game. This approach, added to the God-given talents nurtured by himself and his mentors, has resulted in the supreme displays of skill that have thrilled the world's rugby arenas in the 1980s and 1990s.

All rugby followers will have watched and made their own judgements on Lynagh the player, but the majority can only guess at the person he is away from the public gaze. His natural shyness hasn't made him easy to get to know. Even his team-mates have found him reticent and I had always felt he was quite happy to keep it that way. I was therefore somewhat surprised when he mentioned to me late in May 1994 that he was contemplating a biography of his life. He asked me whether I would put the words down on paper. As I had never done anything like this before, and knew Michael's tendency to say too little rather than too much, it was with some trepidation that I finally agreed to have a go.

The sight of Slack and Lynagh coming to blows would amuse many of our mutual team-mates and I am delighted that during the project, this prospect never surfaced. But that is not to say it was all plain sailing. There was more than one difference of opinion both on matters of memory and of interpretation, but through it all Michael was extremely helpful. It was not always easy for him to address matters that normally he would consider inappropriate for public discussion. Nevertheless, he was prepared to delve into aspects of his life that I felt would help to paint a clearer picture of what makes Noddy tick.

I have not set out to shove my own opinions of Michael Lynagh down readers' throats. There are many experiences he has had during his career that are now shared, and perhaps these will give a fuller insight into his personality. His own thoughts and those of his friends and influences are the substance of the book and I trust that by the final page, readers will have their own appreciation not only of Lynagh the footballer, but also Lynagh the man.

Andrew Slack

1
RARE OULD TIMES

My mind's so full of memories, too old to hear new chimes,
I'm part of what was Dublin in the rare ould times.

Call in at any Dublin rugby club late in the evening, after plentiful jars of Guinness and Smithwick's beer have been consumed by the patrons, and you're likely to hear this song. Sometimes it's tuneful, sometimes not, but you can bet Waterford crystal to a plastic cup that the strains of Pete St John's 'The Rare Ould Times' will float through the club-house rooms before closing time.

Michael Patrick Thomas Lynagh, descendant of the County Donegal Lynaghs, has himself enjoyed some rare old times in Dublin's fair city. None sweeter though than at Lansdowne Road, the spiritual home of Irish rugby, at approximately 3.55 in the afternoon of 20 October 1991, as he plunged through a desperate but ineffective tackle by Irish winger Jack Clarke and scored the most crucial try in the history of Australian rugby – a four-point *coup de grace* that crushed Irish hopes and turned Nick Farr-Jones' Wallabies from also-rans to world champions.

It was the culmination of a strategy which, under the most intense pressure, had formulated in Lynagh's mind just minutes earlier – his composure and his skills jelling perfectly to thwart an Irish ambush.

The Australian World Cup squad had arrived in Dublin the previous Monday, victorious if not entirely convincing in their three preliminary pool matches. Wins over Argentina, Western Samoa and Wales were expected, but the physically taxing demands of three international matches in just eight days had left the Wallabies somewhat wearier than they cared to admit; that those three games had been scheduled in rugby-crazy Wales did little to boost the energy levels.

In Llanelli and Pontypool particularly and, to a degree, in Cardiff, conversation tends to centre around one of three topics. It's about rugby, rugby or, can we beat England in the next rugby international? In Australia, where the game is at best the number two football code in Queensland, New South Wales and the Australian Capital Territory, and little more than a fledgling in the other states, the players aren't used to such obsessive devotion from the person in the street. As a consequence, Wallaby teams touring in Wales have sometimes struggled to cope with the intensity which surrounds the game there. Away from the training paddock and the playing pitch, most Wallaby players on tour are happy to talk about things other than the next ruck or maul they're likely to enter; Michael Lynagh, for one, is far more comfortable dissecting his putting stroke than discussing whether or not his goalkicking technique was perfect in the last game. In Wales, however, at times there seems to be no sanctuary. The pubs, the shops, yes and even the churches, are all likely locations for a quick chat about the next day's game.

It was no surprise then, that the 1991 Wallabies were delighted to be heading for Ireland where, the locals suggest, even when things get desperate, they're never really very serious. The majority of the team had been to Dublin before and knew that while they were there on the business of rugby, the training and games could be balanced by alternative means of amusement. The pubs, the golf courses and the general demeanour of the people would help make the players feel as relaxed as is possible 20 000 kilometres from home and facing the most important fortnight in their sporting lives.

One advantage in being a member of a national touring sporting team is that the patience-testing routine ordinary civilians have to undergo at airports is often short-circuited. Thanks to this, the team was quickly through the baggage area and out into a mild Dublin day, where a luxury coach was waiting to take the troops to their lodgings, the Westbury Hotel in the city centre. It was midday and there was no immediate hurry to get to base, but it was nevertheless rather thoughtful of the Irish Rugby Union to have a police motorcycle escort on hand, just in case a traffic jam blocked progress. But the combination of carrying the Australian rugby team and having a police escort to boot was obviously the equivalent of a red rag to a bull for the driver. Those who were new to Ireland wondered whether they would indeed live long enough to actually play in Sunday's scheduled quarter-final. Prop Tony Daly estimates the bus travelled between eighty and one hundred kilometres an hour on streets not much wider than the vehicle itself. At one stage of this madcap journey, an ambulance was forced to pull over. Nick Farr-Jones, captain of the team since 1988 and one not given to exuberance for the sake of it, was astounded.

'It was as if we had to be at the hotel for lunch and, if we missed lunch, that would be the end of our campaign,' he said. 'The hotel was near the Grafton Street mall and this crazy driver drove straight through it … just up onto the mall and away.'

Usually on tours the team congregates near the back of the bus, but unwilling to miss the driving tactics instigated by Ireland's answer to Nigel Mansell, many of the members moved to the front to peruse the havoc outside. Showing the balance that has made him one of the great centre three-quarters in the game, Tim Horan defied the unpredictable motion of the missile in which he was travelling to capture the adventure on film. His video camera immortalised the journey. Even the heart rate of the ever-composed Lynagh increased a beat or two. 'If this was intended to get us to lunch on time, I was only too keen to volunteer that I, for one, wasn't as hungry as all that.'

It was nothing more than a simple case of Irish bus-driver logic. 'Sure, t'was the quickest way to get there!' Having made it safely – just – the only way to mark their arrival was to follow the old adage: when in Dublin, do as the Dubliners do. That night after dinner Farr-Jones and Lynagh, veterans of the Grand Slam campaign seven years earlier, grabbed a couple of the tyros and took them to one of the many local hostelries for a pint. Guinness is now available world-wide, but even if you can't stand the stuff, it is almost compulsory to have a glass if you happen to find yourself in an Irish pub. If you like the taste you may well think you're dead and in heaven. If you're not so keen, the atmosphere alone generally makes the effort of downing a whole pint worthwhile. Lynagh is a moderate drinker, but whether or not it's his Irish blood, you are far more likely to find him in a Dublin bar chewing the fat than in a similar establishment when he's in his home town of Brisbane.

Although not the captain, Lynagh, with fifty Test caps to his name and the leading points-scorer in international rugby, was a much-valued lieutenant to Farr-Jones. He commanded enormous respect within the team and understood his role as one of the senior members of the side. He recognised the need to help his team-mates understand there was a time to relax and a time to focus. Early in this week it was crucial the players found time to enjoy themselves – nothing that would interfere with the task at hand – but enough to keep them relaxed and happy. And even if pub life was not really Lynagh's favourite form of entertainment, he was aware there were certain social responsibilities he had to fulfil within the team. These were as important to anticipated success as any move that might be called in the heat of battle the following Sunday at Lansdowne Road. A pint of the good stuff wouldn't hurt!

The Wallabies' main enemy was never going to be the Guinness, but there was every likelihood a tendency to underestimate the quality of Irish rugby might be. It was, after all, a bad habit Australian teams had struggled to shake over a long period. In 1979, Ireland had arrived in

Australia for a two-Test tour against a home side that had beaten the All Blacks 30–16 at their last meeting. Flanker Greg Cornelsen scored a world-record four tries in that Eden Park encounter. Ireland were not expected to provide much opposition – their one wild card was European rugby's player of the year from the just-completed northern season – flyhalf Tony Ward.

Ward was a fine player and a goalkicker of stunning accuracy. The Australian press and the players could barely contain their mirth when the Irish Test team was named for the opening international at Ballymore. There was no place for Ward – the number ten jersey went to Ollie Campbell, an unknown from the Old Belvedere club. Later to become a friend and fan of Lynagh's, Campbell is the gentlest of gentlemen but when it came to winning rugby matches he was the deadliest of assassins. He kicked seven goals in the 27–12 victory at Ballymore and then scored all the points as the men in emerald green took out the series two–nil at the Sydney Cricket Ground. On the Wallaby tours of the United Kingdom and Ireland in 1981 and 1984, the Irish were again perceived to be fair game, but although Australia won both those games, later the players nominated the Dublin Tests as the hardest in the tours.

If the World Cup Wallabies were casual in their approach to the 1991 quarter-final the body language of the fifteen men in gold as they ran onto the field was deceptive. To use footballing parlance they certainly looked pumped, more so perhaps after the playing of 'The Soldier's Song', an anthem of the republic of Ireland. This in itself was an unusual occurrence. Rugby is one of the few sports in which the Ireland team is representative not only of the three southern provinces of Connaught, Leinster and Munster but also of Ulster in the north, so it is very rare for any anthem to be played before an international.

To add insult to surprise, there was to be no 'Advance Australia Fair' for the visitors. Scottish referee Jim Fleming moved to halfway to signal time on but the fifteen Australians ignored him, choosing rather to keep him and the Irish waiting as they linked arms and sang their own unaccompanied version of the national song. Experience of those huddles tells me the singing does not offer strong musical competition to the Vienna Boys choir, but in terms of focussing the emotion and passion on the job at hand, it can be useful.

If there was any residue of complacency, it should have vanished before the ball kicked-off by fullback Marty Roebuck even touched Irish turf. Roebuck's kick was perfectly weighted, but with the ball some metres behind him and no contact made by either side, Irish captain Phillip Matthews struck Australia's loose forward Willie Ofahengaue with his elbow. Known as Willie O. to his team-mates, the quiet, church-going, Tongan-born flanker would be in the final of the gentlemen's stakes with Ollie Campbell, but even a Godfearing man can only take so much. The fists started to flail and before a gold jersey was soiled, Farr-Jones' troops had been reminded the Irish weren't there just to make up the numbers.

The first scoring opportunity of the game was given to Lynagh following an Irish infringement; the fact he had been struggling with his goalkicking rhythm so far in the tournament had not been lost on keen observers. As he missed a shot at goal the Australian Broadcasting Corporation's television commentator Gordon Bray opined that 'the fluent stroke is just not there for Michael Lynagh'. Atonement though, was only a few minutes away. From a lineout some forty-five metres from Ireland's line, experienced lock Rod McCall leapt high to get first touch on the ball. His tap was not perfectly controlled and sweeper Tony Daly, the man designated to claim any such untidy ball, was unable to drag it in. It bounced awkwardly for Farr-Jones and despite the attention of Neil Francis, the biggest of the Irish forwards, the skipper was able to shovel a pass to Lynagh. This set in chain a move called by Lynagh as the lineout was being formed.

It wasn't the swiftest service Farr-Jones ever delivered but even though the ball and flanker Gordon Hamilton arrived simultaneously, Lynagh's beautifully soft hands managed to slip it on to centre Tim Horan. The move had been ignited through the skills of a halfback pairing that was on this day marking its thirty-eighth union at Test level: Farr-Jones and Lynagh – the milk and honey of Australian rugby through its finest hours. Originally code-named 'Stellenbosch' after the famous South African University and through the passage of time abbreviated simply to 'S', the move was, as Lynagh explains, nothing new. 'When we played Ireland in 1984, we called the very same move with Mark Ella at flyhalf and myself at inside centre and it worked very well.' Seven years later, with Lynagh now the playmaker at flyhalf and calling the shots, it was a case of when you're on a good thing stick to it.

'I pass to the inside centre who, along with the outside centre, is moving diagonally across the field. David Campese, or whoever the winger might be, comes back inside the inside centre on what is little more than a basic switch pass. It's a move designed to take the opposition defence across, while we bring the open winger back inside on a different angle, hopefully creating a break over the advantage line. When I'm calling moves I like to try and use David Campese as much as possible, because he is a very potent attacking weapon for us.'

That didn't need to be confirmed for the Irish defenders as they streamed across field only to see the world's leading try-scorer spear through them. A despairing grab from a wrong-footed Simon Geoghegan was the only hand that touched Campese *en route* to the tryline.

Lynagh nonchalantly added the two points to give Australia a 6–0 break, but the scene of the try's manufacture was a dismal one for Australian fans. It was only eleven days since Farr-Jones had injured his knee and been replaced in the pool match against Western Samoa. Once he had declared himself fit for the quarter-final there could be no camouflaging any potential weakness. On the international rugby field there are very few places to hide, for a halfback there is none. As Farr-Jones gathered that awkward lineout ball he placed himself in a vulnerable position – no surprise that the arrival of the 198-centimetre 113-kilogram Francis was too much of a strain on a weakened knee.

Australian physiotherapist Greg Craig, an integral part of the Wallaby set-up since 1985, is regarded by many players as a miracle worker but there was no transformation at Lansdowne on this day. Farr-Jones' contribution was finished, with the game not a quarter over. After the conversion, Lynagh trotted over to his captain. There was no change of expression on the flyhalf's face. He camouflaged his disappointment and showed no hint of panic. Only a look which said, that's rugby, let's get on with it. For Farr-Jones, this enforced departure could have been his worst nightmare, but he knew he was shifting responsibility to a most capable deputy. The steadiest hands would be needed to keep Wallaby hopes alive.

'The great thing about having someone like Noddy beside you,' recalls Farr-Jones, 'is that you don't have to give him instructions. I knew he'd been there longer than I had and he knew exactly what to do. When I played with Michael I'd look after the backrow moves and whatever happened in front of me. Basically I knew that once I got it to Noddy it was over to him. He called the shots ...'

Farr-Jones was gone and reserve halfback Peter Slattery got his chance. At least there were no combination problems. Lynagh and Slattery had played together at club and state level for University and Queensland for the previous six years. While they did their best to exercise damage control after the loss of Farr-Jones, there was little doubt the Irish saw his departure as a bonus. They lifted their game in that twenty minutes leading up to half-time and, allied with their ever-present tenacity and spirit were able not only to keep in touch but went to half-time 6–all, thanks to two Ralph Keyes penalty goals.

Any of the experts, and that seemed to be the majority, who'd predicted Ireland would be little more than nuisance value, were making hasty reassessments at the break. Although law changes in 1994 have allowed coaches to come on to the field at half-time in Test matches, this was not the case in 1991. Coaches overcame the communication problem by sending out any relevant messages with the reserves, but on this occasion it was the Michael Lynagh show. Although Farr-Jones limped out to add his encouragement, Lynagh was now the boss. With responsibility came control and he knew what he wanted.

While the romantics would have you believe Australia's rugby success has been built on a run-it-at-all-costs style, this is not entirely the truth. With exciting backline talent like Jason Little, Tim Horan, David Campese and Lynagh himself, it would have been folly to ignore the attacking options at their disposal. But to create such options, a certain amount of unglamorous spade work had to be done. That included control of possession and then sensible disposal by the halves. Lynagh's ability to kick the ball sixty metres, land it on the proverbial sixpence and roll it into touch was, to some of the 'runaholic' newspaper critics, a simple skill, a soft option even. To his team-mates it can often be manna from heaven.

In the opening moments of the second half, commentator Gary Pearse suggested the ideal tactic for the Australians who were running with the breeze at their backs was to 'get the ball into the corners and attack them from the twenty-twos'. Lynagh's first act in that second half was to unleash one of those renowned punts from inside his own half, the resulting bounce giving Australia a lineout two metres from the Irish tryline. 'That's the play you want,' said Pearse. 'Michael Lynagh will have to win this game for Australia.'

From an ensuing play, referee Fleming awarded the Australians a penalty, which Lynagh duly converted, but like a persistent mosquito, the Irish kept frustrating Wallaby hopes of breaking free.

'We'd score a try or kick a penalty, but they'd still be there,' says Lynagh. 'They'd always manage to keep in touch.'

An Irish attack gave them good field position and although a more adventurous team might have released their three-quarter line, Keyes opted to take the simple three points on offer from a drop goal. Despite being right in front and only twenty metres out, Keyes still needed the favourable rebound off an upright before Fleming raised his arm to signal the goal. It was Keyes' third successful kick of the day and two of them had gone, to borrow the billiard term, in-off. Was this the day when the luck of the Irish would snooker one of the tournament favourites?

The best way to negate luck is to create momentum and a decision by Lynagh soon after Ireland had equalled at 9–all gave the Wallabies another crucial score. Rather than take the soft option of an Australian scrum feed on the Irish twenty-two-metre line after Ireland had been caught off-side, Lynagh opted to forgo the territory and use the opportunity to get his forwards doing what they are named to do – go forward. Twenty metres inside his own half, he hoisted a 'Garryowen'. This is a kick named after a club in Ireland; it has the intended purpose of soaring so high that the unfortunate soul unlucky enough to be underneath it some forty metres or so downfield will have half a dozen or more of the enemy thundering towards him at breakneck speed, timing their runs to coincide with the arrival of the ball. Should the kick be perfect and the chase enthusiastic, it gives the receiver, more often than not a fullback, a rather ugly choice. Either he shuts his eyes and rattles off a quick decade of the rosary or he lets everyone discover the coward he is by screaming out the most embarrassing call in the game, '*Yours!*' If he is representing his country and there's a crowd of 50 000 watching, valour usually wins out over common sense.

Lynagh's kick on this occasion was a fraction too far and it was courageously and skilfully taken by Ireland's number fifteen, Jim Staples ... but the Australian cavalry wasn't very long in arriving. Slattery was awarded the ever-crucial put-in to the scrum, and the momentum Lynagh had aimed to create had materialised.

It was time for the sting and the Australian three-quarters had no trouble playing their part. At rugby's top level, a cut pass, where one man misses the player beside him and throws to the next in line, is a very simple manoeuvre and not one that in the modern game opposition defensive lines have major trouble combatting. Nonetheless, the Irish backline pattern this day was curious to the point of non-existence. Sometimes prone to exaggeration, hooker Phil Kearns has suggested the Australian backline tried the move '28 000 times that afternoon, but I guess you couldn't blame them because they kept finding the holes!' Lynagh argues Kearns' mathematics were typically astray but is quite adamant the backs had gone through the move at training at least that number of times.

'We'd studied the video and knew they would be vulnerable to it. At Monkstown training ground we had been through it *ad nauseum*.' Nothing nauseating about it now. Roebuck found the hole, thanks to an ideally placed Horan pass. Jason Little, the man who had been 'cut' by Horan, floated around outside Roebuck in support, took his pass and, with the Irish totally nonplussed, delivered to Campese. He needed no second invitation. With the rhythm very much in his general play, it also returned to his goalkicking and Lynagh then added the conversion to provide another six-point break.

Bzzz, bzzz, bzzz – they wouldn't go away. Yet another Keyes penalty and the Irish were back within three points. While their backline was having its troubles in defence, their attack, when unleashed, was impressive. From a scrum twelve metres inside their own half, they moved the ball wide – not always a regular practice in Irish teams. Staples entered the line from fullback and, just prior to being tackled by Little, dropped the ball on to his foot. It skewed tantalisingly behind a retreating Campese and in front of an advancing Clarke. Like a couple of two-year-old colts chasing Golden Slipper glory in the straight at Rosehill, Clarke and Campese engaged in a bumping duel: nothing illegal but enough to make it impossible for Campese to fall on and secure the loose ball. As one of the game's superstars, and known for his strong opinions, Campese is an obvious target for the press corps after games. He is not always reluctant to apportion blame, be it on others or occasionally on himself. His post-match statement this day, taking the blame for the Irish try was, like several other of his after-game summaries, not totally accurate.

With Campese out of the equation, Clarke showed fine skill and composure to pick up the ball in front of Roebuck and, in the tackle of the Australian fullback, slip a pass away to the supporting flanker Gordon Hamilton. There were forty metres to travel and he did it as though runaway tries against the Wallabies were an everyday event. Covering winger Rob Egerton arrived, but too late. Hamilton had scored, the Irish were in front and the crowd, a good number of whom decided to share the moment with Hamilton by flooding onto the ground, was ecstatic. To add to the theatre of the occasion, Keyes converted from three metres in from the touchline: 18–15 in Ireland's favour.

Not all the crowd was in raptures. Just a dozen or so rows back in the grandstand, at the very end of the ground where the try was scored, were a number of Australian supporters. Among them were former Queensland agent-general in London, Tom McVeigh, and Ian and Marie Lynagh, parents of Michael. Ian remembers.

'Tom McVeigh was behind us and there were a few other parents around and there was this absolute stunned numbness ... The only communication was non-verbal, but after they kicked the goal I can recall asking someone the question ... it might have been Tom ... I said, "How long to go?" and I think he told me about three or four minutes.'

On the field Australian hooker Phil Kearns' reaction was more basic. 'Oh shit,' he thought, undoubtedly not alone in such immediate reflection. His devastated team-mates assembled behind the tryline.

'It's actually one of the few times I remember quite clearly what was said on the field. Normally I don't remember half-time speeches or anything like that, but I guess I remembered this – and I reckon it's pretty accurate – because it was so significant in the end. When Hamilton scored and all the boys were back behind the tryline Noddy just said, "Breathe in guys. Now, forwards, we'll put the ball down there and get good field position. Get the ball and the backs will do the rest." That was sort of it.'

Kearns' recollection *was* pretty accurate according to Lynagh, but the man himself can fill in the gaps. 'When Hamilton scored, I walked across to the referee to find out how long to go. I could formulate a plan from that because the time was a constant. I wanted to give the guys something that was certain, so I walked across and the referee said, "four minutes".

'I didn't want to use any negative words – I didn't say, "Don't panic". I tried to use positive words … so I'd be giving people tasks to do to take their mind off the situation. Before actually describing the plan – the part that Kearnsy recalls – I did tell the guys how long we had, and that there was plenty of time for what we wanted to do, and if they were in doubt, just to go towards the opposition tryline and hold onto the ball.'

Positive, precise and clear – if only his words could have been relayed to the millions of supporters in Australia up in the early hours of the Monday morning watching the game, so they could have shared his composure! Famous French captain Jean-Pierre Rives once suggested that the whole point of rugby is that it is, first and foremost, a state of mind, a spirit. Lynagh had cleansed the minds and the spirit was with them.

As planned, the kick-off was long and Egerton had listened well. At the opposite end of the field to that where he had failed to nab Hamilton, the unglamorous but effective fullback-cum-winger from Sydney University summoned the energy to hare after the kick and apply pressure to the Irish catcher Brian Robinson. With an eye on

Egerton and perhaps an eye on a semi-final berth, Robinson rushed his kick to touch, leaving Australia with a lineout throw just fifteen metres from the goldmine which was doubling as Ireland's tryline.

There is no finer prospector to have in a lineout than John Eales. If a 200-centimetre giant can be described as nimble, then this description fits him. Astonishingly skilful for a big man, he was able to play his part. The Kearns lob was accurate and up flew Eales, seemingly suspended for an age, as he caressed the ball into the hands of Slattery. From there it flew to Lynagh to Horan to Campese, coming back at the covering forwards.

It has been said that forward play is like a funeral – you have to get in front with the family, not behind with the friends. Campese doesn't always enjoy the front pew but on this occasion he seemed to relish the physicality of the clash. No space for jinks and glides and goose-steps, just hold on to that fruit. What had Noddy said? Yeah, go towards their tryline and hold on to that ball, hold it, hold it, hold it.

Good on you, Campo. You were listening and so they all must have been. With the aid of Simon Poidevin first and then the rest of the pack, possession was secured and the platform Lynagh had asked for was constructed: that platform was a scrum eight metres out from the Irish line, to the left of the posts and with Slattery to feed.

On reflection, the Australians will always be grateful to the game's law makers that the changes introduced in 1992 were not in force that afternoon. Eales' leap would have been penalised as he tapped the ball with his outside arm – this is not allowed now – and Campese's retention of the ball would have counted for nothing as the Irish would have been awarded the scrum feed under the 'use it or lose it' rule. But 1991 it was, and the Irish backs were struggling to cope with 'cut two loop', the move that had been used 28 000 times before.

Time for an encore.

Lynagh knew what was needed – others wondered. Tim Horan, that most gifted attacker, suggested a field goal, but the man in charge had no doubts. The execution was sweet. From Slattery to Lynagh, then the miss pass went to a straight-running Roebuck. Despite being hindered by opposite number Brendan Mullin before he had the ball, Little held the pass from Roebuck and delivered to Campese. The Irish defence was again breached, but the cover swarmed. Campese was felled and as the ball hit the turf it bounced backwards. In classic flyhalf fashion Lynagh had chased the ball across field in support, and there he was, to snatch a half-volley with the ease of the wicket-keeper he once was.

He half-hurdled his fallen team-mate and dived for the line.

At the far end of the ground, where Ian and Marie Lynagh were seated, agony had been transformed into ecstasy. Ian's memory is clear. 'I'd seen Michael come around in support but the people had jumped up and there was no full view. I saw him go for the line, and between the gap in the crowd I saw the referee's arm go up to signal the try. At the same time Tom McVeigh behind me saw it and he just grabbed and hugged us. It seemed to go on forever – it really was extraordinarily emotional and I didn't hear any of the silence everyone else spoke of later. All I could hear was this extraordinarily loud noise and cheering. It was one of the longest embraces I'm sure I've ever had and there was a fair bit of passion.'

On the pitch, the Lynaghs' only son focussed his attention on a single blade of grass. 'I recall feeling a huge wave of relief come over me as I crossed the tryline. I noticed that blade of grass and thought what a beautiful sight it was.'

He did not, though, afford himself the luxury of a smile. After being hauled to his feet by jubilant team-mates Horan, Slattery and Little, his look seemed to say, 'Don't be so surprised. That's what was supposed to happen.'

In the dying moments Little dropped an intercept pass which, if it had gone as intended, would have resulted in two things – a certain try and a final score that would not properly have reflected the closeness of the contest. The game and the occasion deserved statistical support: 19–18, here it stands.

Daylight fades early in the Dublin winter. As the players sought the warmth of the dressing rooms, darkness loomed and there was the hint of rain, moisture too on the Australian bench, according to Farr-Jones.

'Spontaneously four or five of the management and reserves broke down, just broke into tears. What amazed me was that when he came off the field Noddy didn't show the emotion we felt. He couldn't seem to work out why we had tears in our eyes and why we were so affected by it.'

Michael Lynagh was still so emotionless, so intense and so in control, on the field at least.

> Ring a ring rosey, as the light declines
> I remember Dublin City in the rare ould times.

2
BROTHER BUCKLEY'S BAND

From Brisbane's Ballymore, the headquarters of rugby in Queensland, it is just a short stroll up the tree-lined streets of suburban Herston to the grounds of the Queensland University of Technology's Kelvin Grove campus. Formerly the Kelvin Grove Teachers' College, this is the Alma Mater of many of those charged with the education of Queensland children.

Marie Johnstone and Ian Lynagh were two of the intake at Kelvin Grove in 1959, and by the time they took up their first teaching posts in the height of summer 1960, they both understood their diplomas weren't the only official documents that would result from that year of study together. It was inevitable the relationship they'd forged at Kelvin Grove in the early part of 1959 would eventually lead to a marriage certificate, which it did on 9 January 1963. Just over nine months later, on 25 October, Michael Patrick Thomas Lynagh was born at Brisbane's Mater hospital; his sister Jane followed him into the world in April 1965.

Marie Lynagh originally hailed from Ipswich, an industrial and coalmining centre near Brisbane. In the last century, it had been earmarked as Queensland's capital. It was also the birthplace of some of the best footballers in the state, and indeed in the country. Mark Loane and Paul McLean, the two giants of Queensland rugby throughout the

1970s and early 1980s, were both Ipswich boys and it was here that Michael Lynagh also began his education.

In the 1930s Marie's mother, Cloris Haenke, became one of the first women to graduate from the pharmacy board of Queensland; she then married Robert Craig Johnstone, a native of Kilburnie, Scotland, who was ten when his family immigrated to Australia in 1910.

Johnstone's interests were as wide and varied as his talents. Even in his sixties he was a much sought-after performer in Gilbert and Sullivan light opera. He loved stage and drama and his son-in-law Ian claims him as 'one of the great joke-tellers'. This apparent love of an audience is not something that seems to have been passed on to his grandson, but those close to Michael Lynagh claim that when he is in comfortable surroundings and with good friends, there is certainly a bit of ham in him. Isabella Franchin for example, Michael's Italian fiancée, says, 'Michael is a great joke-teller.' But even if Lynagh has chosen to hide some of the artistic talents that may have seeped through the generations, there is no question he has demonstrated that his grandfather's renowned skills as a rugby player at the Ipswich Grammar School around the time of World War One have been passed on.

While Marie was a talented runner and swimmer at Ipswich Girls Grammar, any chance of her developing an overwhelming desire to play sport was perhaps quashed by the obsession shared by the rest of her family – mother, father and sister Beth – for the game of golf, a love, if not quite an obsession, her husband and son now share.

'Every Saturday and Sunday I used to go to the golf club while the three of them played. I just putted around on the green to pass the time, and wait for them to finish their rounds. The dinner conversation was usually just a lot of golf talk and while I listened and occasionally contributed, it just didn't interest me.'

Nor apparently, did cricket. Ian is a cricket lover and in the early days of their relationship at Kelvin Grove Teachers' College, he was playing lower grades for the Toombul Cricket Club in Brisbane – a club which, over the years, has had such famous cricketing names as Ken 'Slasher' Mackay, Wally Grout and Jeff Thomson grace its teams. Marie would often travel by train from Ipswich to be with Ian, and as Ian was at cricket, that was where she wanted to be. While he played she would find some shade from the often scorching summer sun and … knit. 'It used to be somewhat frustrating – Marie would knit, and she'd miss all my innings!'

Other members of her family however, were more concerned than Marie with her future husband's conquests on the field. One of the more harrowing experiences for a young man in the early 1960s must have been the visit to a prospective father-in-law asking for a daughter's hand in marriage. Ian recalls such a trip to the Johnstone house in Ipswich.

'When I went out to ask Mr Johnstone if Marie and I could get engaged it was a Sunday. I'd played cricket on the Saturday and he said to me in the Scottish accent that has never left him, "How many runs did you make yesterday?" Fifteen, I said. "If you're going to marry my daughter you'll have to improve on that!"'

Ian Lynagh's grandfather, Patrick Joseph Lynagh, was one of a dozen sons, and had emigrated from Milford, in county Donegal, Ireland; the Lynagh clan eventually ran a dairy farm in Bell at the foot of the scenic Bunya mountains on the Darling Downs, west of Brisbane. Tom Lynagh, Ian's father, joined the radio branch of the Post Master General's department, working in Dalby, Cairns and Melbourne before settling in Brisbane in the 1930s. Tom met his wife Jenny during his time in north Queensland. In later years they would be supportive and loving grandparents to Michael and Jane Lynagh; Jenny claims the famous Noddy kicking style was nurtured in her Kalinga backyard. In Brisbane, Ian was sent to St Joseph's College, Gregory Terrace, in a move that would have much to do with the shaping not only of his own life, but also that of his son.

'Terrace' is a Christian Brothers school, situated no more than a brisk five-minute walk from Brisbane's central business district. In such a location, it draws students from all parts of the city and has, in the Brisbane Greater Public Schools sporting contests, an enviable reputation for producing international sportsmen of the highest quality. World champion 500 cc motorcyclist, Michael Doohan, is an old boy, and while it would be stretching the truth to suggest his skills on a Honda were nurtured on the limited space of Terrace's bitumen playground, there is no denying the school's playing fields in the western suburb of Tennyson have figured in the development of some of this country's finest rugby players. Clem Windsor, Tony Shaw, Bruce Cooke, Chris Handy, Brendan Nasser, Michael Cook, Bill Campbell, Damien Frawley and Mark McBain are a few of the names who have graduated from the red and black of Terrace to the green and gold of Australia.

Ian Lynagh's footballing feats never reached those heights – the zenith of his career came the year after graduating from Terrace, when he played under-eighteen rugby league for the Brothers club in Brisbane and was selected in a couple of representative teams. Injury curtailed any hopes of a prolonged span on the football field. His older brothers, Trevor and Mel, had excelled in the more individual sport of cycling. Trevor carved a name for himself as Queensland cycling champion many times over. The sporting prowess of the Lynaghs is also evident in the feats of Mel's son. Gary Lynagh, Michael's first cousin, was world lightweight double sculls champion from 1991 to 1993.

Ian Lynagh had plenty on his plate in 1963. He got married, started a new teaching job at Villanova College, began studying three nights a week for his Bachelor of Education degree at the University of Queensland, fathered a son and took on a couple of part-time jobs. By the time he reached the final year of his degree he decided to speed things up. Full-time teaching and part-time jobs were now fitted in

(top left)
Marie and baby Michael, 1964.
(Lynagh collection)

(above)
The Lynagh family. Marie, Ian, Michael
and Jane, 1967. (Lynagh collection)

(left)
Kindergarten kid, 1968.
(Lynagh collection)

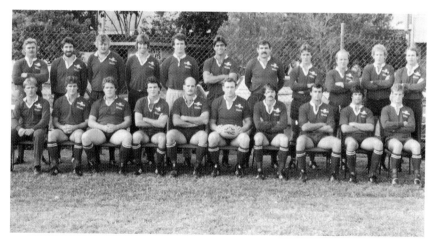

(top)
Gregory Terrace first XV, 1980. Damien
Frawley (*with cup*), Michael Cook (*with
ball*), coach Lester Hampson (*second from
left*), Lynagh (*back row third from right*).
(Lynagh collection)

(left)
Lynagh leads out the Terrace first XV for
the final time, 1981. (Lynagh collection)

(bottom)
The first Queensland team in state rugby's
centenary year, 1982. (Lynagh collection)

(above)
Early days for Queensland, 1983.
(Queensland Newspapers Pty Ltd)

(right)
Help from one of the best. Lynagh gets
some advice from Ireland's Ollie
Campbell, 1983. (Glen Cameron, *Daily
Sun*, News Ltd)

(far right)
Lynagh's first Wallaby tour, France, 1983.
Andrew Slack observes the kicking style
while Duncan Hall and coach Bob Dwyer
confer in the background. (Lynagh
collection)

(above)
On the French tour, 1983. A twentieth-birthday celebration at a restaurant in Germany's Black Forest. (*From back right*) Roger Gould, myself and Michael Hawker shout the birthday boy. (Author's collection)

(top right)
Soaking up the joy of a win over England with coach Alan Jones and Roger Gould, Twickenham, 1984. (Author's collection)

(right)
Grand Slam delight. David Campese, Mark Ella and Peter Grigg with Lynagh in the Murrayfield dressing rooms, 1984. (Lynagh collection)

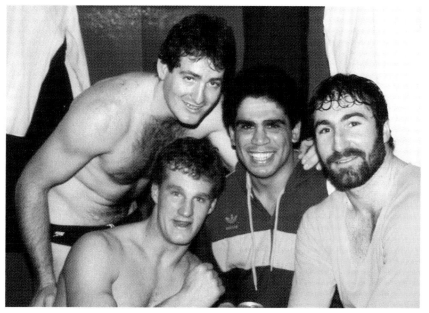

(left)
Peter Slattery, good friend and club, state
and national team-mate, supports the
Lynagh pass, 1986. (Queensland
Newspapers Pty Ltd)

(top)
Hugo Porta left in the wake. Another
Puma pursues Lynagh, Ballymore, 1986.
(Garry Taylor)

(bottom)
World Cup semi-final loss to France,
1987. Despite the result, Lynagh considers
it one of the best games he's played in.
(Presse Sports, L'Equipe)

(right)
Paraguay, 1987. Rugby tours aren't all hard work. (*From left to right*) Michael Hawker, Damien Frawley, Simon Poidevin, Lynagh. (Lynagh collection)

(below)
The Hong Kong Sevens, Australia versus Dubai Exiles, 1988. (Reuter)

(left)
Greg Craig and Mark McBain display their
ancestry at a post-match function in
Edinburgh, 1988. (Lynagh collection)

(below)
Rome, 1988. With Farr-Jones senior and
junior. (Lynagh collection)

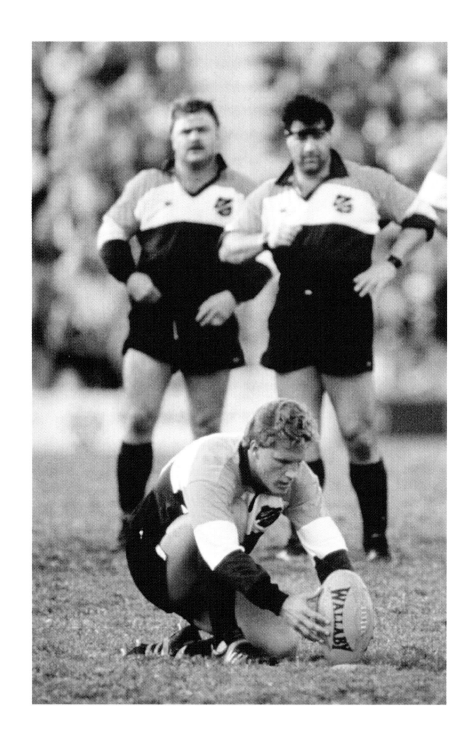

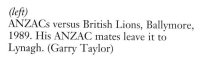

(left)
ANZACs versus British Lions, Ballymore, 1989. His ANZAC mates leave it to Lynagh. (Garry Taylor)

(top)
After the second of his three premierships with University. Ballymore, 1989. (Lynagh collection)

(bottom left)
ANZAC Lynagh gives British Lions intimidator Robert Jones the 'don't argue', 1989. (Queensland Newspapers Pty Ltd)

(bottom right)
Tempo and Noddy, France, 1989. (Lynagh collection)

(above)
French dining, 1989. (*From left to right*)
Peter FitzSimons, David Wilson, Lynagh,
Tim Gavin, Jason Little, Nick Farr-Jones.
(Lynagh collection)

(right)
Yet another birthday on tour. The big
three – Nick Farr-Jones, David Campese,
Michael Lynagh. (Lynagh collection)

alongside full-time study and the parenting of two pre-school youngsters. Energy, it seems, has been handed out in large doses to all members of the Lynagh family.

The family also found time to move into their first house. It was situated in the northern Brisbane suburb of Everton Park, on a block of land Ian and Marie had purchased for £750 before they were married. As conservation was not such a big issue in those days, much of the spare time of young fathers in this new area was spent clearing the trees that flourished around the houses. The difference between the Lynagh family and others was a two-year-old wielding his very own tomahawk. It was Dad's gift. Michael liked having a go at chopping the trees so why not get him a proper tomahawk of his own?

'I don't apologise,' says Ian. 'It wasn't really sharp and he never did chop his or anyone else's finger off. He was always adventurous … Marie was a bit horrified, but generally we approached him with the attitude, "Don't tell him that he can't, tell him that he can. Show him, give him some instructions and let him go." We did watch him very closely but he never did any damage …'

When the cold westerly winds arrive in Brisbane in August they signify one thing in particular – it's Ekka time! 'Ekka' refers not only to the Royal National Show, Brisbane's equivalent of Sydney's Royal Easter Show, but also the Brisbane Exhibition Grounds at which the show is held for ten days every August. But the show is far from the exhibition grounds' only claim to fame. This is the venue where Sir Donald Bradman made his Test cricket debut and where, more than forty years later in 1971, Australia played South Africa in one of the most controversial rugby Tests of all time. Ian took Michael to that game but at the age of seven, rugby was far from a major priority. His fascination with the exhibition grounds revolved totally around the show. However, unlike most other children it was not the merry-go-rounds, the roller-coaster rides or the sample bags which grabbed his attention. It was the tractors.

'Whenever we went to the show,' recalls Marie, 'all he ever wanted to do was head straight for the farm machinery. He'd just sit on the various tractors for hours pretending to drive them, while we just waited until he'd been on every one. He didn't want or need to do anything else.' What some parents on a tight budget at the Ekka would give for a Michael Lynagh!

Insurance agents might think differently though, as this gentle but determined child had crashed two cars into brick walls by the time he was ten. The first incident occurred after the Lynaghs had gone to live in the Haenke family home in Ipswich, and Ian became a daily commuter to Brisbane in his brand-new Austin 1800. The mistaken belief that a packet of chewing gum was hidden somewhere in the car led the three-year-old Michael to investigate. The search was thorough enough for him to manage to release the handbrake. On a hilly drive-way, there was only one way for Michael and the Austin to go – right through Aunty Madeleine's back fence. The result was one ruined fence, one damaged Austin and one cross Michael because he still hadn't found the chewing gum.

Seven years later, and after just one week in a new residence in the Brisbane suburb of Ascot, he was at it again. Although his father refuses to believe he was actually trying to clean the car, this time a Triumph, this was his excuse after he'd managed once again to release a handbrake on a steeply inclined drive. Down it went, across a street which was usually full of playing children. Mercifully on this occasion it was deserted and the only victim was the residence of opposite neighbour Mrs Meibusch. She peeked out to discover a car sitting over her front fence. Her patience was to be further tested a week later. While enjoying the more gentle pursuit of pitch-and-putt golf on the footpath, with his good friend Robert Pozzi, Michael sent a golf ball hurtling through Mrs Meibusch's front window. Regardless, according to Marie, Mrs Meibusch adored young Michael.

After Michael finished his first year of school at St Mary's in Ipswich in 1969, Ian left classroom teaching to enter the field of guidance counselling at schools and the family made yet another move – this time to the Gold Coast. At that time this was the perfect place for a young person with athletic inclinations to grow up. It combined a wonderful climate, long sweeping stretches of surfing beaches and the comparatively slow and casual way of life in a holiday destination.

Both his parents had already noted that Michael was tremendously energetic, and anything in his environment remotely to do with physical activity would seize his interest. Even when he was very young, his physique, the muscular legs and the solid frame, had 'sportsman' written all over it. His report card from the grade four teacher at Star of the Sea convent in Southport told the tale of how he liked to spend his time: 'Michael Lynagh: messy hair, no buttons on his shirt, dirty hands – typical boy.'

You might not get similarly worded reports nowadays but the meaning was clear. Mention was also made of how gentle he was with the girls in his class – certainly a trait not shared by most nine-year-old boys.

Active as he was, he was also a watcher. The powers of concentration he developed to teach himself to swim and surf proved invaluable in his later sporting endeavours. He was never formally taught to swim, and yet by the age of seven he mastered the skill enough to be forever swimming out beyond the breakers. At Main Beach, where the family used to go for their regular beach sessions, the lifesavers were continually bringing him back to shore under the false impression the undercurrents had taken him so far out to sea.

'He used to get upset with the lifesavers,' remembers Marie. 'I'm not in any trouble, he'd say, and they keep coming out and bringing me in.'

Hoping his love of the beach might be channelled in some more structured way, Ian and Marie signed Michael up with the nippers – that group of young surf-lovers who, while being taught the basic disciplines of lifesaving, are expected to spend a fair amount of time in regimented activities on shore. However the beach to this youngster wasn't the sand, it was the sea. He wanted to be out in the water, not running along the beach, grabbing sticks and the like. Those hapless lifesavers who'd spent far too much time rescuing a perfectly safe young Lynagh encouraged Ian and Marie to purchase a surfboard so at least he'd have something to hang on to. By his seventh Christmas he was the proud owner of a handsome red and green surfboard.

It was the beginning of a lifelong love for the water, and surfing in particular. The solitude afforded him by the surf is perhaps its greatest attraction. Nevertheless, for such an eminently recognisable sporting star total sanctuary is impossible – even out behind a lovely two-metre swell.

'Every now and then, a couple of guys might paddle over and ask about something to do with rugby,' says Michael. 'It goes with the territory of being a public figure I guess, but it sure is more relaxing sitting out the back chatting than to be grilled in a restaurant or at some reception.'

The move to the coast also gave him his first taste of team sport, thanks to an old Toombul cricket mate of Ian's. Barry Gibson was teaching at Southport High School and had a couple of young sons who'd taken up soccer with the local side, the Musgrave Hill Rockets. He encouraged Ian to bring Michael along and in 1969 the name M. Lynagh appeared in a team list for the first time. He played three years with the Rockets, from under six to under eight, and in each year made the Gold Coast representative teams.

Peter Hawthorne, the coach at Musgrave Hill, was his first and last kicking coach. Hawthorne knew what he was talking about. His father Frank had been heavily involved in Australian soccer, managing national sides in the 1950s during series against South Africa and China, as well as a team brought to this country by the legendary Sir Stanley Matthews. Lynagh remembers Peter's sons as first-rate players.

Mark was in Michael's team and Don, a couple of years older, still plays as captain-coach of the Merrimac first-grade team on the Gold Coast. According to Peter, Michael was a natural talent.

'All I did was knock a few rough edges off. Keep the head over the ball, follow through in the direction you want the ball to go – that sort of stuff. There was no doubt he was out of the box. He was a star.'

The *Gold Coast Bulletin* for July 1971 backed up that assessment. The newspaper reported the Rockets under eight's 4–0 victory over Coolangatta.

> Rockets' first goal was one of the finest scored in the junior competition this season when Michael Lynagh, playing in his regular centre-half position, crashed the ball over the Coolangatta keeper's head from thirty-five yards out. This was an effort rarely seen in junior play and typified the improvement Michael has shown in the last three games.

Hawthorne claimed the goal was 'just exceptional for a kid of that age'.

After excelling in his first team-oriented pursuit, the omens were good. Three years at Star of the Sea Convent were followed by a fifth-grade year at Aquinas College, a school where rugby league was the winter pastime. Although the school has recently provided some high-quality rugby union teams, it was all league then, as evidenced in the names of some of the students who passed through its doors. Bob Lindner and Paul Hauff were two Aquinas boys who went on to represent Australia in the thirteen-a-side game. The four-stone-seven team in 1973 enjoyed the services of a second row-cum-lock, whose muscular, athletic frame looked likely to serve him well in the rugby league code. Thankfully, for millions of rugby union fans the world over, the physique of this Lynagh boy did serve him well, but not in rugby league.

By this time, Ian had again changed jobs and was a student counsellor in Brisbane at the Queensland Institute of Technology. This meant commuting from the coast – the each-way trip often took three or more hours out of an already full day. Although not a fan of large gatherings where small talk is rife, Ian loves one-to-one conversations. As he is a psychologist they are in many ways his business. On his daily journeys, he would occasionally pick up hitch-hikers – his main motivation simply the opportunity for a chat or maybe to help keep him awake on the coast highway. Marie regularly found herself feeding 'strays' whom Ian had invited home, so she wasn't overly surprised when he walked in one night with another mystery dinner guest.

'I'd picked up this surfie hitch-hiker with a big blond Afro hairstyle,' recalls Ian. 'He told me he'd been thrown out of home in Perth and was now homeless. That turned out not to be quite the whole truth … but anyway I brought him to the house for a meal and he ended up staying for about a year.'

When Michael Chambers eventually told the whole story and revealed that he was actually a Brisbane boy, Ian visited his parents and between them a decision was reached that Michael could stay with the Lynaghs, with the proviso he attended Miami High School, one of the coast's bigger schools. A surfing devotee and with the looks to fit the image, he became the target of a touch of hero worship from young Michael and eventually had a big influence on both the Lynagh children. The fact that he was a school-mate of future world-champion surfer Wayne 'Rabbit' Bartholomew enhanced his image further, and on some Saturday nights when Ian and Marie went out it was Chambers and Bartholomew who babysat Michael and Jane. Rabbit had already established a reputation as a wonderful surfer and the chance to ride his board was a childhood memory Lynagh still relishes.

Although something of a rebel, it was obvious Chambers had taken quite a liking to young Michael and despite the six- or seven-year age difference the pair would surf together and watch each other play football. Lynagh admits that for a time he was the brother he never had, and also the first person outside the immediate family who made him feel he had some ability on the sporting field.

'He always used to tell me I was stronger and a much better foot-baller than the other kids. He really was the first to give me the notion that I could be better than others at football. I think he was pretty wild, but Mum and Dad told him they were the ones making the rules and he had to abide by them. From my point of view though, he was good to me and I liked having him around.' Although they lost touch for many years, Chambers eventually made contact again with the Lynaghs to tell them he had a good job and was planning to marry.

While his years on the Gold Coast had introduced Michael Lynagh to surfing, soccer and rugby league, by the time the family moved back to Brisbane at the end of 1973, it was cricket that was his first and greatest love. 'Soccer and football were just things I did in the winter waiting for the cricket season to arrive.'

Ian played first-grade cricket for Southport in the coast competition and Michael often used to tag along, playing his own matches with other sons on the sidelines.

'I didn't know the first thing about soccer, but I certainly recognised his talent in cricket,' says Ian. 'It wasn't a case of me getting together with him in the backyard and throwing a few balls to him – I don't think I've ever done that. Marie and I were never coaches. Skill was something he developed himself or learned from someone else. We believed our parenting was about process – the process of developing character. He used to hang around when I played, so I guess I was more of a model than a teacher. Even when I was thirty I used to have a cricket ball in a stocking on the clothesline for practice and I'd forever be coming home to find him using it. I certainly can't recall giving him any type of real tuition.'

Although delighted with Michael's inclination, Ian wasn't quite so pleased when he arrived home one afternoon to discover his own Gray-Nicolls bat with its handle sawn in half. A fan of the great West Indian batsman Clive Lloyd, Michael was keen to use the heaviest bat possible and Dad's pride and joy fitted the bill almost perfectly. It was just a bit long ...

In later years, when his talent developed and was officially rewarded with selection in representative under-age teams, Michael would practise non-stop. Peter Philpott was a former Test cricketer who ran coaching clinics and it was at one of these that Michael borrowed the notion of taping a brick to the back of a bat. The intention was to strengthen his left arm, a crucial aspect for any aspiring young batsman. Lynagh would spend hours hitting the ball on the line with the weighed-down bat and then carry on with his normal bat. 'I was always a front-foot player,' says Lynagh. 'It's hard to play back to a stocking.'

His sister Jane could not understand how anyone in their right mind would spend such a large percentage of their life on their own hitting a ball which was wrapped in an old nylon! All the family were amazed that when the stocking broke, as often happened, nothing else did. The windows of their house remained intact throughout Michael's lengthy backyard career.

The family moved to a house in Ascot – one of Brisbane's most established and wealthy suburbs. There was 'old' money aplenty around but the Lynaghs, who hardly fitted into that category, were lucky enough to be in the right place at the right time. They were among the first new people to buy in the street since the 1930s and the welcome they received was an appropriate reminder of why Ascot is often referred to as Brisbane's Toorak.

'Hello,' boomed one of their neighbours. 'Welcome to Royal Ascot – now where are you going to get your help from? We get ours from Hendra.'

'I don't know that we'll be getting any hired help,' responded Marie, declining to add that Ian had been brought up in Hendra.

'What about a gardener?'

'No, actually we've got a gardener, thanks. His name is Michael and he's ten.'

However the Lynaghs grew to love their little three-bedroom English-style cottage in Carfin Street and formed wonderful friendships not only with their immediate neighbours, but with many of the families in the surrounding area.

Early in 1974, Michael commenced what he considers was one of the most important and valuable journeys of his life. It was the first of eight years at St Joseph's College, Gregory Terrace. The day he started also marked the beginning of Brother Barry Buckley's term as headmaster – a tenure which coincided precisely with Lynagh's time at the school. A softly spoken and thoughtful character, this tall Christian Brother had an immense influence on Michael. The seeds of that influence were sown on day one.

'I remember very clearly my first assembly at Terrace,' says Lynagh. 'Brother Buckley made the statement, "You'll only get out of this school what you put into it." That line has stayed with me to this day. Pretty simple stuff, but I decided to put it to the test and my life to date has been rewarded beyond my wildest dreams.' Rugby fans have even more reason to appreciate Brother Buckley's simple message.

Years later, as captain of the first XI in his final year of school, Lynagh won the toss in a particularly crucial match and admits he didn't know whether to bat or bowl. Buckley, a supporter of anything in which Terracians were involved, but a particularly keen cricket supporter, was at the ground this Saturday morning and on asking what choice Michael had made was told that Terrace would be batting. 'I don't know if I've made the right decision.'

'Michael, a decision has been made,' replied the headmaster. 'Now all you have to do is make it work.'

At Lansdowne Road some ten years later, it was precisely those words that went through the acting captain's mind as he conjured up the Wallabies' great escape. When made aware of his contribution to the World Cup victory, Brother Buckley typically deflected any praise, preferring to remember Lynagh the boy.

'Even then, Michael was the type of person that would think a thing through, then be committed to it and go and do it.'

Although he had completed grade five at Aquinas, it was decided Michael would repeat the year at Terrace. The academic standard was not a problem, but Ian and Marie felt he was a little unsure of himself and needed to gain a bit more confidence. It was a good decision for Michael, but an absolute tragedy for any aspiring young bowler in the grade-five cricket teams from other schools. Beware Lynagh the plunderer!

The school had promised a bat to anyone who could score a century in a match; considering the games were only three hours in duration, with an innings for each team lasting a maximum of just ninety minutes, it seemed unlikely the bursar would have to dip into the school purse to pay for many new bats. Wave a challenge at Lynagh though, and in his own understated way he will go at it with an all-consuming passion – to the extent of being pig-headed, suggests his father. But even abundant talent and ruthless determination can't beat the umpire's finger.

Playing against Nudgee College, the other Christian Brothers school in the Greater Public Schools competition and Terrace's traditional rival, Lynagh had played his way to what seemed an inevitable century. Brother Harney, then teaching at Nudgee but later to be primary principal at Terrace, was umpiring when Michael was struck on the pads. Some years later he admitted to Ian he adjudged Michael LBW simply to give relief to the Nudgee fielders in what he deemed was unfair competition. Little did he realise that Michael was ninety-seven at the time!

'Michael eventually made a number of centuries and Terrace gave him his bat,' remembers Ian. 'But I think he's always felt they still owe him one – he doesn't forget things like that.'

On 12 February 1976, his potential was noted in the *Gregory Terrace Newsletter*.

> The sportsman of the week award goes to a primary boy
> Michael Lynagh. Michael, who is under thirteen, normally is
> vice-captain in the under-thirteen A team in the GPS games. As
> the under-thirteen A game against Downlands was washed out,
> Michael played with his class team, grade seven, against CEGS
> and produced two outstanding performances. Firstly he scored
> one of the fastest centuries (109) hit by a Terrace boy (in forty
> minutes). His century included six sixes and sixteen fours. He
> also performed well with the ball, taking six for forty-eight off
> ten overs. Well done Michael!

It was the sort of write-up any twelve-year-old couldn't help but enjoy.

Although he had experimented with soccer and league in pre-Terrace days, there was only one football code that he would play now. It wasn't quite a case of play rugby or else, but you could say students were encouraged to participate and support the school rugby union teams. While there was not quite the same glowing praise for his early rugby deeds as for his summer exploits, Lynagh did make the A teams in the primary grades and in a couple of under-thirteen trial matches. However, a promising youngster by the name of Neil O'Hare had the flyhalf position sealed up and it was back to the forwards for Michael.

'In the trials that year,' Michael says, 'I was put in a relatively weak team and I ended up spending the whole afternoon making cover-defence tackles. The team coach, who must have read somewhere that number eights are supposed to do cover-defending tackles – he had probably been a fan of some of the great rugby league locks of the past like John Raper or Ron Coote – decided number eight was the spot for me.'

Lynagh concedes his experience up front wasn't especially memorable. 'I was probably the loosest forward in the history of the game. I can't say I particularly enjoyed having my ears rubbed off the side of my head and I always seemed to find myself standing back beside the fullback having a chat about everything but rugby.'

His dislike for the position didn't go unnoticed and he was moved downwards and outwards – down to the Bs and out to flyhalf. The next season was spent in and out of the A team playing flanker, number eight or inside centre, but mostly at flyhalf in the Bs.

If progress up the Terrace rugby ladder was slow, the same could not be said of his cricket prowess. In 1978, at the age of fourteen, Michael was selected in the first XI. Despite those impressive bowling figures in primary school, he had honed the skill of wicket-keeping and initially made the first XI as a batsman-keeper. As a wicket-keeper he had received support and encouragement from Barry Maranta, a well-known Brisbane businessman and the person regarded as the main driving force behind luring Greg Chappell from South Australia to play for Queensland in the Sheffield Shield. Maranta's son Michael, later to play Sheffield Shield cricket himself for Queensland, was the opening bowler for Terrace on the day Lynagh made his first XI debut. The match was against the Church of England Grammar School, better known as 'Churchie', where the pitches and facilities were, and still are, so highly regarded that Australian teams and overseas touring sides often preferred to practise there rather than at the Brisbane Cricket Ground.

Greg Chappell was a childhood hero, but while he had scored a century in his debut Test, Lynagh's dreams of a similar beginning to his first XI career quickly turned sour. The first ball from left-armer Maranta was a prodigious inswinger and went past a diving, out-stretched Lynagh hand for four byes. Great start, thought the glove-man. 'Come on Michael,' he muttered to himself, hoping the next ball would provide a better result. The crafty Maranta bowled an outswinger. Oops – too crafty. Both batsman and keeper played for the inswing. Four more byes. Churchie none for eight, with two balls gone.

There had been another contender for the team's wicket-keeping role; Roger Forbes was overlooked for the job but as an excellent opening batsman was selected for the team. While Churchie made this flying start without a bat being laid on ball, Forbes was standing helplessly at first slip. 'I'm sure he was thinking he would have taken those two balls,' said Lynagh. Unfortunately, any pondering Forbes may have been doing was soon rudely interrupted.

'The third ball was Michael's straight one,' recalls the wicket-keeper. 'I had it covered until it took the edge of the bat and flew to my right. I thrust a hopeful glove at it, but it caught the outside tip of my index finger and then flew straight into the mouth of Roger, at first slip, knocking out his front tooth. To suggest I was ready to retire from first XI cricket and return to the tranquillity of the under-fourteens is an understatement.'

Happily, things took an upward turn from then and Lynagh remained the Terrace first XI stumper for the rest of the season. When Maranta wasn't terrorising opposing batsmen, he took up residence at first slip beside the tyro. Not quite the shy, retiring type, like fourteen-year-old Lynagh, Maranta's competitiveness and aggression was reasonably obvious to anyone within earshot. Not many GPS batsmen that season weren't given hints by Maranta on how to improve their technique, and long hours in the field beside him helped Lynagh grow up.

His sporting maturation, though, took many turns. As he had at the Southport Cricket Club, Michael would go to Ian's club matches whenever school commitments allowed. By now Ian was playing for University club in the third-grade side captained by Dr Cam Battersby, a leading Brisbane surgeon and cricket administrator, who managed the 1994 Australian tour of South Africa, the last undertaken by Allan Border. One weekend, in a match against Easts, University had batted on the Saturday and were due to field on Sunday. Ian fell ill overnight and rang Battersby to inform him he was unable to play but suggested his son might be a capable replacement. Battersby was unconvinced that a fourteen-year-old could keep wickets against grown men but, without a viable alternative, he relented and allowed Michael to play.

Within a few overs, the skipper was pretty satisfied with himself. Michael had performed with distinction taking three catches. The Easts captain was less than impressed and complained that a substitute fielder was not allowed to keep wickets. Battersby complied and young Lynagh was moved to the gully where the ball followed him – another two catches. No substitute fielder can be placed in an attacking position said the Easts captain, as his batting lineup disintegrated about him. Banished to deep fine leg to keep tempers cool, Lynagh was unable to avoid the spotlight – yet another catch.

Many times after that performance Dr Battersby would suggest Ian was looking a smidgin pale and it might be wise for him to take the weekend off and let Michael fill in.

'Are you feeling sick Ian … please?'

Cricket however, was about to take a back seat. At Oregon State University, where Ian had earned the chance to study for his doctorate in psychology, there is not a great deal of interest in the game. In August 1978, Ian, Marie, Michael and Jane set off for the United States, Ian to fulfil his professional ambitions and his two teenage children to do some growing up, albeit in different directions.

3
HANG TIME

Jane Connor has brown eyes, dark hair and olive skin. Michael Lynagh, her brother, has blue eyes, blond hair and fair complexion. Jane is vivacious, outgoing and effervescent. Michael is composed, quiet, shy to the point of timidity. Jane is a risk-taker, occasionally radical. Michael is rule-bound, usually conservative. A stunningly attractive mother of two, Jane has been calling things as she's seen them since she first learned to talk.

'Michael and I didn't really speak much to each other when we were growing up. I don't think he particularly liked me,' says Jane. 'While I think we're pretty close now, I wouldn't call him out of the blue to shoot the breeze. He's not that kind of person. You don't just call to chat to him. If you've got something to say you call.'

Michael's perspective is little different. 'We somehow grew apart, and the relationship was pretty stormy during our teens. We didn't get on very well at all,' he says. 'Looking back on it, it's quite sad and I know it disappointed Mum and Dad a lot.' Ian and Marie Lynagh raised two very different children, but one trait is shared – they are both competitive. Growing up, these individual characteristics asserted themselves and a reasonably volatile cocktail was mixed.

'He was always incredibly interested in sport,' recalls Jane, 'and as I was often the only other one around and was a bit of a tomboy I used to get sucked into his games. We'd inevitably end up fighting and I would always be the one in tears.'

As Jane couldn't quite grasp the appeal of cricket, and Michael had his stockinged ball anyway, most of their sporting contests were football-oriented. Usually it was Strudwick versus Raper, Valleys versus Redcliffe. Ross Strudwick was a former St George rugby league player who had once represented Australia in a World Cup. He moved to Brisbane and linked with the Valleys club which was within walking distance of the Lynagh home. He became one of the most dominant personalities in Brisbane league during the 1970s and was credited with nurturing the early career of Wally Lewis. Redcliffe's Ron Raper was the brother of Australian league great John, and had a far more reserved image than Strudwick. Michael made the rules. Michael was Raper and Jane was Strudwick.

'He always had to be someone,' says Jane of her brother. 'We played tag, but it would sometimes turn violent. He'd shove me on the footpath and then say, "I was just pushing you into touch."' Michael constructed obstacle courses around the cul-de-sac where they lived, making use of the neighbours' driveways, their garden patches and any other available hazards. The pair would ride their bikes through the course but Jane complains that big brother was not only contestant, but referee as well.

'He'd pull me up and say what I was doing was against the rules. It was always by the rules, but they were his rules and I never got to make any. He didn't like to lose – still doesn't.'

But if Michael ran the show in those Carfin Street squabbles, it counted for little at Crescent Valley High. In August 1978, the Lynaghs arrived at Corvallis in the state of Oregon, on America's north-west coast. Located in a very rich agricultural centre in Willamette Valley, the rural town of Corvallis was perceived to enjoy an increased level of sophistication, thanks to its links with the Oregon State University. The family moved into a large house left temporarily vacant by a North Korean professor, and Michael and Jane immediately began school at Crescent Valley High. It was the first time they'd been at the same school and if Ian and Marie were hoping this, together with a change of scene, might bring the pair closer together they were mistaken.

'If anything,' recalls Jane, 'it drove us further apart.'

'Jane has always dared to be different and I was happy to be part of the crowd,' says Michael. 'In America, it was initially uncomfortable for me. At school, everybody knew we were different. We spoke differently. Everyone would ask you to say a particular word just so they could hear your accent. Jane revelled in that – she liked being the centre of attention. She liked being the one doing the entertaining while all I wanted to do was blend in.'

Like it or not he was the centre of attention in one person's eyes. He had hardly unpacked his bags when a boy from the house opposite introduced himself and offered Michael a share of his paper run. They teach them to chase a dollar young in the United States and this junior entrepreneur was prepared to offer the newcomer one of his 'franchises'. Although not yet fifteen, the businessman of the future could sense it was not in his best interests to accept the offer.

'This guy was a year or two older than me and probably thought he could take me for a bit of a ride,' remembers Michael. 'All that I would have been doing was working to make money for him … the real reason though, was that it was too early in the morning and far too cold.'

Lynagh decided that to overcome the alienation he felt in a strange new environment he would resort to something that had always made him feel comfortable and would also present a challenge – team sport. The experience and success of three years of soccer at Musgrave Hill made the decision obvious: join the soccer team. But some backyard activity with a friendly neighbour altered his plans. Alan Bromley, a Crescent Valley High school-mate, had invited Michael over for a 'throw of the footy'. The Aussie didn't need to be asked twice. The American gridiron football is smaller and narrower than the rugby version and tiring of continually throwing it to Bromley, Lynagh decided to test his kicking skill with this odd-looking ball.

'Goddam, how did you-all do that?' exclaimed the surprised recipient, after Lynagh had punted it all of twenty metres. 'Can you do that again?'

'Sure thing,' replied Lynagh. 'You want it left foot this time?'

Bromley was no longer just a neighbour. He was Lynagh's self-appointed manager. 'You've got to try out for the team. I'm taking you to see coach Fagan tomorrow.'

It was the time when O. J. Simpson was at the height of his first and more comfortable stint as a household name in America, and the sports-loving Lynaghs enjoyed learning the ropes of the new game. Just as it is difficult to live in Melbourne and not at least pretend to support an Australian Football League team, it's tough work residing in the United States and having no interest in gridiron. Fortunately, it was a good time to be a football follower in Corvallis. One of the early matches Ian and Michael attended was the defeat by Oregon State University of the much vaunted University of California Los Angeles for the first time in an age.

So Michael had some idea of the machinations of the game when he arrived at practice the day after Bromley's 'discovery'. By the time he had encased himself in the combination of pads, guards and helmet required for this brutal sport, about the only visible body parts were two blue eyes. The helmet could have passed as a leftover from the 1960s space program and Michael was a bit bemused at the amount of protection needed when all he was going to do was kick. But the borrowed gear didn't affect his performance. His first practice kick was a torpedo punt that soared very high in the air. 'Hang time' – the term used for the amount of time a ball stays in the air – is an important element in American football. The longer the ball is in the air the more time your own team has to advance downfield. This boy knew a thing or two about 'hang time'. The ball cleared the expectant catcher's head and landed some forty-five metres downfield.

'What's your name boy?'

'Lynagh sir, as in ocean liner.'

'We play every Thursday and train every other afternoon,' said coach Fagan. 'Now go and get your gear together Lynagh.'

Although it took him some time to get used to the rule in American football that says you can be tackled when not in possession of the ball, he soon became a valuable member of the side. Lynagh was good news for the Junior High team, but it could also be said that the Junior High team was even better news for Lynagh. Once again, team sports had helped him get through a difficult time. He learned to cope with the idea of being different, and if he needed confirmation that he was an outsider, it came from an unlikely source – his geography teacher.

'He was a southern man, with a real "get down you-all" accent,' remembers Lynagh. 'He didn't shave very often, drove a Mustang and usually smelt of a heavy night. He asked me where I was from and I said Australia.'

'Ain't that an island off Mexico, boy?'

Ian sees Michael's stint in the American football team as the catalyst in a change in his attitude towards competitive sport. While he had always loved sports and games there was now a harder edge. 'It was the first time I'd seem him so determined about getting into a team,' says Ian. 'Actually I think he was more determined about getting one of the uniforms! He really wanted a helmet too and … the school presented him with one when he left to come back to Australia. He still has it.'

The confidence that his spell in the football team had given him translated into what for a quiet, respectful lad like Lynagh, was a very bold statement. Terrace's headmaster Brother Buckley was visiting America and spent some time with the Lynaghs.

'I'm going to try out for the first XV when I get home, Brother,' said Michael, momentarily forgetting his normally conservative approach to such things. The long and occasionally rocky climb to rugby fame had begun.

While Ian remained in Oregon to complete his studies, Marie, Michael and Jane returned to Australia for the start of the 1979 school year. Jane found it difficult to settle back into routine after the American experience, but Michael slipped back into life at Terrace and Ascot as though he'd never left. However that first XV seed which had been sown in America was ready to sprout. Marie remembers a phone call Michael made to Ian soon after they'd got home. 'Although he wasn't really in the football limelight he spoke to Ian and said, "By the time you come back I'm going to be in the firsts." It was his big goal.'

But the trials weren't for a few months and meanwhile there were some bowling attacks, both of the Greater Public Schools and back-yard variety, with which he had to deal. Michael had met Phillip Pozzi some years earlier at one of the Peter Philpott cricket camps and, discovering they lived in the same area, they struck up a friendship which has endured through hundreds of backyard 'Test' matches, touch games and assorted other sporting adventures. Phillip's younger brother Robert, and neighbours Jamie Douglas, Morgan Windsor, Bob Needham and, later on, Tim and Matthew Fynes-Clinton, helped form a merry band of mates.

During school holidays in the early years of World Series Cricket, the lads would assemble at the Fynes-Clinton tennis court. They'd play normal 'Test' matches all through the day and, when night fell, would momentarily retreat to the various houses, gather all the bedside lamps they could muster, attach them to the tennis court walls and continue on with the 'day-nighters'. Like Lynagh, the Pozzis attended Gregory Terrace and the three would more often than not spend the afternoon after school playing in the Pozzi's rather confined backyard.

The usual rules existed – over the fence, you're out, snick into the trampoline, you're out, on to the road, you're out, into a window, you're dead. While Michael was rarely a peacemaker when it came to relations with his own sibling, he was usually the arbitrator in the regular disagreements between the brothers Pozzi.

'Michael would make a century and then 200, we'd get tired and I would start fighting with Robert,' says Phillip. 'Michael would come and separate us and then he'd go on batting and we'd get tired again and Michael would have to go inside and tell Mum the boys were fighting again and he was going home. He'd come back the next after-noon and go on to 300 runs!'

Thousands of hours of cricket on the lawn took their toll and the scuffed turf where the batting and bowling creases were marked remains to this day as a permanent reminder of those battles. When Michael wasn't clouting cricket or golf balls, kicking footballs or riding skateboards there was only one other place you'd be likely to find him: in his room playing music.

'He was really into music,' remembers Jane. 'After playing sport all day he'd just go into his room and listen to records for hours. He'd bought a guitar in America and occasionally played along with a Steve Miller record. Even at fourteen or so he was a bit ahead of his time.'

The Pozzi brothers shared his musical tastes, which were certainly a long way from the mainstream pop music that appealed to most teenagers. 'I suppose you'd have called it alternative. Brisbane band the Saints and the Numbers from Sydney were two of his favourites and they weren't playing the stuff most kids of his age enjoyed.' Lynagh's love for music has not diminished and Jane claims that if sport had not consumed his life, he would have somehow got himself involved in the music industry.

But the sweetest music this fifteen-year-old heard in his first term back at Terrace was when the name M. Lynagh was called out to attend a meeting of first XV hopefuls. Thirty-five boys were to be chosen for a three-match tour of New Zealand, after which coach Lester Hampson would name the team for the GPS competition.

'This meeting was a turning point in my rugby career,' says Lynagh. 'Lester was quietly spoken. In fact he didn't say much at all, but after hearing what he had to say I knew I wanted to play in his team. I worked on my fitness and my speed.'

Hampson was a Terrace old boy who had coached Queensland under-nineteen sides and had been 'recruited' to coach the school's under-sixteen A side in 1975. He took over the first XV the following year and coached them for six successive years, winning five premierships in the years 1977 to 1981. In the forty matches played in that time the Terrace firsts lost just two matches. Not coincidentally, Michael Lynagh played in many of those games. In 1979, Hampson was searching for a replacement for his star flyhalf and goalkicker Michael Maranta – the same boy who figured in Lynagh's sticky start to his first XI career. Maranta had finished school and a couple of perceptive parents mentioned to Hampson that this young Lynagh lad showed some promise. Hampson took little convincing.

'From the first time I saw him, I knew he was something special,' says Hampson. 'The thing I remember is he had the softest hands. Often a halfback might fire a bullet pass out to a flyhalf and you'd hear the slap as the hands met the ball. You'd hear nothing when Lynagh caught it. His ball-handling skills were superb – he really stood out.'

Schoolboy trial matches can often become an exercise in chaos control. Scores of young hopefuls, some with next to no chance of graduating to the top teams but keen to try out, are run on and off during the games, while coaches and parents form their opinions. Sadly, coaches and parents aren't always on the same wavelength. No variance of opinion on Lynagh, according to Hampson. 'The potential was there for anyone to see.'

So three months after returning from overseas, Lynagh was back on an international flight, this time as part of the Gregory Terrace first

XV squad travelling to New Zealand. His first outing was against the Papatoetoe High School and two of his team-mates on that day, Michael Cook and Damien Frawley, would also graduate later to Wallaby ranks. By the end of the tour there was no doubt who would be wearing the number ten red and black jersey for the 1979 season. Lynagh will never forget the day he got the news.

'I rushed home from school, ran straight into the house and telephoned my father in America. I wanted him to be the first to know. I then walked into the garden and told my mother.' The exhilaration Lynagh felt at elevation to such lofty ranks was understandably difficult for a fifteen-year-old to contain, but once on the field, youth didn't equate to immaturity.

'When you come into the first XV, and you're up to three years younger than some of the others, you are very much the junior,' explains Hampson. 'But Noddy never played like that. Nor did he try to be the star. He did as he was told. Always in control, he found his feet quickly and showed an old head on young shoulders. He was just so mature – you didn't have to worry about him being one of the lads smoking behind the dressing rooms.'

But it was the pipe-smoking Hampson who'd have been excused for fuming after the first GPS competition match of that season. There are no finals in the GPS system. The nine participating schools play each other once and the team with most premiership points at the end of the season takes the title. There are no second chances, although a shared premiership is an occasional by-product of the system. One loss can, and often does spell the end of premiership hopes, so it was a rather forlorn Terrace first XV that trudged off the playing fields after being beaten 13–11 by Ipswich Grammar in the opening game of the season.

Terrace's fifteen-year-old flyhalf had performed creditably though. He missed a couple of conversions, including one which struck an upright, but contributed a second-half field goal, which coming at that time gave his team the lead. It was a skill which Hampson encouraged and, while in his senior rugby career Lynagh has not been a prolific kicker of field goals in the mould of South Africa's Naas Botha or England's Rob Andrew, on the odd occasions he does choose the drop-goal option, the result is usually three points.

It was more than the odd occasion in these early days – five field goals in as many matches testify to that. However, if Lynagh's performance had lit a spark of hope in his first outing, he put on a veritable fireworks display in the second.

'He was simply brilliant,' recalls Hampson. 'He did everything the rules of rugby allow you in terms of scoring. Tries, penalties, field goals and conversions – he got the lot. He was so confident. He took a quick twenty-two metre dropout and I must admit, as coach, it shocked me. Fortunately it shocked Churchie too. We scored and ended the game with a 27–9 victory.'

The team remained undefeated after that initial setback and as Ipswich suffered a couple of losses, Terrace secured the premiership. It was an impressive beginning for Lynagh, and further accolades were to follow with his selection as captain of a Queensland under-sixteen team to play at a carnival in Perth. There were also Queensland and Australian schoolboy sides to be chosen that year but, despite pressure from outside, Hampson encouraged Lynagh to stick with the younger age group. He felt there would be plenty of opportunities ahead and there was no need to throw his young star to the wolves at that early stage.

Even with the perfect vision that hindsight affords, it is difficult to state categorically whether keeping him out of the big time actually helped Lynagh's development – but it didn't hurt. Certainly he appeared relaxed about involvement with the under sixteens – more perhaps than he may have been at the open schoolboy level, where seventeen- and eighteen-year-olds dominated the teams. In fact he was so relaxed that he took his first step into the representative rugby arena lying down ... literally. Queensland junior rugby union identity Roy

Elmer was the under-sixteen coach and just prior to running on for the first match, after all the necessary warming-up had been completed, he suggested that the boys go and rest under a tree to relax and get comfortable. 'Wake up Noddy, we're on,' was the next thing Lynagh remembers. Living up to his nickname, the skipper had fallen asleep.

Although Queensland only finished third in the carnival, Lynagh was named captain of an Australian under-seventeen team that was to tour New Zealand the following May. Jeff Sayle, the man credited with much of the success of the famous Randwick rugby club, was coach, while future Wallabies Brett Papworth, Greg Martin and Cameron Lillicrap were included in the side with Lynagh. So although Terrace team-mates Cook and Frawley secured places in the Australian Schoolboys, a team Lynagh might have made, Hampson's advice paid its own dividends.

The laconic Cook who, as inside centre played beside Michael during two seasons of first XV football, at club and state level and also in one of Australia's best wins of the 1980s – over France at the Sydney Cricket Ground in 1986 – has always been a fan.

'He was just brilliant – that's the only way to wrap it up. For someone so young to come into a first XV and cope with the nerves and show such great vision was astonishing,' says Cook. 'He's an intense person, but I admire him because of the enormous pressure he's performed under. When you think about it, in almost every game he's played, since he was fifteen at Terrace right through to his thirties, he's had the responsibility of the kick-offs, the line kicks, the twenty-two dropouts, the goal kicks and any field goals that are required. He directs the traffic, often captains teams and then plays well himself.'

As someone who once deputised for an injured Lynagh as flyhalf in an interstate match in 1988, Cook knows what he's talking about. 'I know if someone came up to me and said I had to do the line kicks, I'd worry. I'd think, I have to kick for the line today. I hope I put them all out or otherwise I'll look a proper goose. To have to put up with that kind of pressure constantly isn't easy and I reckon he's handled himself marvellously well.'

If the time in America had encouraged Lynagh to play first XV football, Cook believes the under-seventeen tour to New Zealand gave him the notion he was much more than just another first XV footballer. 'I remember after that trip he seemed a little more intense and serious. He realised that he deserved to be up in that company,' says Cook. 'I think he's very ambitious and even then would have clearly mapped out what he wanted to be. He'd have had visions then of becoming the Australian flyhalf and doing it for a long time.'

The Wellington under-seventeen team probably had similar visions. In the third match of the New Zealand tour, the Lynagh-led Australians defeated the home side 39–14, with the captain again pulling out the full bag of tricks. He kicked a conversion, a penalty, a field goal and scored a try. Ever happy to let his deeds do the talking, on this tour Lynagh's job was far from over when the full-time whistle blew. The burdens of captaincy on a rugby tour include a fair bit of speech-making and, as he was far from a big talker in normal circumstances, the idea of public speaking even then had little appeal. Nothing has changed. Despite countless invitations, some of them potentially quite lucrative, which continue to come his way, Lynagh largely shuns speaking engagements. As a sixteen-year-old in New Zealand there was no choice – the captain of the team spoke after each game and that was that. According to Greg Martin, the experience did him good.

'In those days he was even quieter than he is now,' claims Martin. 'Even as the nominated captain, he was very reserved. But as he made more speeches, it seemed he came out of himself a bit more and it increased his overall confidence. He wasn't ever going to be like some of the wild New South Wales country boys we had on that trip, but by the end of it he had come out of his shell a bit.'

The team won all five matches including the 'Test' against New Zealand at Christchurch. The match was a curtain-raiser to a

Canterbury provincial game in which All Black Wayne Smith was playing. After the match Michael first met the man who later became a
much-respected opponent, a team-mate in a World XV and the coach
of Lynagh's Italian club Benetton. Although the under-seventeen side
won the match with a comfortable 25–16 tally, it would have been
more convincing had Lynagh's kicking not been astray. Not one who
forgets criticism easily, Lynagh recalls the words of a New Zealand
television commentator at the time. 'Lynagh couldn't kick the skin off
a rice pudding.'

On his return from that tour it was straight back to the pressure of
the first XV and Lynagh himself began to wonder if he was getting too
big for his own boots.

'I didn't play particularly well for the firsts in 1980,' he says. 'I'd hurt
my knee and I began to wonder if after the under-seventeen tour I
started to play the star a little. I'm not that kind of person, because
modesty has always been very important to me. Perhaps I'd failed to
work as hard on my game as I had the year before. Also other schools,
having seen me in that previous year, started to talk about me and kept
a closer eye on me during the matches.'

However, Lynagh was back to his best well before season's end and
the report in Brisbane's *Sunday-Mail* newspaper for 27 September 1980
gave him top billing when Terrace defeated Brisbane State High
School 12–0, to claim their fourth successive premiership.

> Man of the match was Terrace's backline general Michael
> Lynagh who masterminded the attack with skilful variation from
> the flyhalf position. Lynagh, though heavily spotted early on,
> put his stamp on the game, driving High back with raking touch
> finders.

For a more detailed, and unquestionably more colourful description of
matches, the *Gregory Terrace Newsletter* was not to be outdone. Sports
master Brother Ryan would write about the first XV matches employ-
ing a different theme each week. Even for Terrace parents who didn't

love rugby, it must have made enjoyable reading. His report on 1 August 1980 of that 12–0 triumph over State High was a Ryan classic.

> This game was the power-laden, boiler-room struggle that we have come to expect from Terrace–High School clashes in recent years … Casting off with a long deep kick on the final leg of their quest for the 'golden fleece' of an undefeated GPS premiership, Frawley and his rugbynauts immediately mounted immense pressure on their opponents.
>
> Repeated kicking duels slowed the momentum of the attacks but eleven minutes into the game, Michael Lynagh was able to weigh anchor as he winched the undefeated premiership three points closer with a spot-on field goal … It took the good ship, 'Terrace Rugby' precisely two minutes to reach the high seas. Dave Morganti set most of the sheets 'bellying' with the stiff tail breeze as he gathered the ball at the back of a lineout and made a clean break … Seconds later the craft was under full sail as Paul Facey, snapping up the ball from the break down, was impelled irresistibly across the tryline by a combined 'heave-ho-me-hearties' shove from several Terrace forwards. As Michael Lynagh's conversion kick sent the ball sailing between the posts, the prow of the vessel was ploughing and surging towards the land of fortune … it was no easy voyage from this point on. At one stage a daring, but rash buccaneer attempted to decapitate Matt Scanlan but the fellow was forced to walk the plank to the tune of a Michael Lynagh penalty goal. Despite the adversities of their journey, and there were reefs and squalls, our plucky lads remained undaunted and their line unbreached as they met fire with fire and attack with attack throughout the see-sawing and scoreless second half. Jubilation at 'four in a row' erupted among the ranks of the Terrace faithful, who lined the shores as the final whistle blew, and the gallant, unbowed ship sailed proudly into port. The weary captain, crew and pilot retired to drink the delightful draught of satisfaction that is proper to those who have striven, sought and found without yielding.

Who said 'Terracians' were passionate about their rugby?

Despite the fame Lynagh had acquired at school, the backyard sporting contests with friends continued. In the winter he and the Pozzi brothers, together with any other local who cared to join in, would assemble at nearby Oriel Park and touch games involving twenty or thirty boys of all ages would take place. They christened themselves the O Park boys. Much later, one afternoon in 1983, Lynagh was selected on the Wallaby reserve bench for a Test match against Argentina, and decided to warm-up for the occasion with a game of touch with his mates before heading off to Sydney. A twisted ankle resulted, and it was a very sheepish Lynagh who arrived at the Australian training camp the following day to tell team management he had tripped on a gutter during a training run. His life membership of the O Park gang was placed on notice when a couple of the 'committee' noticed the newspaper report on Lynagh's withdrawal from the Test squad and the excuse given. When he passed by the area during one of his trips home from Italy in 1994, Lynagh noticed the O Park tradition lives on – only the names and faces have changed.

It was no surprise when in 1981, his final year of school, Lynagh was named captain of both the first XI and first XV. The cricketers were pipped for the premiership but it was to be five in a row for the rugby. Unfortunately for Lynagh, his contribution was cut short one winter's afternoon on the Gold Coast. The Southport School is beautifully situated on the northern end of the Gold Coast, not far from where the Lynaghs had lived less than a decade earlier. The school buildings are reminiscent of those you might expect to find at Rugby school in England, although the view over the Southport broadwater is some-what more scenic and the weather far superior. Rowing sheds are situated on the canals which lap up to the edge of the many playing fields the students have at their disposal. In short, it is an idyllic setting, but Lynagh couldn't have given a tinker's curse for aesthetics on this particular day. It was the sixth match of the season and after making a break, Lynagh was tackled heavily by future Australian rugby league player Peter Jackson. His collarbone was broken in three places and the dream of leading Terrace to glory was shattered along with it. Also gone, it seemed, were his chances of making the Australian Schoolboys tour to Great Britain later in the year.

'It was a depressing three weeks to the end of the season,' remembers Lynagh. 'By this stage at school, the rugby matches were the most important thing for me. It was all-consuming. When I left school I naturally came to realise there were other things than playing rugby but because of the close-knit family unit at Terrace, it seemed the most crucial thing was to play well for the first XV.'

As Brother Ryan might have said, the Terrace ship was able to sail to port without its navigator. The team was successful in its last three matches to secure the premiership, while Lynagh was afforded the honour of leading the side out for the final match against Brisbane Boys College. It was an emotional moment for someone who loved the school from the first moment he set foot on its grounds.

The collarbone healed quickly enough for Lynagh to take his place at the trials in Sydney for the Australian Schoolboys team and, although far from being at his fittest or sharpest he performed well enough to confirm the already glowing reputation he had established. He was billeted for the trials with Matt and Brad Burke and when all three were selected, Peter Burke, a former league international and a publican who knew a thing or two about partying, put on a shindig of the first order for his two sons and the visitor. When the trio arrived at Cranbrook School the next morning for uniform fittings, their faces matched rather nicely the bottle-green Australian blazers they received.

Although Lynagh's major achievements at school had been of a sporting nature, he had not neglected the more academic aspects of his education. By the time the Australian Schoolboys team departed Sydney on 10 December 1981, he knew that he had worked hard enough to ensure entrance to the University of Queensland on his return. Exactly which course he was going to choose was yet to be decided. For him there were more urgent priorities.

The 1977–78 Australian Schoolboys team had set a yardstick that was unlikely to be matched. The Brazilian and Hungarian soccer teams of the 1950s and 1960s might care to differ, but rugby buffs would argue a more freakish assembly of footballing talent has never been assembled. Among their numbers were the Ella brothers, Wally Lewis, Michael O'Connor, Michael Hawker, Tony Melrose, Tony D'Arcy and Chris Roche. Their record of sixteen matches for sixteen wins with a points total of 553–97 gives statistical clout to any argument. As the 1981 team set off under the captaincy of Steve Tuynman, manager Martin Pitt tried to dilute any comparisons with their famous predecessors.

'We are a more physical team than the 1977 one,' he said. 'We may not have many Ellas in the team. In fact, at this stage, there are no stars. All the twenty-seven players are of equal ability which will give great depth and flexibility.' However, when Tuynman's side thrashed Irish Schools 24–0 (six tries to nil), in the fourth match of the tour, sports writers acclaimed it as superior to the 1977–78 squad.

One of the greatest moments in international rugby contests is when a packed house at Murrayfield, the home of the game in Scotland, unites as one to sing the adopted Scottish anthem 'O Flower of Scotland'. Lynagh, as much as anyone, enjoys the moving renditions that precede international games in Edinburgh, but it hasn't prevented him from making that Scottish flower wilt once the whistle blows. One of his affairs with Murrayfield guided the Wallabies to Grand Slam history three years later, but the seeds of the romance were sown on the Schoolboys tour, when he was man of the match in the 34–0 hiding of Scottish Schools. Five goals and a try from the flyhalf helped enhance the side's claim to be 'the best schoolboy rugby union team to leave Australia'. The Schoolboys waved the Aussie flag while, at the same time, the 1981–82 Wallabies, under the leadership of another Terrace old boy Tony Shaw, were struggling to make a mark.

John Morton, a renowned sports journalist in Brisbane and at the time sporting editor of the now defunct *Telegraph* wrote in the editorial for 12 January 1982:

> Don't condemn those luckless Wallabies too much. Their pack, it seems, was even lighter than that of the Australian Schoolboys side now rampaging on an unbeaten trail through the British Isles. And the Schoolboys successful kicker, Michael Lynagh, of Brisbane's Gregory Terrace, is a round-the-corner kicker just like those blokes from Ireland, Wales, Scotland and England who booted goal after goal against the Wallabies in those Tests best forgotten.

Morton's point about the kicking style was well made. Paul McLean, who had such trouble raising the flags on the Wallabies tour, used the style favoured by just about every Australian goalkicker from both rugby codes up to that time. It entailed lying the ball at an angle of about forty-five degrees on a mound of sand, walking straight back and kicking it on the point. Lynagh was the first kicker of note in Australia to use the 'round-the-corner' style and yet, within a decade of his rise to prominence, there was hardly a kicker in the land using the McLean technique.

The Schoolboys tour finished with a 13–9 win over Wales and a perfect record from the ten matches and, within a couple of days of returning to Australia, Lynagh found his name beside that of McLean in the Queensland squad for the upcoming 1982 season.

Lynagh had arrived home with one unexpected piece of baggage. In his first week at Gregory Terrace, almost eight years earlier, he was at cricket training with grade six. As usual he was with people a year or two his senior. One of the boys had fallen asleep in class and been scolded by the teacher. By the time he arrived at cricket, his class-mates were ridiculing him and calling him 'Noddy'. The young Lynagh thought this was a good way to make his mark, so he joined in the teasing. The subject of this ridicule took offence at the little upstart and asked him how he'd like to be called Noddy. The focus of everyone's attention now became Lynagh, and within a week there was hardly a teacher or student at Terrace who didn't know Michael Lynagh as Noddy. When Lynagh finished school he was hopeful he could leave the name behind.

'I thought I'd finally get back to being plain old Michael, but with me on the Schoolboys tour was Damien Kelly, a good friend and a fellow Gregory Terrace player. He kept calling me Noddy and all the guys picked it up.'

The Australian sporting public love referring to their heroes by their nicknames. Rugby league personality Paul Vautin is better known as 'Fatty' while Allan Border is more often than not, plain old 'A.B.'. Similarly, when speaking of Michael Patrick Lynagh, even those who have never met him tend to use the sobriquet. Before the 1981–82 Australian Schoolboys had even left Britain's shores to return home, every Brisbane rugby club was clamouring for the services of the youngster known as 'Noddy'.

4
SHADES OF RED

For many years rugby union in Brisbane was the sole preserve of the private schools. Even in the mid-1980s, many senior clubs still relied on the old boys system, wherein tradition largely dictated where a graduating schoolboy might continue his rugby. The result of such exclusivity was that the cream of the cream would gravitate towards one of three senior clubs – Brothers, Greater Public Schools Old Boys, known simply as GPS, or University. The so-called district teams like Souths and Wests, which made up the rest of the competition, were left to pick up the playing crumbs. The record of premiership successes quantified the imbalance. In the thirty-six premierships contested from the end of World War Two until 1981, the season prior to Michael Lynagh's senior debut, Brothers and University had each won fifteen flags, GPS two, Teachers two, while Souths and Wests had both enjoyed just one season of glory.

Now however, times and thinking have changed. As rugby moves slowly if inevitably towards open professionalism, clubs in all major centres enjoy a far more structured recruiting process than ever before. Souths have become the trendsetters of the 1990s. Recruitment from schools outside the normal GPS or TAS (The Associated Schools) net has secured it not only a swag of premierships, but also the kudos which goes to any club that has enjoyed the services of a number of the game's superstars, men like Jason Little, Tim Horan, Garrick Morgan, Troy Coker and Sam Scott-Young. With players of that ilk, success is assured, and by the end of 1994 Souths had won four successive Brisbane premierships and established itself, alongside Sydney's Randwick, as the élite club in Australian rugby.

But Souths was never an option when Michael Lynagh returned from Britain at the end of 1981. Although every club hoped against hope that a player of Lynagh's calibre might opt to wear its colours, realistically the choice was always going to rest between University and Brothers. Brothers had done its share of wooing and felt there were several points in its favour. Tradition was one: historically its player base had come from the rugby-playing Catholic schools such as Nudgee and Gregory Terrace. Geography was another. The Jack Ross Oval, headquarters of the Brothers club, was within walking distance from the Lynagh home in Ascot, while the presence in the A-grade team of players such as Tony Shaw, himself a former Gregory Terrace first XV player and an Australian captain, would surely carry some weight.

Brothers, which at that time was enjoying a run of success that reaped five premierships in as many years, hadn't counted on two things. One was the capacity of Lynagh not to sacrifice clear thinking to haste, while the other was the Loane factor.

Mark Edward Loane, known to his team-mates as the 'dogmatic doctor', was the main character in Queensland's resurgence after a long period in which New South Wales had completely dominated the Australian rugby scene. In 1976, as a twenty-one-year-old medical student, he led Queensland to the most significant victory in its history – a 42–4 shellacking of the Blues at Ballymore. The changing of the guard had taken place, and while Queensland basked in the immediate glory, the result was of long-term benefit for the game in both states. The Blues had been shaken out of their complacency and the Maroons had discarded an inferiority complex. Australian rugby was the winner on that day.

Like most other rugby football followers, Ian Lynagh was a fan of Loane. 'I didn't like the aggro that was associated with Brothers at that time,' says Ian. 'And I had always admired Loane, and the way he played football. I remember talking to Michael about him.'

John Ryan, a former Terrace school-mate of Ian's and the Queensland team manager and selector at the time, helped set up a meeting between the University club president, the Lynaghs and Loane. Loane was the dominant figure in the conversation.

'I had very little idea who he [Lynagh] was,' recalls Loane. 'I'd heard he was a pretty good player but typical of University, we weren't impressed by anything very much. He might have been the world's best player, but we didn't know, and for that matter, didn't care too much either.'

Despite the fact that much of his spare time was consumed with sport, Lynagh had left Terrace with an impressive academic record, and his intention to complete a Human Movements degree at Queensland University helped Loane construct his case. Even if he didn't care for the business of recruiting, he didn't see why Brothers should have what Uni could get.

'I proffered the advice that his degree was probably more important than anything,' Loane says. 'Rugby would fit in better with his studies if he stayed with University.' The practicality of this argument was hard to counter when much of the Human Movements course would take place within a short distance of the University club oval. With tongue pressed only lightly in cheek, and speaking a language not uncommon for the highly intelligent ophthalmologist he is, Loane recalls, 'From the outset Michael appeared to be very much an individual and I certainly had an inkling his type of individuality would be swamped by the monolithic tribalism of Brothers.'

So it was to be University. The next problem to be solved was whether he should go straight into senior ranks or spend a year at colts level to prepare. Again, Loane was an influencing factor.

'Mark drew himself up to his full height and he appeared almost twice the size of Michael,' says Ian. 'He said then that if Michael was going to play grade football and if he got the ball, people of his build and perhaps even bigger would be trying to hit him with all the strength they had. Having seen that, I was secretly hoping it would be enough to convince Michael a year in the colts mightn't be a bad thing. Loane had made it clear what he'd be getting into but he didn't push it. He let him think about it. Michael came back the next day and said he'd like to give the seniors a go.'

Before he made that decision, the Queensland selection panel had already given its blessing by including him in the state squad. His first training session at Ballymore helped make up his mind. He was thrust into a backline which included Paul McLean at fullback and first-class players such as dual international Michael O'Connor and the prince of wingers, Brendan Moon.

'I still remember that first Queensland squad training run,' says Lynagh. 'Paul [McLean] called for the ball to be moved simply along the backline and it was just the smoothest machine I'd ever been involved in.'

University coach Geoff Davies, a graduate of the famous Welsh club Llanelli, was only too happy to welcome Lynagh to the first-grade ranks. Davies had played with two of the game's most respected flyhalves, Barry John and Phil Bennett, and rated Lynagh 'at least their equal at the same age'.

So on 7 March 1982, Michael Lynagh made his senior debut. As flyhalf for Souths, I had the dubious pleasure of marking the highly acclaimed newcomer on a very wet and uncomfortable afternoon – uncomfortable for me anyway. I recall being badly deceived by a Lynagh sidestep and ending up on the wrong end of a pretty thorough beating. My diary for that day records it simply. '... Went out to St Lucia and played University in absolutely atrocious conditions. They beat us 17–0; Michael Lynagh made a superb debut.'

My opinion was shared. The next day the match report in the Brisbane *Telegraph* by rugby journalist Wayne Smith began,

> Michael Lynagh, University's rookie rugby union five-eighth has got 'it' ... 'it' being that indefinable something extra which separates champions from merely talented footballers ... In years to come the hundreds of hardy spectators who braved the rain and the mud will fondly recall the discomforts when they recount the tale of how they saw Lynagh make his debut in senior football.

In the years since that first match Lynagh has, to put it mildly, not always seen eye to eye with the offerings of Smith the journalist, but the relationship at least began on a friendly note. And if Loane had appeared a touch blasé at the arrival of the new boy at training, that attitude disappeared when the games began. 'It was the most impressive first-grade debut I've ever seen,' he said at the time. 'As far as I'm concerned, he's a godsend ... and not only for University.' Coincidentally, University's seventeen points that afternoon were scored by just two men; Loane notched two tries and Lynagh kicked three penalty goals.

It was a significant match for Australian rugby. Along with Lynagh, several other players who later made great contributions to the game nationally began their first-grade careers. They were 1984 Grand Slam hooker Tom Lawton, who played for Souths, his opposite number, David Nucifora, later a member of the successful 1991 Australian World Cup squad, and colourful Wallaby fullback Greg Martin.

Deposed national coach Bob Templeton was in the crowd, along with fellow Maroons selector John Ryan. Templeton was also Queensland coach. Their attention was focussed directly on the University number ten. Knowing the incumbent Queensland flyhalf Paul McLean was nearing the end of his career, Ryan whispered to Templeton during the game, 'The king is dead, long live the king.'

A Queensland team was to be named for the opening match of the
season some three weeks later, and Lynagh's claim had been staked
emphatically. He had enjoyed a dream start but he was just an apprentice and nobody at University questioned that Loane was very much
the master. Wallaby hooker Bill Ross had returned to the club after a
season spent studying at Oxford University and he knew the ropes.
Loane was boss. Listen and obey, and if you want to disobey, do it
damn discreetly. Lynagh hadn't yet learned the rules.

The first few rounds of the Brisbane club season are played in
March and that can mean high temperatures and humidity to match.
University's second premiership game was against Redcliffe and it was
on an awful, muggy Brisbane day, when merely counting to ten would
have caused any normal person to burst into a lather of perspiration.
Mad dogs and Englishmen would not even consider it; only rugby
players dare go out in the Queensland sun at times like this.

University had secured a comfortable winning margin three-quarters of the way through the game and with only a few practice matches
under their belts the University players, bar one, were looking to get
through to full-time in cruise control. That one exception though, was
the skipper. The Red Heavies, as University men are known, received
a penalty outside goalkicking range and everyone but Loane was ready
for Lynagh to find touch with one of his long, raking, punt kicks,
thereby enabling the players to have a slight breather as the lineout
formed.

'Loaney didn't see it like we did,' remembers Ross. 'He wanted to
keep the pressure on Redcliffe by kicking an up and under with all of us
bursting our boilers to chase the kick. His adrenalin was flowing but
you can be damn sure it wasn't contagious and if the up and under had
eventuated, Loaney would have been the only one chasing it.'

The on-field conversation between Loane and the new chum in the
number ten jersey caused the University forwards to stare at each other
in disbelief. Loane – University, Queensland and Australian captain, a

twenty-seven-year-old doctor with twenty-six Test caps to his name was being defied by Lynagh – an eighteen-year-old first-year Human Movements student, playing his second A-grade game.

Loane to Lynagh: 'Put it up.'

Lynagh to Loane: 'No, I'll kick for touch.'

Loane: '*Put it up!*'

Lynagh: 'I'll put it out.'

Loane: '*PUT IT UP!*'

Lynagh then terminated the dialogue by thumping the ball into touch. 'I remember thinking at the time that here's a kid who thinks from within,' says Ross. 'He doesn't take a lot of advice.'

Loane's immediate rage at such action eventually subsided into resignation. 'I knew then that he was certainly an individual, because at that stage I think I was the Queensland captain too, and I'd have thought my authority might have had some consequence. I realised that as is the nature of most geniuses, he was making his own rules. It was obvious my opinion was going to worry him very little. It was such a profound dismissal of any form of authority that I, for once, was lost for words!'

However, Lynagh's on-field confidence was not matched away from it. He had the utmost respect for Loane and his authority, but had acted on impulse – an impulse that most agreed later resulted in the correct decision. That did not comfort him greatly as he sheepishly exited the field after the victory, all the time looking for some way to unobtrusively depart the scene and avoid the wrath of Loane. No such luck, University club's dressing rooms aren't very big. The skipper sauntered over to the young gun.

'In one way I admired what you did out there,' said Loane. 'But don't do it again. I'm the captain and right or wrong, what I say, goes. No problem?'

'It was a very good lesson for me,' says Lynagh. 'I was used to doing what I wanted on the field, but one of the great things rugby teaches you in being part of a team, is to respect that team's authority. I was confident of myself once the whistle blew, but I was also naïve and innocent and ignoring Loaney was proof of that I guess.'

Away from the field, there was no question much of his behaviour was that of a respectful, well-mannered, properly brought-up young Christian gentleman. But boys will be boys. Around the university campus, Lynagh gravitated towards those friends he had made during school days. Former team-mates and opponents like Brisbane Grammar School old boys, Greg Martin and David Nucifora, as well as Terrace colleagues, Michael Cook and Damien Frawley, were part of the crowd.

A giant of a man, Frawley was of country stock and invited Lynagh to taste the pleasures of rural life on one of his jaunts back home during a university break early that year. Out they went to Frawley's grandparents' property at Cunnamulla in south-western Queensland. Frawley's cousin owned the pub in nearby Eulo and the young city slickers rolled up one night to have a few quiet drinks with some of the locals. This is not a part of the world where much store is placed on airs and graces, and the pair slipped with some gusto into both the ambience and the grog.

'Noddy's an inoffensive bloke who'd rather do you a good turn than a bad one,' says Frawley, 'and you do sometimes feel as if you have to be on your best behaviour when you're around him. But I've seen another side of him a few times, and the night at the Eulo pub was one of those times.' At the end of a hard night's drinking, they returned to the Frawley property in one of the patron's dust-covered utilities. 'Noddy was so full he was trying to throw stubbies through the back window of the ute. He couldn't work out why they were bouncing back!'

Lynagh acknowledges that Frawley's recollection was accurate but claims he only tried to throw the stubbies out the back window because he hadn't been able to work out how to wind the side windows down! It is not the sort of behaviour that he recalls with any sense of pride or fond nostalgia. Nor would some of his more recent friends believe him capable of such antics.

The centenary year of Queensland rugby was 1982, and accordingly there were many special games and events organised for the code's flagship – the Queensland team. Administrators were praying the big names in the game would be available and ready to do their best for the Maroons all season. Those hopes foundered from almost the first day, thanks to the absence of fullback Roger Gould, one of Australia's most charismatic and talented players at the time. No one loves a good time better than Gould, and if rugby briefly had to take a back seat then so be it. The Wallaby tour of the British Isles finished in January and Gould decided a sojourn in Argentina, where he'd made some acquaintances on the 1979 tour, would be worthwhile. Queensland would have to survive without him for a month or two.

Paul McLean, who had moved to fullback in the last game of the British tour to accommodate the selection of Mark Ella at flyhalf, was the obvious choice to cover for Gould, temporarily at least. So when the Queensland selectors named the state XV for the opening game of the centenary season against New Zealand province Wairarapa-Bush, McLean was at fullback and Michael Lynagh was chosen at flyhalf for his senior representative debut. Within six months Lynagh had exchanged the red and black of Terrace for the red of University and now he wore the maroon of Queensland for the first time. They were all shades of red that suited him well.

It was a significant match in more ways than one, with hardbitten frontrower Stan Pilecki becoming the first man to play one hundred games for Queensland. At thirty-five, Pilecki was from a different generation than Lynagh, and in terms of skills the pair were poles apart: old-school Pilecki – bash, barge, tons of courage, and new-wave Lynagh – all silken skills and finesse.

The code was beginning to change in an attempt to cope with the greater competition for spectator dollars. Wider coverage and growing interest in games such as basketball meant winter spectator sport was no longer restricted to league or union. Queensland rugby officials had learned a thing or two about promotion and had received plenty of publicity some years earlier through a paid newspaper insert urging spectators at the Ballymore interstate match to 'Boo a Blue'. These inserts developed into something of an art form, each new one trying to outdo the previous effort in its cleverness. The one that graced the bottom of the sports pages of the *Courier-Mail* in the days leading up to the Wairarapa game stated 'Nothing could be fynagh than to cheer for Michael Lynagh'.

Those responsible for the match program also took a liberty with spelling: the number ten for Queensland was recorded as 'Lynah'. As the only player in the Queensland XV who had not played Test rugby, certainly he was the most likely candidate for a mis-spelling. By half-time the quality of the Queensland players was obvious as they raced to a 28–3 lead. Lynagh was enjoying himself and a more comfortable first forty minutes at this level of the sport would have been difficult to imagine. To all intents and purposes he might have been back at Tennyson, running the proceedings for Terrace, as he had done just one season earlier. The second half was more of an education; the Queenslanders failed to build on the foundations, and Wairarapa-Bush displayed some Kiwi grit before Queensland eventually prevailed 32–9, quite convincing figures. However, Brian Lochore, the visitors' coach and the man who took the All Blacks to success in the inaugural World Cup in 1987, claimed some success in that 'we won the second half'. He was highly impressed with the newcomer Queensland had unearthed, but he could hardly have predicted that in four years he would be coaching him in a World XV team.

Despite the disappointing second half from the Queenslanders, the critics seemed satisfied. 'Michael Lynagh fitted in neatly at flyhalf, in a sound, at times clever debut that suggests he will be wearing a

Queensland jersey for a long time to come,' Wayne Smith wrote in the Brisbane *Telegraph* of 5 April 1982. Lynagh had passed his entrance exam with distinction but the real test was six days away.

Queensland named an unchanged team for the clash with Sydney at the Concord Oval (now the Waratah Stadium), and Lynagh found himself face to face with Mark Ella, the man recognised as one of the true superstars of the game. The Sydney backline featured the entire Ella trio. Centre Gary and fullback Glen joined Mark, and while Randwick supporters had always been wondrous in their praise, not only of the Ellas' individual skills, but also of the mutual telepathy they appeared to enjoy on the field, this was the first time viewers north of the border had seen it so amply demonstrated at representative level. With the Sydney forwards dominating their opponents, the backline, superbly served by halfback Peter Carson, was on the front foot all day. Although the loss of Paul McLean through injury had been a blow for Queensland prior to the match, the Maroons still entered the game as firm favourites. A 25–9, four-tries-to-nil hiding rocked the punters. As Lynagh's last defeat of that magnitude had been in the under-fourteen B team at school, he was hardly used to the situation. Nevertheless he recovered from a shaky start to be one of the few Maroons whose reputation escaped unscathed. In his reflections on the game written on 11 April 1982, Frank O'Callaghan, the *Courier-Mail's* rugby writer and a man whose love of the game had earned him the nickname Frank O'Rugby, could find words of praise for only one Queensland back.

> It all began badly with young flyhalf Michael Lynagh kicking into touch on his first two kick-offs. Not that Lynagh played badly. He impressed many, notably Australian coach Bob Dwyer, and he had the distinction of scoring all Queensland's points – a lovely, angled, thirty-metre field goal and two neat penalty goals. His inexperience surfaced at times, but overall his was a good effort.

The Queensland Rugby Union was not too proud to admit that many of the advances made in the game from the early 1970s onward had come about because of increasing contact with New Zealand provincial teams, Canterbury in particular. Apart from the occasional shock result, the All Blacks had dominated trans-Tasman contests since the war, and Queensland officials had decided it was time to learn something from them. Regular tours of New Zealand, where it was guaranteed the rugby would be of the highest quality, provided an invaluable education for young talent. To show its gratitude for the role the New Zealanders had played in the development of rugby in Queensland, the QRU invited a New Zealand XV to play a match in the centenary year. It was an All Black team in all but name. Fittingly scheduled for Anzac Day, the Kiwis were far too good for Queensland in a match that Lynagh believes alerted him to the fact he might not be quite ready for constant exposure to that level of rugby. After Roger Gould returned to Brisbane, Lynagh made the twenty-one-man squad for a three-match tour of New Zealand, but with Gould at fullback and McLean back at flyhalf, Lynagh's only other Queensland game for the season was the mid-week outing against Hawkes Bay in Napier. It was however, the only win Queensland had on the tour.

It was a useful learning process for Lynagh. Things at first-class level were not proving as stable as they were at school. In those four games he played for Queensland in 1982, he partnered three different halfbacks – Tony Parker, Guy Sanders and Mick Arnold. It is unsettling for even the most experienced player to cope with a different man beside him in each match, and for a tyro like Lynagh it made that initial foray even more difficult.

'I realised after those first four games I wasn't quite strong enough,' remembers Lynagh. 'I would rather have been playing in the other games but the rest of the season was still a good experience. I was happy to be part of the bench and learn from people who'd been there, and when I came back to play semi-finals for University, I was a much more confident player; 1982 was a perfect grounding.'

Lynagh wasn't the only rugby figure who'd been on trial that season. After the 1981–82 Wallaby tour of Britain, national coach Bob Templeton had lost his job and was replaced by Bob Dwyer, the coaching supremo at the highly successful Randwick club, home to the Ellas and numerous other outstanding players. One of Dwyer's main tasks when he came into office was to choose which flyhalf would suit his purposes best for the upcoming Test matches against Scotland and New Zealand. With the Ella versus McLean debate one of the most vexing problems in the early 1980s, there was no way Lynagh was even part of the equation. Consequently, he was only an interested onlooker when Dwyer's first Australian team ran on to the Ballymore ground with Mark Ella at flyhalf and, more controversially, his brother Glen at fullback. Queenslanders were incensed. They could perhaps understand the preference for Mark, but Glen's selection instead of either McLean or Roger Gould was too much for them to handle. Elements of the Ballymore crowd decided the best way to voice their disapproval was to boo any time the ball came near Glen. The boos were perhaps directed at Dwyer and his fellow selectors but it made the behaviour no less reprehensible. As a Queenslander, Lynagh cowered in embarrassment.

The 12–7 defeat by the Scots meant changes for the following week's Test at the Sydney Cricket Ground and, almost inevitably, McLean and Gould returned to the playing XV while both Ellas were relegated. The new-look Australians thrashed Scotland 33–9 but shockwaves followed after full-time, when eight of the Queenslanders announced their unavailability for the six-week, three-Test tour of New Zealand that was about to begin. Irresponsible sections of the press interpreted the withdrawals as a protest at Dwyer's selection policies but they actually marked the beginning of the end of amateur rugby as it had been in Australia. Players who had been touring almost non-stop for the previous few years decided to call a halt so that families, studies, professions and mortgages might take priority over rugby. Add to that the lack of appeal of six weeks of hard rugby in damp, cold New Zealand and suddenly the Wallaby team was forced to take on a whole new look. The mass pull-out woke up a few hibernating administrators and gave a hint at the direction the game needed to follow.

Lynagh was a member of the Australian under-twenty-one side which played the New Zealand Colts in a curtain-raiser to that second Test against Scotland and, with McLean's withdrawal from the New Zealand tour, he looked close to a good thing. However, although his under-twenty-one team-mates David Campese and Steven Tuynman were selected in the Mark Ella-captained squad, there was no room for Lynagh. Tim Lane, the man he had kept out of the Queensland team earlier in the year had leap-frogged him to earn a berth in the touring party.

If Lynagh had wanted to blame anyone for his omission he might have pointed the finger directly at Bob Templeton, then his state coach and one of the guiding lights throughout his entire career. Although he had lost the Australian coaching position, Templeton was retained as a selector and, after watching Lynagh's progress for most of the year, felt best qualified to decide his immediate rugby fate.

'He was obviously a very talented young kid and we could break his heart by sending him on what looked like being a very arduous tour. I felt very strongly about it. Both Dwyer and John Bain, the chairman of selectors thought he should go, but I was insistent that they were trying to rush him too much. We talked about it and eventually we all agreed he'd be better off left at home. We could have taken him but we'd have been running the risk of destroying his confidence.'

Lynagh was disappointed, although not shattered, but looking back years later he believes he could have handled it. Not surprisingly, Templeton holds the alternative view. 'In 1983 I thought he was a lot more assured in what he did. He'd had time to become accustomed to the pressure of senior football and I think in hindsight that we did the right thing.'

After retiring from Test football in triumph after the second Scotland match at the Sydney Cricket Ground, Paul McLean looked likely to step down also from his Queensland duties in 1983. Although Lane had enjoyed a moderately successful tour of New Zealand, there was no doubt who the Maroons' flyhalf would be. But before the rigours of first-class rugby were again thrust upon him, Lynagh enjoyed a January tour of the British Isles with University. Most of the games were against other universities or district teams. This was not the five-star, all-expenses-paid tour that the game's élite players are used to now. It was pretty basic stuff. Team members had to pay for some of their own expenses and, when not billeted, hotel accommodation generally included cold food and cockroaches. But a bad room doesn't stop a man dreaming.

'We were staying in a particularly nasty little hotel in Cardiff across the river from Cardiff Arms Park,' recalls Lynagh. 'There were leaks in the roof and I was sharing a room with five others and sleeping on a camp stretcher. Whether it was the snoring, the leaking or the cold I don't know, but I remember getting up in the middle of the night and staring out the window at the Arms Park and thinking that my rugby dream was to play on that ground for Australia.'

The dream was realised later the following year when Australia beat Wales on the Grand Slam tour. After he scored a try at the river end of the ground during the first half of the game he remembered the grubby little hotel and his dream.

Queensland halfbacks could have been forgiven for their notion that playing inside Michael Lynagh could be a career-threatening prospect. After three different partners in his four games with the Maroons, Lynagh faced the first Queensland trip of 1983 to Fiji and New

Zealand with two more number nines, Peter Lavin and Paul Johnston, neither of whom had worn the state jersey before.

A 48–24 demolition by Fiji in Suva and another sound beating by Counties in Pukekohe meant a less-than-memorable trip for Lynagh, but the second game against Western Province in Nadi made it all worthwhile. Greg Martin, Lynagh's close friend from school and university, made his state debut in that match but Nadi is memorable for other reasons. As Lavin was chosen for the opening game against Fiji, Johnston was due to partner Lynagh in the halves for the Western Province clash. Johnston was a fine player and was in some ways unlucky not to have a far longer representative career. In other ways he was lucky to have one at all.

Training facilities are not always everything they might be in Fiji and the day before the match, the team was forced to practise on a nearby airstrip. Not a disused one – we were only allowed on it between flights! Fortunately it wasn't overly busy that day. As a first-time tourist, Johnston was enjoying the attractions of the Coral Coast and had thrown himself wholeheartedly into the holiday routine. Coach Templeton though, is no tourist. During the Wallaby tour of Argentina in 1979, when some of the team organised a trip to the famous Iguazu falls and invited Templeton to join them, his response was, 'Bring me back a postcard and I'll read it under the shower!' Templeton was there for the rugby and nothing else. As Lynagh recalls, being forced to train at the local aerodrome had hardly enhanced Templeton's mood but it became even blacker after one exchange with the budding halfback.

'Bob had been trying to get Johnno to perfect this blindside move where the halfback puts a chip kick behind the defending winger, but Johnno just couldn't get it right,' recalls Lynagh. 'Eventually, after doing it more than a dozen times, Tempo said to him that he'd have to come back in the afternoon and practise some more. Tempo has heard a lot of excuses from players over the years but even he couldn't believe it when Johnno said, "Sorry Bob, I'd love to but I've already booked a scuba diving lesson."'

Match day, however, put a smile on Templeton's face thanks to a 26–0 victory, and the sight of craggy prop Stan Pilecki stripped to his underpants hosing himself down in the front of the old wooden grandstand. The extreme heat and the lack of a dressing room had forced Stan into such action and the steam arising from his ample frame was reminiscent of the scenes at a stable after early morning trackwork.

The retirement of McLean and Loane, the big two, as well as the defection of Michael O'Connor and Tony D'Arcy to rugby league, meant 1983 was a mixed season for Queensland. Wins over New South Wales and Canterbury were the highlights, and although Templeton believed Lynagh was a more composed player that season, he himself wasn't so sure.

'I felt under pressure a lot of the time and wasn't really confident in my own mind. The press didn't help along the way either,' says Lynagh, hinting at the prickly relationship with the media which, he claims, has been an ongoing problem during his career. 'I was trying to play mistake-free rugby and while that was successful to some extent, it also meant I wasn't trying anything. I'd get the ball and end up being a bit hesitant.'

What some journeymen players would give to enjoy Lynagh's hesitancy! He contributed twenty points in a 44–0 win over North Auckland as the Maroon machine began to crank up, and he was the pivotal figure when Australia's under twenty-ones beat a New Zealand Colts team 26–18 at Pukekohe. The New Zealand side included Grant Fox, a man whose career over the next decade in many ways mirrored Lynagh's own. Fox would soon earn Lynagh's respect but when the Argentinian touring team arrived in Australia in the second half of 1983, it included a man who had already won the young Queensland flyhalf's admiration.

Hugo Porta almost single-handedly carried the soccer-mad South American nation into the rugby spotlight through magnificent individual performances all over the world. Australians first took close notice when he booted three field goals, two with his right foot and one with his left, as he spearheaded his team to a highly unexpected victory over the Wallabies in Buenos Aires in 1979. Queensland was scheduled to play the tourists prior to the first Test, and the prospect of a one-on-one with the great man was, at that time, the most exciting prospect of Lynagh's fledgling career.

The flyhalf contest turned out to be no case of master versus apprentice. It was clearly older lion versus younger lion. Argentina won a pulsating game 34–28, but for Lynagh, who had played superbly, there was great satisfaction in the personal duel he won. The great Porta had been restricted to a mere twenty-one points. Lynagh had notched twenty-four. That Porta himself was glowing in his praise of his young opponent after the match was the forerunner of some significant news.

Unaware the Australian Test team was to be announced after the game, Lynagh ignored the post-match festivities at Ballymore, instead opting for a few quiet drinks with state and club team-mate Duncan Hall, before staying the night at the home of friend and well-known Brisbane hotelier Kim Weller. When Lynagh was woken from his early-morning slumber by a radio news bulletin announcing the Australian rugby team for the first Test against Argentina, he listened with understandable interest.

'Gould, Campese … Ella captain, ho hum … Roche, Poidevin, yeah, yeah, Hall vice-captain … and there's a new face in the squad; Queensland's teenage flyhalf Michael Lynagh has been named in the reserves.' Yahoo!

The new Wallaby hopped out of bed and raced into Hall's room to tell him the news. 'Duncan, you're vice-captain and I'm in the reserves,' he gleefully announced. The experienced Hall had been through all this before. 'Yeah, good on you Nod. Well done. What's for breakfast?' For Lynagh, the announcement of his name in a senior Australian squad for the first time is one of his most treasured memories. Apart from the delight at being included, logic suggested also that he was a near certainty for the Wallaby tour of France and Italy later that year.

Australia won the Argentine series two–nil and, although Lynagh failed to get a sniff of the action, he was duly selected for the tour to France. Before departure there were more decisions to make. Already his reputation had spread beyond Australia and he received the first expression of interest from an Italian club – something which was to become an annual ritual. The Belluno club invited him to stay on after his Australian team commitments were completed, while there had also been an offer from a team in San Francisco. Again Mark Loane's counselling was to prove valuable.

'He suggested that I had plenty of time to do those things and that first I should establish myself in Queensland and Australia. Playing for your country was the most important thing and if I could do that, Loaney reckoned all the other opportunities would flow on. He said I could always go to Italy in six or seven years, when I would still be only in my mid-twenties. He was off the mark. It took me eight years!'

In mid-October Lynagh set off from Sydney as a member of a Wallaby touring party for the first time. The team included other newcomers like Tom Lawton, Nigel Holt, Jeff Miller and prop Ollie Hall, later to gain fame of a different sort through his acting roles in the *Mad Max* movies. The three Ella brothers, David Campese, Simon Poidevin and Michael Hawker ensured the side would lack nothing in class.

Six days shy of his twentieth birthday, Lynagh made his Wallaby debut where eight years later he would begin his career with the Italian club Benetton. The rugby ground at L'Aquila is a converted cycling velodrome, and more closely resembles an ancient Roman coliseum than a modern sporting facility. On a freezing night, the concrete terraces were a far from inviting prospect and a meagre crowd of 2000 saw Test rugby's most prolific scorer notch his first points for Australia.

Lynagh contributed a field goal, a penalty and two conversions in the Wallabies' 26–0 defeat of Italy B.

After another match in Italy, the team moved to France for the main leg of the tour and Lynagh was an onlooker in the first game. It may have been just as well. Later to be dubbed the battle of Strasbourg, it was a brutal affair, which a courageous Wallaby team won 18–16; it was a clear illustration to the new boys that the next five weeks would be no picnic. If the aggression and skills of their opponents were some of the hurdles they'd have to overcome, others became evident during Lynagh's first game against a French police XV in Le Creusot. Graft and corruption were alive and well within the refereeing ranks.

Lynagh had kicked three penalties before a sideline conversion of Duncan Hall's try levelled the scores at 15–all. With just moments to go Lynagh received a perfect pass from halfback Dominic Vaughan and, as he'd done so often for teams in the past, slotted the field goal. As the ball soared through the posts, he began to head back to halfway for the anticipated re-start of play. However the congratulations of his team-mates were cut short when the referee, who obviously followed the logic that he had to live in the town, signalled no goal. I was stand-ing beside the referee at the time and the flight of the ball could not have been mistaken. Welcome to France.

Language difficulties, combined with the hard rugby and refereeing interpretations had earned French tours a notorious reputation and David Hillhouse, the sole survivor of the previous Wallaby tour to France in 1976, was presented with a medal by his team-mates at the conclusion of the 1983 tour in recognition of the fortitude he showed by volunteering to go through the ordeal twice.

'Even though I was pleased to be on the tour,' recalls Lynagh, 'expe-rience has since taught me that French tours at the time were organ-ised to make life hard for the touring team. The All Blacks experienced the same problems, but I've been back twice on Wallaby tours in 1989 and 1993 and they were both fantastic. The organisation has improved markedly and now, far from being one of the worst tours to make, it's one of the best.'

Lynagh's playing contribution in 1983 came to an abrupt halt at Agen in the final match leading up to the first Test. With inside centre Michael Hawker carrying a niggling injury, there had been some press talk that Lynagh was being considered for his position in the Test match. A collarbone broken in four places just one minute into the Agen game put paid to those speculations. Long bus trips were the norm on the tour and the extreme pain of his injury wasn't eased when Lynagh woke the next day to the realisation that an eight-hour trip to Clermont-Ferrand was on the itinerary. Thankfully, there was a break *en route* for lunch at a quaint countryside café. Feeling somewhat brighter, thanks to a painkiller and a glass or two of wine, Lynagh was quite chirpy when he lined up for a team photograph with the manager of the restaurant. Little did he know the team's pyrotechnics expert, Brendan Moon, had a little firework display prepared for the locals. Just as the photographer called '*fromage*', a row of bungers exploded beneath the feet of some unsuspecting Wallabies. Lynagh was near the action and the fright caused him to throw both his arms skyward and jump out of the way, which is all very humorous if you've got two healthy wings!

Against the odds, the Wallabies drew the first Test but were unable to improve on that and lost the series after a 15–6 defeat at Parc des Princes in Paris in the second Test. The team moved to Toulon for the final game against the French Barbarians and it was during this sojourn on the French coast that Lynagh received a fillip from an unexpected source.

It seemed the Australian flyhalf jersey would belong to Mark Ella for as long as he wanted it, and as he was only four years older than Lynagh, there was every chance he would be around for much of Lynagh's prime time. However, during a few drinks with his captain in the bar at the Toulon hotel, Lynagh was let in on a little secret.

'Mate, next year is going to be my last.' Ella said to a stunned listener. 'I'll go on the Wallaby tour to the British Isles and then the number ten is all yours.' Lynagh admits to being quite excited at the news, figuring that if he could maintain fitness and form in 1984, the following season could hold big things for him. But the real excitement was going to come sooner than he thought.

5
FROM KILCOY MAIDEN TO
MURRAYFIELD MARVEL

The North British Hotel, Princes Street, Edinburgh. Time: five o'clock on the morning of 9 December 1984. The shrill ringing of the phone rudely interrupted the deep sleep of room-mates Peter Grigg and Michael Lynagh. Thirteen hours earlier the pair had been key figures in the most significant victory in Australia's rugby history. The 37–12 win over Scotland at Murrayfield stood with earlier defeats of England, Ireland and Wales to achieve a unique Grand Slam. Relieved of the goalkicking duties midway through the ten-week tour, Lynagh had been reinstated as the team's sharp-shooter for the Scotland game, and obliged with a record-equalling twenty-one points – eight successful kicks from nine attempts.

R-r-ring. Grigg rolled over and stuck his head under a pillow. Noddy'll answer it. And sure enough, despite the early hour and that little pest in his forehead doing all the hammering, Lynagh lifted the receiver. He answered as politely as if he had been rung at his office in mid-afternoon.

'Hello, Michael Lynagh speaking.'

The voice on the other end belonged to a middle-aged female. 'Hello, Michael. I'm sorry, I don't know what the time is over there. I'm ringing from Adelaide. I stayed up and watched the rugby last night and I went berserk when you came on for the first kick. I jumped up on my chair and yelled, "What's this Jones bloke doing, has he gone mad? Doesn't he know Lynagh can't kick?" By the end of the match, I had tears in my eyes. I'm sorry Michael. I just had to ring and tell you.'

'Thank you. I appreciate the call,' replied Lynagh, and replaced the receiver ...

By the end of Australia's rugby commitments in 1983 the numbers weren't looking good for Bob Dwyer. In his two years as Wallaby coach, twelve Test matches were played. Only five had been won, three of those against the relatively weak rugby nations of Italy, America and Argentina. Finally, on 24 February 1984, the decision was made. Alan Jones, who had lifted the unfashionable Manly club to victory over Randwick in the previous year's Sydney club grand final, was appointed Australian coach. Although the forty-one-year-old had managed New South Wales teams in previous seasons, most of his prospective players knew little about him, either as a person or a coach. It was not long before all that changed. Jones had big plans.

Michael Lynagh was unaware of the machinations behind the election of Australia's rugby coach. Dwyer was out, Jones was in. So what? On the French tour, no great bond had been forged between Dwyer and the back-up flyhalf.

'I listened to him but he didn't really influence me greatly in those days,' recalls Lynagh. 'I never got particularly close to him and there was no doubt I learned more from the senior players like Mark Ella, Brendan Moon, Michael Hawker and Roger Gould. I watched them all closely at training and listened to them talk. They were great value.'

Nor did he pay much heed when Gould alluded to the fact that Dwyer was going to face a challenge on his return home; Lynagh's priorities were getting his broken collarbone properly healed and making a bid for the Australian team to go to the Hong Kong Sevens. The elevation of Jones didn't alter those plans. Lynagh's ambition to be selected for Hong Kong had been fuelled by Michael O'Connor, a former Queensland team-mate and later to become a dual international. 'It's the best tour you'll go on,' O'Connor told him. A distaste for the drudgery of pre-season training was a big factor, too. Throughout February, while his club-mates were being driven on by the ever-vigilant trainers, who screamed at them if the tenth four hundred metres wasn't as quick as the first, those selected for the University sevens team would practise the abbreviated game in the middle of the oval.

'While the others were running around the park, we got to play sevens,' says Lynagh. 'Basically it was just touch, except you got tackled. It was hard work, but much better fun than the alternative.'

Geoff Davies, Lynagh's first University club coach was a sevens expert and tutored Lynagh on the finer points of the game. Although normal rugby rules applied, a very different tactical approach to that used in the fifteen-a-side version was required. Initially, Lynagh played sevens as he would any normal game of rugby. He kept going forward, passing quickly, supporting the ball and committing himself in defence. Ten minutes of advice from Davies straightened him out. Possession was the key in sevens rugby. If he had to run backwards – not done in fifteens – to obtain it, that was all right by Davies.

He explained the subtleties, likening the process to a soccer player who dribbles the ball while a defender shadows him. Once the defender commits himself, it's time for the player with the ball to explode into action. Lynagh learned quickly enough for Mark and Glen Ella, two of the game's best exponents, to suggest he would make an ideal replacement for former Fijian Qele Ratu, who had retired after representing Australia in Hong Kong the previous year.

The Redcliffe sevens tournament was the last selection trial before Hong Kong, and despite University's 14–12 semi-final loss to eventual winners Fiji Police, Lynagh had performed well enough to reach his first goal for 1984. He was the new boy in a very experienced Australian side. Captain-coach John Maxwell had tasted success in both the 1982 and 1983 tournaments and the tried and tested core around him included the Ella brothers, both on their sixth visit to Hong Kong, Brendan Moon and Chris Roche on trip number four and David Campese, there for the second time.

But before Lynagh could test O'Connor's theory on Hong Kong, he had some local matters to attend to. The first match of the club season is traditionally a replay of the previous year's grand final and as Brothers had beaten University 30–15 in the 1983 premiership-decider, these two clubs prepared to do battle again. Lester Hampson, Lynagh's Gregory Terrace mentor, was now coaching University and at the Tuesday night training session during the week of the match, he announced the first-grade side. Although it was the start of Lynagh's third season in the club's top team, he was still very much one of the pups. Only lock Sean Tweedie was younger than him. It was a surprise for everyone when Hampson announced the new captain – Michael Lynagh. In March 1984, Jim Tucker in the Brisbane *Daily Sun* speculated that history had been created.

> Wallaby five-eighth Michael Lynagh became possibly the youngest first-grade captain in Brisbane rugby union history when he was handed the reins at University last night. Lynagh, just five months past his twentieth birthday, was a surprise choice ahead of Queensland skipper-elect Chris Roche and for-mer captain Andy McIntyre.

That University beat the defending premiers 35–3 suggested the captaincy duties sat easily on his shoulders.

In the space of a fortnight, rugby's roller-coaster ride took Lynagh from captain and decision-maker to the most junior member of the team. Now he was in Hong Kong with the élite of the game and at a welcoming cocktail party at the Hong Kong Hilton he met Alan Bond, who six months after the America's Cup was at the height of his fame. This was high-rolling stuff for the young man, and although he had been involved with most of his colleagues on one level or another over the past two seasons, he felt privileged to be there. But Maxwell and his merry men weren't in the business of treating new boys with kid gloves. A first-timer in Hong Kong does as he's told and, at the insistence of veterans Maxwell and Moon, Lynagh fell into line and agreed to take the Star ferry to the shopping mecca of Kowloon, on the Chinese mainland. 'Don't forget your camera, Noddy,' said Moon.

Business commuters and tourists alike throng to the ferry terminal and, never ones to let a chance go by, the rickshaw drivers gather in their hundreds to descend on the unsuspecting tourist. Noddy was okay though. Maxy and Brendan were there. They knew the ropes.

'Give us your camera, Nod,' said the captain-coach. 'Stand by that rickshaw and I'll get a photo.'

With the photo duly taken, and not so much as half a buttock even touching the rickshaw seat, Lynagh thanked the driver for the twenty seconds of his time and walked off.

'Forty dorra, prease. Forty dorra.'

'What do you mean, forty dollars?' said Lynagh. 'It was only a photo.' Lynagh departed with the rickshaw driver scurrying after. By now, old hands Maxwell and Moon were on the Star ferry, congratulating themselves on having nabbed another new chum.

Lynagh eventually relented. The rickshaw driver was $40 better off and the young Australian a little bit wiser. The tradition of the 'rickshaw rort' continues to this day. On his first Hong Kong trip, Tim Horan fell victim to ringmaster Lynagh, while in 1994 Jason Little perpetrated a similar act on rookie Wallaby scrumhalf George Gregan. It had become obvious to the rickshaw drivers that Australian rugby players were easy meat – George's inexperience cost him a hundred!

After two successive tournament wins, Australia was bundled out of the 1984 competition in controversial circumstances. The multiculturalism of the event was clearly illustrated by the fact Australia's first match was against Kwang-Hwa, while a Korean referee who didn't speak English was in charge of their second match with Canada. Several injuries, combined with language difficulties, meant Australia played a man short for the last few minutes of the game, and the always-enthusiastic Canadians held the tournament favourites to a 12–all draw. With nothing in the rules to clarify the situation, the winner was decided on the flip of a coin. Ever since an ugly incident in the very first tournament in 1976, the Hong Kong spectators have loved to hate Australia, so it was a hushed crowd that greeted Maxwell and Canadian skipper Jim Donaldson, as they strode to the halfway line to toss. When Donaldson called correctly, the tournament favourites had been ousted and both the crowd and the Canadian team went berserk. Lynagh's first Hong Kong experience had been enjoyable, if not successful. No matter, his talents were to take him there eight more times over the next decade.

Australian sport was beginning to adopt a slightly different face by the mid-1980s. Skills and fitness remained the basic building blocks but sports science and methodology had increased awareness of how optimum performance might be achieved. When Queensland departed for a three-match tour of New Zealand in April 1984, there were two Lynaghs in the touring party. At the invitation of coach Bob Templeton, Michael's father Ian, now a sports psychologist, who had been working with rugby league and basketball teams among others, accompanied the squad. As something quite new, his methods were viewed with a deal of suspicion by many members of the team. Hefty second-rowers couldn't all see how lying prone on the floor, closing their eyes and practising a meditation of sorts was going to win them much lineout ball. For others, Lynagh senior was a useful sounding board and a worthwhile accomplice in the quest to improve their footballing skills.

If performance was a yardstick, the younger Lynagh seemed very relaxed about his father's presence. It was after the opening match of the tour, a 31–12 win over North Auckland at Whangerei, that

Lynagh's growing stature as a player was first taken seriously outside Australia. In rugby terms, the boy had become a man. D. J. Cameron, one of New Zealand's most respected rugby writers, had seen enough to place the Queensland flyhalf in some exalted company. He wrote in the New Zealand *Herald* on 30 April 1984:

> With his crisp action, balance and smooth swing-through, Lynagh looked the best goalkicker in these parts since Naas Botha departed in 1981, and if anything, he seemed to have more control than Ollie Campbell. However, unlike the non-tackling, short-tempered Botha, Lynagh did his share of the hard work, and showed a canny awareness of when to pass and back up ... It was a most impressive performance and if the news is not rattling around the Wallaby bush telegraph by now that Mark Ella faces a stern challenge, it soon will be.

Ella face a challenge? Kiwis might fly! Mark Ella would wear the number ten jersey in any Alan Jones-coached team. Jones and his predecessor Bob Dwyer might have had their differences but in the early 1980s Ella's star shone brightest and no coach would think of entering a Test match without him. Jones though, had made it abundantly clear he would not be sending an Australian team onto the field without a recognised goalkicker. Lynagh was unquestionably the best in the country and this provided the puzzle that the media throng loved to tackle. Ella will be there, yet Jones has all but guaranteed Lynagh a place. Where though? He can't put him at inside centre ahead of Michael Hawker, nor at fullback instead of Roger Gould. Or can he?

A big season lay ahead for the Wallabies in 1984. Entrée was a short tour of Fiji. A Bledisloe Cup three-Test series against New Zealand was main course while dessert would be served in the British Isles with an eighteen-match tour during the northern winter.

Jones' entry to the Wallaby scene had been a hurricane of fresh air. Never operating at anything less than full throttle, he spoke to players constantly, letting them know his expectations for the year. 'We must be unapologetic in the pursuit of victory,' was the catchcry. Apologies weren't his strong suit. There were none for Mark Ella when he surprisingly lost the captaincy for the tour of Fiji. Lynagh was too smart to fall into the trap of thinking the loss of the captaincy might put Ella's place in the team in jeopardy, but he was getting rather impatient. Ella's assurance in France six months earlier that he was soon to retire was cold comfort.

Nevertheless another Wallaby tour was an extra feather in the cap and away from rugby responsibilities, Fiji was certain to be a haven for Lynagh's leisure pursuits of surfing and golf. He'd seen the brochures: idyllic islands basking under a constant blue sky. But the brochures had fibbed. It didn't just rain. It pelted down every day and regular training sessions took place in ankle-deep mud; it was easy for the players' moods to turn as dark as the tropical rainclouds that hung overhead incessantly. It was in this less-than-ideal environment that he was chosen to make his Test debut. Michael Hawker's wedding coincided with the Fiji trip and his unavailability saw Lynagh fill the inside centre position in the one-off Test. It wasn't quite the dream debut he'd envisaged. A rain-sodden National Stadium in Suva is a far cry from Cardiff Arms Park. In the 16-3 Australian victory, Lynagh was little more than a bit-player. 'I just recall how terrible it was. I hardly touched the ball because of the conditions.'

Although history was to prove him anything but a one-Test wonder, the possibility of suffering that ignominy may have preyed on his mind when he returned to Australia and was duly dropped for the first Test against the All Blacks. 'People say I've never been dropped, but in fact I was … and after my very first match!'

Despite Jones' earlier promises about goalkicking, the side chosen for the Test saw Lynagh replaced by Hawker, and the kicking duties allocated to David Campese and Mark Ella. Sitting on the reserves bench alongside another rising star named Farr-Jones, Lynagh watched Australia's 16–9 defeat of New Zealand. With personnel unchanged for the second Test at Ballymore, the Bledisloe Cup looked to be Australia's as they rattled to a 12–0 lead after just twenty minutes. Some inexperience from the Wallabies, a committed New Zealand display and a whistle symphony from English referee Roger Quittenton combined to turn things around. The All Blacks won by four points and a series-decider was set up at the Sydney Cricket Ground a fortnight later. In the meantime, Queensland faced the tourists and suffered a morale-rocking 39–12 loss.

Losing dressing rooms are never much fun but it was a particularly gloomy scene that afternoon. There was an almost tangible depression as Jones entered. While trying to keep chins off the ground, he camouflaged his own concerns. How could his Australian players re-group and challenge the New Zealanders in six days' time? While he pondered, Lynagh tried to wind down.

Lynagh's intense approach to rugby has a kick-back. He finds it impossible to come off the field, win or lose, and slip straight back into normal mode. 'When I see replays of television interviews I've done straight after games, I find it hard to believe it's me,' he says. 'I'm always talking and thinking really quickly. My arousal level is way up because that's how it often is on the field and I can't just switch it off straight away. So I've got myself into the habit of taking a very long shower after a match and just soaking up a bit of time. That helps me become less fidgety or agitated and I make more sense when I have to speak to anybody, be they family, friends or media. As a result, I'm normally the last one out of the rooms after a game.'

Most of the players had retreated to the condolences of acquaintances outside when Jones noticed Lynagh. Discarded strapping, empty drink containers and muddied gear lay on the concrete floor. The coach and the kid sat on the wooden benches.

Jones had a favour to ask. He wanted him in his Test team. 'Noddy wasn't in great shape after the match but we had to go up and pick a Test side so I told him my thoughts,' recalls Jones. 'I said to him,

"Mate, I reckon Dave Burnett, this Irish referee we've got in Sydney, will just blow and blow and blow, and I think you should play. You don't know me all that well but it's my view and my practice to discuss these things with players before I pick them." I told him that Mark Ella would definitely play but he [Lynagh] could play fullback. When he asked me what Roger Gould would think of this idea I replied that I would speak to him, but as he'd played for Australia for years, I was sure he would volunteer for anything that was in the best interests of winning the series.'

Lynagh was taken aback by the approach. 'I'd never played fullback before and I was scared I'd let the side down,' he remembers. 'Besides, Roger was playing very well and with the All Blacks very adept at putting up the high ball, there was nobody in the world better at catching it than Roger.'

He knocked back the offer of a Test jersey and, although his reasons were team-oriented, he admitted some thoughts of self-preservation were in his mind. 'If I went and played a shocker, and missed all the goals, how long would it have taken me to recover, and would I ever get a chance again? It might have been different if it had been the first Test and not the third.'

So he stayed on the bench while Campese and Ella shared the kicking. The predictions of a penalty shoot-out proved accurate. New Zealand won 25–24, and retained the Bledisloe Cup.

'This is the Melbourne Cup Michael, not some bloody maiden race in Kilcoy.' Share his views or not, there can be no question that Alan Jones has a way with words, and he enjoys making frequent analogies with the sport of Kings. After the bitter disappointment of watching the Bledisloe Cup snatched from the grasp of his team, firstly at Ballymore and then the Sydney Cricket Ground, the Wallaby coach was, like the players, anxious to atone. Those gut-wrenching losses to New Zealand would be largely forgotten if success could be achieved on the ten-week tour of the British Isles. There were many things in the Jones blueprint for success which, in his rather emphatic style, he trumpeted to anyone who cared to listen. However, one aspect of the plan he kept largely to himself and a few senior players was the role he wanted, indeed needed Michael Lynagh to play.

The thirty-man Wallaby squad landed at Heathrow on 10 October – just fifteen days short of Lynagh's twenty-first birthday. There was a classic London fog to greet the touring party, but as we all soon learned, nothing was going to cloud Jones' single-minded, purposeful approach to the task at hand. Not three hours after trudging wearily through customs, everyone was on the rugby pitch. By no means was it a 'stretch your legs, get the fatigue out of your system' session. This was the real McCoy.

Thirty different personalities means thirty different reactions to this kind of shock, but for the main part the players all seemed to understand where Jones was coming from and, despite the obvious difficulties, gave their all. Lynagh tried to give more than that, but even for the gifted, perhaps especially for the gifted, trying too hard can lead to problems. Whether it was his keenness to impress, the jet lag or both, Lynagh's silky skills deserted him, and in those early days of his Wallaby career it didn't take too much to dent his confidence. When he was down his face told the story and, not slow to interpret such signals, Jones made a beeline for the man he wanted as one of his trump cards.

'What's your problem?' inquired the coach.

In a rare departure from his usually tactful and diplomatic manner, Lynagh blurted it out.

'It's Mark Ella this, Mark Ella that,' he complained. 'Am I supposed to be a part of all this?'

'Do you know anything about horse-racing Michael?' asked Jones.

'No,' snapped Lynagh.

'Well, I'm going to tell you something about it.' Out came the reference to the Melbourne Cup, along with the information Lynagh most wanted to hear. 'We've got to put our best team together for the Tests. Mark Ella will be in it, let me erase any doubts in your mind about that one. However in this muck games can be won and lost on goalkicking. You're our best goalkicker, so put two and two together. Now stop dropping your lip, shut up and get on with it. I don't know where you are going to play, but you'll be there!'

Jones was chasing four 'Melbourne Cups' – the four Test matches against England, Ireland, Wales and Scotland. It was a case of the first Saturday in November for Melbourne Cup number one. At Twickenham on 3 November he needed his thoroughbreds to produce their winning form.

Economic and social realities mean that long Wallaby tours of the British Isles are a thing of the past, but from the turn of the century they have been the most sought-after prize for an Australian rugby player. The first official Wallaby touring side was chosen in 1908 and spent six months away, playing thirty-one games in England and Wales. The trip coincided with the London Olympics, and the Wallabies beat a British team, the single other entrant, to win Australia's only Olympic gold medal in rugby.

While today's team carries a toy wallaby on tour, the 1908 side had a far more exotic mascot. With quarantine regulations less stringent in those times, team members managed to bring a carpet snake with them to England. 'Bertie' was a much-loved member of the team, and when he died in Wales during the course of the tour, there was strong suspicion he had been 'done in' by a reptile-fearing Taffy.

In 1927, the Waratahs, a team comprising Sydney players, except for Newcastle halfback Sid Malcolm, toured the British Isles and France and set the standard for Australian teams of the future through their exciting, fifteen-man, running style of rugby. The legendary Cyril Towers, grandfather of Pat Howard, Lynagh's Wallaby team-mate, was one of the stars of the tour.

The arrival of the second official Wallaby team to tour Britain coincided with the outbreak of World War Two, and all matches were cancelled. Further tours of between three and six months' duration took place in 1947, 1957, 1966, 1975 and 1981 – the most successful was that by the Third Wallabies in 1947–48, who won three of their four internationals in the United Kingdom. The 1981 Wallabies arrived with great expectations but failed to fulfil their promise, winning only one of the Tests. In Britain at the same time as Tony Shaw's 1981 Wallabies was the successful Australian Schoolboys team; included in that squad were five players who would be returning to the UK just three years later with the Eighth Wallabies. Ian Williams, Cameron Lillicrap, Matthew Burke, Steve Tuynman and Michael Lynagh were destined to be part of the most successful Australian team ever to tour Great Britain.

Alan Jones' immediate call to arms of his troops on landing in England should have surprised no one. After all, he had suggested to the players that the tick they placed on their customs and immigration forms should not be in the 'holiday' or 'other' box but rather alongside 'business'. But the coach realised the players would need some space. There were seven days before the first fixture and, after four intense training sessions, the team members were given Saturday afternoon and Sunday off to do whatever they wished. 'Chilla' Wilson, a Brisbane gynaecologist and former Wallaby captain, and as amiable a character as you could meet, was the team manager. The only conditions he imposed on the players when they set off for twenty-four hours respite from rugby was that they should not end up in hospital or gaol and that they should be back at St Ermins Hotel, the London base, by Sunday evening.

It is always a shade disappointing not to be selected for the first match of a tour, but Lynagh wasn't overly bothered at missing a spot in the opening game against a London Division side at Twickenham – the home of rugby. However an injury to utility player James Black earned

Lynagh a call-up at inside centre, outside Mark Ella – a hint of things to come.

'Although we had a number of inside centres in the party, my selection there in the first match gave me a clue as to what might happen,' remembers Lynagh. 'Alan had told me at that early training run at Lensbury that I'd probably be in the team, but I didn't really want it to be fullback. Brendan Moon, who usually didn't speculate aloud, also told me I was being "more than considered" for the Test number twelve, so I was starting to get a bit excited.'

Lynagh kicked four goals in the 22–3 win and generally distinguished himself. Not so distinguished was the post-match speech by Steve Williams, team captain for the day. He made the usual perfunctory noises of gratitude to the referee and opponents, before suggesting to the caterers he had tasted 'better goulash at a refugee camp'. It wasn't exactly complimentary to the beef Wellington, and although some of the officials, not to mention the cook, were aghast, the comment sent both teams into uproar.

There was little to laugh about in the next match against South-west Division in Exeter. At his favoured position of flyhalf, Lynagh was one of the few Australians to play well, scoring all the Wallabies' points in the 12–all draw. Lynagh came on as a replacement in the third match against Cardiff and when his name was read out for the next game against Combined Services, Matthew Burke suggested to him he was on the 'iron-man tour'. Lynagh didn't mind. 'Non-players had to do all the extra training, so I was only too happy to play. I'd much rather keep fit by playing than training.' A try, and six conversions from eight attempts produced a personal haul of sixteen points and further definitive evidence that he was a commodity this team could not do without.

Another commodity every touring rugby party needs is a 'baggage-master' – a title that understates the value of a man who becomes a vital part of the team. For over two decades, Graham Short, an electronics repairman from Bournemouth, has been involved with All Black and

Wallaby teams in this capacity and has become a close friend to many of the great rugby players of recent times. His responsibilities include organising the mass of clothing and other assorted equipment that is a necessity on these tours, and ensuring that if the team is in Edinburgh one day and Cork the next, so too is the gear. What sort of studs do I need for this ground? Ask Shorty. Where are my boot-laces? Ask Shorty. What's the best nightclub in this town? Ask Shorty. I've forgotten my mouthguard and there's only two hours until kick-off. What'll I do? Ask Shorty.

But apart from being a trouble-shooter, Shorty's other strength was his thoughtfulness. Lynagh's twenty-first birthday fell on the day the team arrived in Aldershot to prepare for the Combined Services match. A four-hour bus trip with a nagging hangover wasn't the way Lynagh had envisaged celebrating his coming of age, and arriving at the Seven Hills Hotel in Surrey, he was musing over the disadvantages of spending birthdays away from home. He grabbed his bags and trudged off feeling slightly sorry for himself when, on opening the door of room 124 he noticed the bottle of Moët and Chandon waiting for him on his bed. Shorty had rung ahead from Cardiff to ensure the surprise was in store, and an accompanying note read, 'You didn't think we'd forget did you? Happy birthday.'

A cake was provided at dinner and the Champagne was opened at the hotel bar. Shorty, Nigel Holt and Matthew Burke were only too happy to drink a toast to the man Holt had already dubbed 'boy drunk'. Lynagh's temperate drinking habits and the fact he didn't need ten pints to make him feel tipsy were enough ammunition for Holt. As the players filed out from the dining room they each dropped in and shared a drink with the birthday boy.

Although touched by the gesture, Lynagh was even chirpier when the team was announced for the final match before the first Test against England. It is always pretty easy to predict the make-up of a Test side on tour: rule out anyone who is in the preceding mid-week game and you just about have it. The non-selection of Lynagh for the night game against Swansea and the choice of Hawker as flyhalf pointed to the certainty that Lynagh would be required at Twickenham on Saturday.

The Swansea match was played on the St Helen's ground made famous by West Indian cricketer Sir Garfield Sobers, who had once struck every ball of an over from Glamorgan spinner Malcolm Nash out of the ground for six. The Australia–Swansea match was a night fixture and even Sir Gary might have struggled to find the middle of the bat when, sixty-seven minutes into the game, the lights went out. With the Wallabies leading 17–7, referee Laurie Prideaux kept the players on the pitch for six minutes in the dark before abandoning the game. Some of the crowd demanded their money back, while one admitted to being delighted he could tell his grandchildren he was there the night the Wallabies turned into All Blacks! While the players were disappointed their game had been cut short, no one complained during the speeches at the after-match function when James Black maintained the spirit of the occasion by turning off the lights in the function room.

Players hate being kept in the dark about team selection, and so the side for the England game was announced by manager Wilson the first thing next morning. The great surprise was not the selection of Lynagh at inside centre – the writing had been clearly on the wall for some time – but rather the demotion of Lynagh's University club-mate Chris Roche for David Codey. Nick Farr-Jones too was to make his first appearance for Australia in a Test.

It was the game Lynagh terms his real Test debut. Fiji was fine, but this was fair dinkum. As he lined up for the singing of the national anthem, flanked by Farr-Jones and Simon Poidevin, the phone was ringing at his parents' home in Brisbane. Jill Pozzi, mother of Robert and Phillip, Michael's two childhood mates, rang the Lynaghs to share her excitement at seeing him on the television screen. Ian and Marie

recall it as one of their fondest memories in Michael's long and distinguished career.

'Before the England game I wasn't nervous,' Michael claims. 'One of
the things Jones brought in was that we prepared for the game really
well. We trained hard and we analysed our opposition. And we trained
to combat their strengths and attack their weaknesses. We'd done it all
at training so when it came to game time we knew where we were
heading. This is what we're strong at – this is how we're going to do it.
If you've played the game before you get there, there are no surprises.
That's why I wasn't as nervous as I probably should have been.'

Australia won the match 19–3, with Ella, Lynagh and Poidevin all
scoring tries – the only downside of the afternoon was the broken arm
suffered by Brendan Moon, a good friend of Lynagh's and one of the
game's best wingers. That apart, Lynagh's day had been fruitful.
Stephen Jones, the *Sunday Times'* rugby correspondent was impressed
with his first viewing. In his article on 4 November 1984 he wrote:

> His try sealed a remarkable afternoon for Lynagh. He had been
> brought in to kick goals but proceeded to fire almost every kick
> wide of the posts. At the same time he provided the rich com-
> pensation of an authoritative performance in the centre.

He was pretty happy with himself the next morning, as the players
wound down with a game of touch. He reflected on the win and how
good it felt to be a part of the Wallaby picture. He was looking forward
to the next Test against Ireland in six days' time – his only wish was for
a better success rate with his goal kicks.

Jury's Hotel in Dublin is situated some five hundred metres from the
Lansdowne Road rugby ground and apart from its proximity to the
action, it also has a very Irish feel about it. The sign in the car park
advertises the fact that the dining room is open twenty-three hours a
day. The Wallabies could never discover what happens for the other
sixty minutes!

Lynagh roomed with Farr-Jones and on the morning of the Test, the pair jogged to the ground for a kick on the back oval. Lynagh couldn't miss. Every one straight between the posts. Farr-Jones was impressed. Lynagh looked to have taken that form into the game by opening the scoring with a forty-metre drop goal, but when he notched a penalty late in the match to seal Australia's 16–9 victory, it was his only successful kick from five attempts. A 20 per cent success rate doesn't keep you in the job at this level. Nor does it prevent you from becoming an easy target yourself. On the way to training for the next match against Ulster, the team bus drove past a disused rugby field where the decrepit goalposts leant at a forty-five degree angle. 'Stop the bus,' screamed Ella. 'Give Noddy a go at those – he might get one!'

Lynagh was concerned with his inaccuracy at both Twickenham and Lansdowne Road but, satisfied with his general play, wasn't too worried as the tour moved on to Limerick. Halfway to a Grand Slam, Jones was beginning to warm to his task. The intensity was increasing and his patience with some of the players' foibles decreasing. One particularly heavy drinking session at Bunratty Castle outside Limerick was seen by Jones as potentially damaging to the task at hand, and in circumstances like that he does not hold back. The team meeting the following morning saw Jones at his acerbic best. The playmakers of the previous night cowered as he launched into an angry tirade. He berated those who were perceived to be lacking in commitment, urging them to be aware of how they should take care of their bodies. As the team filed onto the bus for training, Chris Roche, who was not the most enthusiastic Jones listener, whispered, 'The only parts of my body that are sore are my bloody ears!'

Jones had given plenty of thought to Lynagh's lack of success with the boot and during a delay at Shannon airport while the team was waiting to fly to Wales, he confronted the youngster, getting straight to the point. 'I'm thinking of taking the goalkicking from you,' he said.

According to Jones, Lynagh was immediately on the defensive, but Lynagh's recollection varies. 'I wasn't overly concerned at not doing the kicking. In fact, when Alan told me I would definitely be in the team, I saw it as a stamp of approval. I was being picked for my foot-balling ability alone and not the fact that I could kick goals.' He felt a wave of relief at one burden of responsibility being lifted from him. It didn't mean though that he did not want the goalkicking role back. He was speaking to his father regularly and together they discussed what things might have been affecting his kicking.

'I was kicking well mid-week because when I played in those games I generally played flyhalf,' recalls Lynagh. 'At inside centre I was play-ing at a lot higher arousal level because of the extra tackling required. Dad had looked back at the Ireland and England games and said that although I was striking them okay they were still just missing, and he felt it was because I'd been rushing them – a consequence of this high arousal level. He thought having the break from kicking was a good idea and he sent me this tape telling me what I should be doing. It basi-cally came down to doing everything in slow motion.'

The Wallabies were staying in the coastal town of Porthcawl for the Welsh Test and Lynagh and Burke, the team's surfing freaks, roomed together. Three years earlier the previous Wallaby team had been snowed in at Porthcawl, and Parramatta winger Mick Martin gained some notoriety by going for a swim. His resultant hypothermia was well publicised and dissuaded the two 1984 surfies from actually getting wet. Certainly there was no chance of a quick dip on the morn-ing of the Test as the heavens opened and torrential rain fell. Although not overjoyed at the thought of playing in the slop, Lynagh was thank-ful he did not have to worry about the goalkicking. That was Roger Gould's problem.

Miraculously, the weather improved. Australia played superbly. Lynagh scored his second try in three Tests and Gould snagged five out of seven. Life was sweet.

Touring rugby squads can often be divided into two distinct teams – the main fifteen that play the important games and the others who become a sort of support staff. This tour was no different, with the mid-week team happily referring to themselves as the 'green machine', and aware that in no small way they were contributing to the overall success. Spirit was high. While Jones was known to occasionally explode, berating anyone guilty of sloppiness, he could also overdo the praise. The team broke into spontaneous laughter at a team meeting following the Welsh Test, when Jones singled out the experienced winger Peter Grigg for his good form.

'You're on fire Griggy,' he enthused. 'You're playing better than you can!' Whatever Grigg did for the rest of the tour, no matter how mundane or simple, team-mates were there to remind him that he was playing 'better than he could'.

Three Melbourne Cups were in the cabinet and the fourth was up for grabs at Murrayfield. Lynagh had enjoyed his rest from goalkicking but was refreshed, ready, and perhaps mindful of the fact that the last time he had been at Murrayfield he had kicked five goals and scored a try for the Australian Schoolboys.

For one of the few times in his life, Jones was unsure which course of action to take. Gould had been a runaway hit in Cardiff but there was no doubt Lynagh was the team's best kicker. At training, Jones explained to Lynagh that he wished to do some individual work with him. 'We're going to get some bad ball against Scotland,' he explained, 'and we are not going to be able to use it, so it will probably be a good time to have a drop at goal.' The ball was rolled behind Lynagh a dozen or so times. He turned, gathered and snapped at goal. Jones was observing closely. Not for the reasons he had just given, but rather to judge if the rhythm was back in Lynagh's kicking. The field they were training on was something of a bog, but Lynagh kept banging the ball between the posts. There was the answer.

Back at the team hotel, Jones bumped into respected *Sydney Morning Herald* sports writer Jim Webster, who asked which kicker would be used in the Test. Before Jones could answer, Webster said, 'If I were you I'd let Lynagh kick for goal.' Jones thanked him and then went to Lynagh's room. He had a general chat about the following day's match with Lynagh and room-mate Peter Grigg, but when Jones left, Lynagh followed him into the hallway.

'Who is kicking for goal tomorrow, Alan?'

'I've absolutely no idea Michael, but if I were a betting man, I'd have a few bob on a bloke named Lynagh. I wouldn't worry about it though. I'd just go to bed.'

The coach and captain checked the state of the field and the weather conditions early on the Saturday morning and returning to the hotel, Jones sought out Gould.

'Mate, would you have any problems if we give Noddy the goal kicks this afternoon?'

'Jonesy, you can give 'em to Mother Teresa if you want, as long as she kicks 'em and we win!'

Irish referee Stephen Hilditch awarded Australia the first kickable penalty of the game. The success or failure of this one strike might determine the Wallabies' fate. It was not the most difficult kick Lynagh had ever faced: twenty-six metres out and fifteen metres to the right of the posts. It wasn't quite bread-and-butter stuff, but it should not be missed. The pressure was on the youngest player on the pitch.

'I remembered what Dad had been saying,' says Lynagh. 'I just went into slow motion as I lined up that kick. You are much more able to perform a fine motor skill with a low arousal level. Goalkicking is like asking a golfer to run between shots, tackle somebody, pass a golf club to someone and then sink a six-metre putt. It's the same sort of thing and it's not easy to do. Preparing for this particular kick, I dug the hole for the ball very slowly and deliberately, just to ensure I was slowing myself down.'

Slowly, slowly, slowly … bang. The ball did not deviate a centimetre as it travelled between the uprights. 'That kick was pretty monumental for me,' says Lynagh. 'I'd rate it one of my best ever.'

By the full-time whistle, Lynagh had equalled the Australian points-scoring record. Eight successful kicks from nine attempts reaped him twenty-one points and Australia's 37–12 win had afforded the Eighth Wallabies rugby immortality.

Rugby journalist Norman Mair did not hold back in his report in the *Scotsman* on 9 December.

> It is no fun watching Scotland being beaten, let alone thrashed. Not normally – but on Saturday the rugby of the Wallabies transcended mere patriotism and left anyone with a real feeling for the game enchanted. The crowd saluted them rather as they used to rise to Don Bradman after he had butchered the England attack.
>
> 'Poetry and murder lived in him together,' said Somerset's Scotsman, R. C. Robertson-Glasgow, of the Don and so might we say of the Wallabies who took Scotland apart at Murrayfield.

After Sunday's early morning call from his Adelaide fan, Lynagh set off with the team to celebrate. A kindly local opened his bar to the Wallabies, and Lynagh found himself in a drinking team with props Andy McIntyre and Cameron Lillicrap and lock Nigel Holt. This was esteemed company, and on the drinks menu was a particularly powerful little Scottish cocktail called 'sheep dip'. A couple of these, interspersed with the odd tequila slammer had Lynagh feeling no pain. The 'boy drunk' had graduated.

That night the team was to leave Edinburgh and travel to Cardiff for the final two games of the tour against Pontypool and the Barbarians. The team assembled at the train station to catch the overnighter to Bristol. By this time, Noddy was somewhat tired and emotional. As he attempted to retreat to his sleeping compartment, he found the way in the narrow aisle blocked by the not-so-narrow figures of Tom Lawton, Holt and McIntyre. A little playful pushing and shoving, and a short time later Lynagh was on the floor. 'Doormat' came the call from Roger Gould. Any frisky Wallaby within earshot came rushing down the aisle, and with no regard for the health or well-being of Australia's latest record-holder, traipsed all over the prone figure of Michael Lynagh.

From hero to doormat in twenty-four hours; rugby can do that to you.

6
BLEDISLOE BLISS

Warmth, beautiful warmth; a Grand Slam was one thing but a rolling surf under a generous sun was another. The Eighth Wallabies arrived home five days before Christmas 1984, with civic receptions and other trappings of triumph awaiting them. Michael Lynagh hightailed it to the coast. The tour had brought unparalleled success but it didn't take away from the fact that it was in many ways a chore. As one who takes responsibility so seriously, there was never a chance for Lynagh to fully relax until the tour was completed. Only the beach could provide that relaxation. It was less than a month before training for the coming season would begin, and all Lynagh wanted in that time was his surfboard, the use of his parents' beach unit on the Gold Coast, a television to watch the summer of cricket and the company of some of his old school-mates.

The routine was standard: a few hours in the surf, a couple of beers at the Broadbeach Hotel beer garden, games of touch footy in the park or on the beach and the odd evening of night-clubbing. This was the perfect wind-down from a year of achievement and the ideal curtain-raiser to any further challenges that 1985 might bring.

It should have been a boom year for rugby in Australia. Thanks to the Grand Slam, the code had gained unprecedented coverage and excited far greater public interest than ever before, but if appetites had been whetted, there was meagre fare on offer. The international program at home was limited to visits by Canada and Fiji. Australia, recently crowned heavyweight champion, was up against a couple of bantamweights. Any chance to capitalise on the Wallabies' newly won popularity was lost.

Administrators were trapped between a rock and a hard place. Experience in 1976 and 1982 had taught them that Wallaby teams returning from long tours of the British Isles generally suffered a let-down the following season. Subjecting them to a rigorous home campaign involved high risk. Not only was there the chance of jaded players performing poorly, but the mass withdrawals from the 1982 Wallaby tour of New Zealand had alerted authorities to another concern. As an amateur game, rugby was bleeding its top players dry. Players involved in all matches for both state and country could be expected to spend anything from four to six months each year away from family, study or work. With not a cent of compensation paid at state level, and the princely sum of about $20 a day offered as expenses while on national duty, players and officials realised there was a limit to the number of sacrifices that could be made.

Rugby's marketing men were also dismayed at Mark Ella's retire-ment. Even before scoring a try in each of the internationals on the Grand Slam tour he had been the code's most marketable figure, and at the age of twenty-five had a potential minimum of five years left at the top level. But Ella was not to be dissuaded. He left in some-what controversial circumstances, writing in the *Sydney Morning Herald* on 6 April 1985 that he would find it difficult to continue playing under the coaching of Alan Jones. His claim that Jones' methods made it hard for him to enjoy his rugby resulted in a widely held perception in the rugby community that Jones was, wittingly or other-wise, the man who drove the much-revered Ella out of the game. Ella's conversation with Michael Lynagh in a Toulouse hotel late in 1983 suggests this was not the case. Ella had decided before Alan Jones even applied to coach the Australian team that 1984 would be his final year in the game.

Lynagh had relished playing alongside Ella and, although disappointed that a player of his stature should leave the game so soon, was only too willing to take the opportunity offered. He was champing at the bit to get that gold number ten on his back. Ella himself had few doubts about the quality of his successor. In the *Sydney Morning Herald* on 15 June 1985, the morning of the first Test against Canada and Lynagh's first as Australia's flyhalf, Ella wrote:

> I wouldn't argue with his being the best five-eighth in the world right now. In fact, I think that in the next eighteen months, he'll become one of the world's best rugby players, regardless of his position, and will remain there for just as long as he wants.

As his Test debut against Fiji a year earlier had been a low-key affair, so too was the match with Canada. The most significant feature was that the game marked not only Lynagh's first Test as flyhalf, but the beginning of a halfback combination with Nick Farr-Jones that became the linchpin of the Australian rugby machine on another forty-six occasions.

To offset the paltry offerings at home, there was a one-off Bledisloe Cup Test against New Zealand scheduled in Auckland. The closeness of the series between the two sides twelve months earlier, and the Wallabies' subsequent victories in the United Kingdom, meant the match was billed as a world championship. Retirements and injury had robbed Australia of a number of experienced backs including Ella, Roger Gould, David Campese and Brendan Moon, and the All Blacks won a lacklustre game 10–9 to maintain the tradition of close matches between the two countries. For both Lynagh and Farr-Jones, it was the first time they had confronted the All Blacks and also their first taste of defeat in the international arena. After the game the pair sat together on the bus journey from Eden Park back to the team hotel in Takapuna on Auckland's north shore.

'Nick and I tried to work out what had gone wrong,' remembers Lynagh. 'We agreed that going into the match we'd held the All Blacks in awe because so many people had told us how tough they were, but we agreed it wasn't anywhere near the ordeal we thought it might be. Australia had lost that game rather than New Zealand winning it and we made a little agreement with each other that it would be the last time. There was a full series the following year and we now knew what we were up against and wouldn't be so hesitant. We were disappointed about the loss but in many ways it just made us very keen for the twelve months to roll by so we could get back and have a crack at them.'

After the glories of the previous season, Lynagh had been given an early lesson that things didn't always go according to plan in the hurly-burly of international rugby; 1985 was a 'nothing' year – meaningless victories against second-tier rugby nations and a one-point loss in the only game that mattered.

The wear and tear of four years in representative rugby was also beginning to take its toll. Some of the finest goalkickers in world rugby have been known to go to some trouble to avoid any undue physical confrontations in the course of a game, but Lynagh was no shirker. He had broken the ring finger on his right hand in training during the week leading up to the Bledisloe Cup match, but despite the discomfort took his place in the side. His knees were also giving him trouble and when he returned to Australia, underwent an arthroscope to repair torn cartilage, which ruled him out of the Fijian series.

He recovered in time to help his old club University force a berth in the Brisbane grand final. University hadn't won a premiership for six years and went into the match against Wests as narrow favourite. However, an incorrect ruling from Kerry Fitzgerald, the world's leading referee before his premature death in 1992, denied victory to the students. Fitzgerald ruled a field goal to Wests' Tim Lane as fair, but all at the ground saw what the television replay later confirmed – the ball had gone under the crossbar, not over. The resulting three points were enough to get the Bulldogs home to a 10–7 victory.

University was not the type of club to hold a grudge. 'We invited Kerry to a pre-season cricket match at the club the following January,' recalls Lynagh. 'There were all sorts of prizes on offer, one of which was a six-pack of beer for anyone who could hit a six over the crossbar of the goalposts at the end of the field. We told Kerry that as he found it tough to distinguish the difference, he'd get the six-pack even if it went under.'

Most of the class-mates with whom Lynagh had begun his Human Movements course at the beginning of 1982 were by this time ready to enter the big wide world with a couple of impressive looking letters after their names. Lynagh had spent more time on rugby endeavours than at lectures, and although he enjoyed university life when he was there, the course he had chosen was at this stage in his career more a time-filler than anything else.

He had finished school at the end of 1981 armed with good enough results to provide him with several career options. Law was considered, but he wasn't convinced about actually becoming a lawyer. He had always been good at economics at school and maintained an interest in that subject, but was unsure if it appealed as a full-time profession. Sport was his great love, and the four-year Human Movements course, previously known as Physical Education, was about sport.

'A few of my friends were doing it and I was happy to do something that involved a fair amount of activity, but realistically I had little idea where I was heading professionally. Although at the start of 1982 my studies were number-one priority, by the middle of that year, and certainly by the start of the next, things had changed. My concerns and goals then became almost exclusively rugby-oriented and I never seriously considered pursuing anything in the physical education line. The only line I was really interested in was the goal line!'

Lynagh was a tap on the head for any rugby invitation and Human Movements could get along without him. So in November 1985 he found himself in Dubai for a seven-a-side tournament when most of his class-mates were suffering exam pressure. Noddy would defer ...

and defer ... and defer. But if he ever found himself in Australia long enough to actually sit for an exam, there was little chance he'd fail. His pride made sure of that.

If the 1985 rugby program resembled a famine, 1986 was a veritable feast. In the 1990s complaints abound that top-level rugby has become too time-consuming for amateur players, but the enormous time commitment is not something that has just occurred. Lynagh's 1986 itinerary is evidence of that. On New Year's Day he left Australia with the Queensland team for a one-month tour of the British Isles and Europe. He was back in time to play in the Hong Kong Sevens tournament, before jetting off to Britain once more, this time as part of an invitational World XV. All this was prior to the season proper in which, aside from state commitments, he would be involved in Test matches against Italy and France, a two-match series against Argentina and then the big one – a three-Test, seven-week tour of New Zealand from July to September.

While the Wallabies have come to expect five-star treatment when they travel, this is not always the case with provincial sides. Queensland arrived in London for their pre-season tour on a bleak morning and were shuffled off to the Hyde Park Towers Hotel. For a person travelling alone with no more than a couple of handkerchiefs for luggage the rooms were adequate. For a representative rugby team in which hefty beasts with lots of luggage are the norm rather than the exception, the rooms were a joke. Within twenty-four hours, management had arranged a move and the side moved to a nearby hotel with rooms where a cat could at least be swung.

But if accommodation in London was bad, Amsterdam was worse. When rugby teams arrive at new locations, there is always great anticipation about who your room-mate might be for the next few days. Snorers and smokers are to be avoided at all costs and if you happen to be of average build you avoid rooming with one of the many giants that are generally among the party. The quickest some players move on tour is when a bus arrives at a new hotel and they scurry into reception to secure the key before their mate, so as to nab what is usually the only double-bed in the room. (However, when you are rooming with a person twice your size, physical threats usually confine the smaller person to the single bed. Early possession counts for little.)

On arrival at the Queensland team's hotel in Amsterdam, the room lists were read out: Cook and Martin, Slack and Gardner, Lynagh and Frawley. Lynagh was delighted. A good friend from school-days, he knew Frawley's habits weren't too disconcerting and he would have been only too happy to sacrifice the double-bed to allow the far larger frame of Frawley some comfort.

What double-bed?

'The room was so small,' recalls Lynagh, 'that Frawls used to have to put one leg out the window and stand on the bed to get dressed. He couldn't fit into the bathroom and if he wanted to get changed I had to leave the room.'

As most of the other rooms were of similar dimensions, the players soon worked out that the less time they spent in them the better. Lynagh, Frawley and indeed the majority of the side, became regular customers of the Bulldog Bar – a local establishment where two blackboards revealed not only the prices of the various beers on sale but also the cost of the different forms and quality of hashish and cannabis available. Although not interested himself in experimenting, Lynagh did gain some amusement from the antics of some of the bar's local patrons. Before the tour, each player had been given a bright red-and-blue striped woollen jumper and, as the bitterly cold weather dictated, rare was the occasion they were not worn. With the amount of time the team spent in the Bulldog Bar it was inevitable the heavy and varied scents that wafted through that cosy retreat would remain temporarily trapped in the thick Australian wool.

The Queenslanders defeated Holland 54–4, and less than twelve hours after celebrating at their favourite Amsterdam haunt were in the customs area at Milan airport. The distinctive jumpers were a big hit with the sniffer dogs, and the local police must have thought they had stumbled across a uniformed team of drug-smugglers. The dogs eventually confined their attention to team-members Ross Hanley and Michael Cook and the laughter that initially broke out when the dogs bailed up the pair soon turned into looks of concern on the faces of team management and players. No, they couldn't have been that stupid ... could they? As one of the team duty boys, and therefore responsible for the supposedly smooth running of the day's activities, Lynagh was damn sure that if two of his team-mates were to be locked up for smuggling drugs, his reputation as a duty boy would be severely dented! He and team manager John Breen accompanied the two suspects to a room where every last item of their luggage was thoroughly searched. Toothpaste tubes were squeezed dry, gifts intended for loved ones unwrapped and checked, every last item gone through with the proverbial fine tooth comb.

There was generous applause from their team-mates when Cook and Hanley eventually emerged, without handcuffs and swearing that the first thing they'd do when they got to the hotel would be to throw those wretched woolly jumpers in the rubbish bin.

The weather for most matches on the tour ranged from cold and wet to extremely cold and extremely wet, but Lynagh's confidence at provincial level was by this time sky-high. The game against Ulster in Belfast was played in the worst circumstances imaginable. Many of the older players, who had suffered some atrocious conditions in their time, claimed they could remember nothing to match it. The rain fell in horizontal sheets, such was the strength of the freezing cold wind. Ulster had been unbeaten in their previous seventeen matches, but thanks to two Lynagh penalties, Queensland upset the locals to record a 6–4 win. Lynagh considers his second goal as one of the most memorable of his career.

'We were awarded a penalty fifteen metres out from the line and just to the right of the posts. In normal circumstances a very straightforward kick.' Nothing, though, is straightforward when you are kicking into a howling gale. 'I took my normal walk back and then came in and hit it absolutely as hard as I could. It went through the posts and the touch judges' flags went up. However by this time the wind had got hold of the ball and it came back around the goalpost and landed parallel to me and thirty metres to the left!'

The full-time whistle was the sweetest of notes and sacrificing sportsmanship for common sense, the entire Queensland team forewent the normal obligatory handshaking with the opposition and raced to the dressing room. Without removing their muddied boots, jerseys or shorts the players stood under the hot showers until the warmth gradually returned to their bodies. For flanker Jeff Miller, it took longer than most. A case of hypothermia was not one of the dangers he'd considered when first warned of the hazards of rugby! Lynagh rates the conditions as the poorest he has played in, but my own diary notes from that day suggest his play was not affected. 'We won the game 6–4 in by far the worst conditions I have experienced – I even wore gloves. Slatts and Noddy though were superb.'

Midway through the tour, Lynagh learned he had been selected in an overseas squad to play two matches in Britain in April as part of the centenary celebrations of the International Rugby Board. The squad included nine Wallabies, eight All Blacks, six South Africans and two Frenchmen. With South Africa's Naas Botha and New Zealand's Wayne Smith also in the twenty-three-man outfit, Lynagh played only in the first game against the British Lions at Cardiff. With team-mates such as Serge Blanco, Patrick Esteve, John Kirwan, Murray Mexted and Schalk Burger, he understood he had been afforded quite an honour.

Officially at that time, South Africa was very much out of the inter-national sporting scene, but aware of the passion the South Africans had for their rugby, the Australian and New Zealand players were very curious about their Springbok team-mates. One thing Lynagh quickly discovered was that if South Africa were to ever re-enter the legitimate rugby brotherhood, they would not lack for size.

'I remember we assembled for the distribution of gear and called out our shorts sizes. Even the Springbok backs were big, but prop Flippie Van Der Merwe was unbelieveable.' Lynagh ... 34, Mexted ... 40, Farr-Jones ... 36, Blanco ... trente-huit, Lawton ... 46, Van Der Merwe ... 52!

While he was pretty impressed at the physical presence of the South Africans, Lynagh was also taken by the intense and conscientious attitude the All Blacks in the squad showed during training sessions. It is impossible to dull the competitive nature of international sportsmen, but tours of this nature usually include a slightly more laid-back approach to training. In all honesty, they are often junkets. Not so, seemingly, for the All Blacks. They appeared very serious indeed.

'First of all I thought the All Blacks were just gearing up for the Wallaby tour of New Zealand later that year, but it wasn't until the happy hour after our second and final game that they actually let us in on the secret,' said Lynagh. 'They were going straight from London to South Africa for an unsanctioned tour of the Republic.'

The New Zealand Cavaliers played a four-Test series against South Africa, and caused a huge uproar within official New Zealand rugby circles. The barks of the administrators though, proved far worse than their bites; the players involved were given only a one-match suspension on their return home. For his part, Lynagh wished his team-mates from across the Tasman well, even though he harboured reservations about such a tour. From both an ethical and a rugby standpoint, he felt it was not the right thing to do. He also believed it was none of his business and therefore kept his opinion to himself.

What had delighted him was the attitude of the All Blacks toward himself and fellow Wallabies in the team. 'Up to that point, the only time we really met these guys was on the field and at after-match functions. Naturally, the competitive nature of Australia versus

New Zealand sporting contests makes it pretty difficult to forge great friendships and a certain distrust can develop. However, we all got on really well, with all parties making attempts to break down any barriers that might have existed. It went some way to showing we are not as different as some people might like to pretend.'

Social niceties aside, his business was helping Australia win rugby games and that meant the next few months would see him working overtime. As well as games against Argentina and Italy, a single Test against the French was included in the Wallabies' build-up to the Bledisloe Cup series in New Zealand. On their day the French are capable of producing an ethereal style of rugby, one that even the best Australian or New Zealand sides cannot match; they play as though there is a musical vibration to the game. When the 1986 French tourists met Queensland at Ballymore, they played like an entire orchestra. Their 48–9 win over one of the world's top provincial sides was labelled as the ultimate rugby performance. Coaches waxed lyrical about the skill and panache displayed. Some suggested conventional coaching videos would become passé. Budding youngsters need only watch a replay of the France–Queensland match to learn how the game should be played. For the Queenslanders, particularly Lynagh and those others who would be confronting the French for Australia the following Saturday at the Sydney Cricket Ground, the replay was more a horror movie than a coaching video.

Once again Alan Jones had a chance to triumph against the odds. 'Alan was really excited at the thought of the challenge of turning things around in six days,' remembers Lynagh. He wasn't quite as excited about the loss of brilliant inside centre Brett Papworth, another of Lynagh's former Australian Schoolboy team-mates. Papworth's climb up the senior representative ladder had been stalled by a wrongly held belief that his tackling was suspect. Just as he convinced the doubters of their error, injury intervened and he was ruled out of contention for the French Test. However, there had never been question marks over the defensive capabilities of his replacement. Michael Cook had been nailing opposition inside centres to the floor since his first XV days at Gregory Terrace. He might not have possessed the lightning-quick sidestep of Papworth, but there was no doubt the French midfield would have their work cut out finding a passage past him. Since he had played beside Cook at school, club and provincial level, Lynagh had just the recipe to erase any nerves the new boy might have been suffering in his Test debut.

Australia won good possession in the opening moments of the Test and, as usual, the Farr-Jones pass to Lynagh was swift and precise. Up she went. Spectators still searching for their seats would have had time to get to the top of the Bradman Stand and back again by the time this Garryowen started its descent. Underneath it stood Serge Blanco, one of the game's most exciting players. As he had been chasing Lynagh's Garryowens since he was sixteen, Cook was well-versed in the art. The timing was spot-on, and as Blanco took the ball he also took the full force of Cook's ninety-odd kilograms. The match was won in that phase of play. The confidence France had extracted from the Queensland game suddenly counted for nothing, while the Lynagh and Cook combination erased any negative thoughts that might have been lingering in the minds of the Australians. There was of course, much work still to be done in the remaining seventy-nine minutes, but the early psychological battle had been decided.

Under pressure, the French tendency towards indiscipline surfaced and Lynagh showed his gratitude by booting a record twenty-three points, taking Australia to a 27–14 victory. True, the French scored three tries to one, but it was a well-deserved Australian win and one in which Lynagh had conducted proceedings. Despite this, the fact that Australia had managed only one try initiated a spirited debate on whether rugby authorities had the scoring system right. With field goals and penalty goals worth three points and tries, at that time, only worth four, there was a widely held belief that an imbalance existed.

Teams were encouraged to play for the penalty rather than the try, which lead to a more stagnant style of rugby.

No doubt there was merit in the eventual decision in 1992 to raise the value of a try to five points; Jones however, had argued vehemently with International Rugby Board representatives that to devalue the penalty goal was to belittle the rare skills of players such as Lynagh.

'Lynagh is very quick, has lovely balance, is a good runner and passes the ball beautifully,' says Jones. 'But the point is that kicking is a remarkable skill, and the aim of the game is to win, while the subsidiary objectives are both to entertain and leave people coming off the paddock so they've enjoyed the game.'

Jones' debates with administrators were always an entertaining sideshow. This one was no exception.

'Before making these decisions in smoke-filled rooms, why don't we give everyone six balls each?' suggested Jones in his typically provocative manner. 'We'll go out and line them all up on the twenty-two-metre line, within spitting distance of the posts. We can all have six kicks each and if we all get three out of six, I guess we would have to say it's pretty easy to kick for goal. However I'd venture to say most of us would score nought. This is a skill of the game and the laws of the game should reward skill.'

With South Africa out of the picture, Australia's search for undisputed champion status was almost complete. The Wallabies had beaten England, Ireland, Wales, Scotland and France in their most recent clashes with those countries and now only the All Blacks remained. An easy series victory over Argentina, in which Lynagh equalled his French feat by again scoring twenty-three points in a Test, was followed by the big one – a full series against the All Blacks in New Zealand.

The Wallabies assembled in Sydney for a three-day training camp before departing for New Zealand. Lynagh was not looking forward to this camp with any relish. Normally, the training sessions at these pre-tour affairs are numerous, arduous, lengthy and occasionally pointless. Lynagh could handle the numerous and arduous aspects but he has always argued that any training that takes three hours can be done more efficiently in two. He was subsequently delighted when he realised training was confined to once a day and it was short, taxing and purposeful. The players really didn't need any extra motivation, but on the Saturday afternoon before departing for the Shaky Isles, the team went to the Sydney Cricket Ground to watch their rugby league cousins take on and beat New Zealand – all good, healthy, psychological points-scoring.

Although they knew that a 6.45 am wake-up call was scheduled on the Monday morning, Lynagh and a few other golfing fanatics in the side congregated on Sunday evening to watch the live telecast of the British Open from Turnberry. When Greg Norman sank the final putt to snare his first major championship, little did the Shark know there was a bunch of Wallabies riding on his back. There was time for just over three hours' sleep before setting off for our own major championship, but it had been a great weekend for Australian sport and the 1986 Wallabies were determined to keep the flag flying.

Lynagh was left out of the first game on tour. Fullback Andrew Leeds made an auspicious debut for Australia kicking seventeen points as a rusty-looking Wallaby outfit drew with Waikato 21–all. That match in Hamilton was played under sunny skies and on a firm pitch. It didn't take long for the damper reality of touring life in New Zealand to settle in. Down it came the next day – in bucketfuls. It didn't stop for three days and on the morning of the match against Manawatu in Palmerston North, the impossible happened. The rain got heavier!

It was the sort of day where all sensible lads stay indoors, but locals tend to frown on international touring sides who fail to show up for their scheduled fixtures. The match turned into the slow-moving chess game that rugby can become in those conditions, but the closeness of the scores maintained the interest. Two penalties apiece had the scores locked at 6–all when, with only a minute to go Australia received a penalty twenty-two metres out and fifteen metres to the right of the posts. In those conditions no kick is easy, and since he had slotted just two from his previous seven attempts Lynagh knew this one was far from a certainty. He also knew he had to give it a go. Unfortunately, this was not a piece of thinking prop Enrique Rodriguez appeared to share. Before the captain or goalkicker could grab the ball and calm things down, 'Topo' had taken a quick tap and hurtled headlong into the opposing defence. *Topo* is Spanish for mole, and his fellow Wallabies were ready to bury their Argentinian team-mate two metres under, when the referee awarded another penalty against the home side. Topo was off the hook, and although time was up on the clock, Lynagh had the chance to secure an Australian victory.

The ground was waterlogged, it was cold and windy and the ball was an oval ball of soap. The home supporters provided a chorus of catcalls and whistles and the angle of the kick was anything but a cinch. 'That's the sort of pressure I like,' said Lynagh afterwards. Some might argue there lurks a masochist beneath those curly golden locks but Lynagh sees it differently. 'If you're the goalkicker, it's the sort of situation you like to be in. I never thought of missing it and it was the best one I hit all day.' The final tally of 9–6 in the Wallabies' favour was his reward.

Lynagh might well have got used to kicking in the rain because there were to be only two Saturday matches for the rest of the tour when rain didn't fall. Neither of those coincided with the Test matches. The sun shone during the week but it was certain that when the grey clouds gathered, the weekend was at hand. Nevertheless, the Wallabies approached the first Test in Wellington with an undefeated record. A telegram from Sir Donald Bradman on the eve of the match alerted the team to the interest back home, and although there was also a message of good luck for the players from Prime Minister Bob Hawke, it paled into insignificance beside that from the Don. Lynagh has enormous respect for exceptional sporting figures who, in his eyes, carry themselves with dignity away from the field of play. To be in the thoughts of a legend such as Bradman gave Lynagh and his team-mates a great boost.

Wind is the one thing that can mar a rugby game more than mud and slush and rain, and no place on the rugby atlas is more likely to provide a healthy breeze than Wellington. One of the local radio stations even calls itself Radio Windy. Despite a good recent record there, Australian teams rarely enjoy playing in the wind tunnel known as Athletic Park, and when Lynagh, clad in mittens and beanie, inspected the playing surface on the day before the match, it seemed obvious the Wallabies' hopes of playing a free-flowing game would be stifled by the conditions.

Friday's gale turned into a solid downfield southerly on Saturday and after winning the toss, the Australians opted to run with it at their back. Opinion varies on whether running into or with the wind is the better option, but as captain, I was firmly of the belief that we should use it while it was there. After all, the wind might ease in the second half. And even if it didn't, there was always the danger in having the elements with you in the second forty minutes that the team's intensity would drop, believing the conditions would do all the work. Certainly there was enough confidence in this Australian team to defend against anything in the second forty minutes.

Nevertheless, the nine points accumulated by half-time was not anything like a comfortable buffer. Lynagh converted a David Campese try and then added an ultimately crucial forty-seven-metre penalty to complete the first-half scoring, but by windy Wellington standards a 9–0 lead was chicken feed.

The All Blacks quickly used the wind to their advantage in the second half, nailing two penalties and getting to within three points of the Australians. Lynagh was under heavy pressure from the New Zealand backrow and we decided that Farr-Jones should divert some of that pressure. In tandem with his forwards, Farr-Jones used his strength and skill to exploit the short side and it was from one of these forays that the Australian backs manufactured a try for winger Matthew Burke. Despite a New Zealand try, which left Australian supporters with some well-chewed fingernails over the final ten minutes, the Wallabies hung on for a 13–12 win. It had not been Lynagh's finest Test match but even so, his first-half goals were the difference between winning and losing. Although Farr-Jones was undoubtedly Australia's man of the match, the contribution of Lynagh hadn't gone unnoticed.

'If he was a cricketer,' remarked one of his team-mates, 'he would be one of those blokes who, when he was out of touch, would still be able to make a century – even if it wasn't as pretty as usual.'

Not afraid to use the thoroughbred comparison when applicable, coach Jones decided his star 'colt' Lynagh could do with a spell. He would play no more games before the second Test at Dunedin in a fortnight. The Wallaby wagon rolled on to Buller on the west coast, where the pressure was a little less intense and Lynagh and a few of the the other crucial men in the Test XV could afford to relax. Piet de Groot was the most revered player in the local side, and it wasn't because of his rugby ability. Big Piet was the world coal-shovelling champion, and in those parts that was a mighty impressive addition to your curriculum vitae.

The Wallabies won 62–0, and although those few days on the west coast were used as a wind-down time, Jones didn't let any slackness creep into the side. There were a number of players in the touring party who were there more for the experience than as legitimate contenders for the Test side. Rod McCall, a young lock from Brisbane, who later was to play a significant role in Australia's successes in the 1990s, was one such rookie. In later years, the man known as 'Sergeant Slaughter' was a far cry from the shy type he appeared on this, his first Wallaby tour. Rarely short of an answer these days, he had no response then to Jones' inquisition after a couple of training sessions did not measure up to the standard required.

'Slaughter, when we assembled in Sydney a few weeks ago, did the ARU give you half a blazer? No they didn't. Did the Adidas man only give you one boot? No, he didn't. Did you only get half a tie when you got your number ones? No you didn't.' Jones raised the volume. 'Then Slaughter, can you tell me why you're only giving me 50 per cent on the training paddock?'

McCall might not have seen the funny side at the time, but it gave his team-mates quite a laugh.

After a somewhat disjointed first-Test effort, Jones was searching for a more expansive display in the second Test at Carisbrook in Dunedin. As usual, his assistant coach Alec Evans had the Wallaby scrum in great shape, but although a dominant scrum is a crucial factor in winning rugby matches it wouldn't secure victory on its own. 'A big serve might get you through the first couple of rounds at Wimbledon,' argued Jones, 'but you can be sure you won't be meeting the Duchess of Kent if you don't have any other shots in your repertoire.'

They suspend play if it rains at Wimbledon. If they did this in Dunedin you'd rarely see any rugby at all. Any plans of a grandiose, free-flowing game were sunk in the mud and slop of Carisbrook. The match turned into what the football commentators nowadays refer to as an 'arm wrestle' – a close physical encounter where ball movement is at a premium. In the closing moments it appeared it was going to be another occasion on which Lynagh would be called in to act as his team's saviour. Trailing 13–9, the Wallabies scored what seemed a legitimate try to number eight Steve Tuynman. Lynagh would have the chance to convert from wide out and give Australia not only their first victory in Dunedin in eighty-three years but also an unbeatable two-nil lead in the series. The Bledisloe Cup would travel to Australia. But Welsh referee Derek Bevan had other ideas. To the disbelief of the Australians and the unrestrained joy of the New Zealanders, Bevan ruled no try. Lynagh managed to kick a penalty soon after, but all too late as the All Blacks ran out 13–12 winners. Amazingly it was the fourth consecutive match between the two sides in which a single point was the winning margin.

David Campese, who was playing in his preferred position of full-back, found the wet weather very detrimental to the way he had hoped to play the game but although he bore some criticism for his fragility in the difficult conditions, his good mate Mark Ella came out in his defence, insisting Lynagh should share the blame for the Dunedin loss.

In his book *Path To Victory* Ella wrote:

> David Campese had a bad game in the second Test and blew some chances, but it was wrong to put so much of the blame on him. It just happened that a lot of his mistakes happened out in the open. At Campo's request, I went home and broke down each mistake that was made on a video of the Test. Whether the forwards had erred or the backs? Campese certainly wasn't the only offender, and a lot of our problems stemmed from Michael Lynagh, who for once was out of touch.

Lynagh agreed it had not been one of his better performances, but while some of his team-mates were absolutely shattered at the result, he kept the loss in perspective. 'I certainly was very disappointed, but by no means devastated. I never had any doubts that we could beat them in the next Test.'

Alan Jones was perhaps more annoyed than devastated by the loss and made the mistake of finding problems where they didn't exist. At the function after the Test, Nick Farr-Jones and Simon Poidevin were chatting cordially with Brian Lochore, the All Black coach. As members of the international side which Lochore had coached earlier that year, both Farr-Jones and Poidevin had become mates with the very likeable and highly respected Kiwi farmer. It was nothing more than friends exchanging social chit-chat but to Jones it must have seemed an indication of a lack of commitment to the cause. As captain of Jones-coached sides for three years, I believe this was Jones' single biggest mistake. He turned a meaningless conversation into an issue, and in so doing permanently damaged the relationship between himself and one of his most valuable players. Lynagh distanced himself from the drama.

'I think Alan had cranked things up since the Grand Slam but it was basically the same *modus operandi*,' says Lynagh. 'There were a few strange things and that problem after the Dunedin Test was one. Nick is a very outgoing person and after games he has always been very friendly with the opposition. He sees it as part of the game. With Alan it is warfare really. They're the enemy. You don't fraternise with them until the war is over. I think there is some common ground in the middle but at that time I just stayed out of it.'

In keeping with his penchant for providing the unexpected, Jones announced to all those who had played in the Test that they could have the Monday off and go and vent their frustrations on the golf course. All but one, that is. He summoned Lynagh to his room. 'Mate, I'm going to take the pressure off you,' announced the coach. 'You beauty,' thought Lynagh. 'He's going to tell me to go and play golf rather than train.'

'Against Southland, I want you to be fullback and captain.'

'Sorry. I thought you said you wanted to take the pressure off me!'

Lynagh had never played fullback nor captained Australia. Jones' interpretation of releasing pressure was obviously far different from his own. Jones failed to understand Lynagh's lack of enthusiasm for this latest honour. 'Look, I'm giving you the opportunity to captain your country,' he said. 'It'll give you a chance to chime in from the back, have a look at what's happening in front of you, and just get some perspective from a different position.'

'I appreciate the honour of the captaincy but I don't think playing fullback helps ease any pressure,' he responded. 'Besides there are other blokes here chosen as fullbacks who should be playing fullback.'

Unhappy or not, Lynagh led Australia in its best performance of the tour, accounting for Southland 55–0 in Invercargill, and showing just what could be done given a dry ball and a firm surface. Attention began to focus on Eden Park; the two remaining matches against Bay of Plenty and Thames Valley were only skirmishes in the march towards the real battle. Before the Thames Valley game, Jones managed to get most of New Zealand offside by his inflammatory comments about the hotels allotted to the Wallabies in the tiny town of Thames. For locals in a town like this it is often the honour of a lifetime to host international sporting teams. Unfortunately, some of these places don't have the large and well-equipped establishments such teams have come to expect. In Thames, they didn't have a hotel big enough to accommodate the whole team. With just three days to go before one of the most important matches in Australia's rugby history, the Wallabies were not even staying together; the team was split up between the town's two hotels. There was no doubt it was an unsatisfactory arrangement. Jones had made his feelings clear on these matters prior to the first Test in Wellington. 'When players are putting money through the turnstiles and playing for the enjoyment of the game, they're entitled to a decent room and a decent feed.'

None of the 1986 Wallabies disagreed with this sentiment. However, while Jones' criticisms were aimed more at the New Zealand rugby administrators who had set the itinerary, his less than complimentary remarks about the hotels in Thames were taken somewhat to heart by the good folk of the valley and the Wallabies became public enemy number one.

Even his greatest detractors don't argue that Jones can be a first-class motivator and there was no doubt he did a sterling job for the Thames Valley team on this occasion. Although one of the weaker teams the Wallabies faced on tour, they came out like the All Blacks themselves. Lynagh had been seconded to commentate for a local radio station and was perched atop the caravan that doubled as a grandstand when play began. He got a bird's-eye view.

'Thames Valley kicked off and the ball went behind our winger Peter Grigg. He dived on it and the whole Thames Valley pack went over the top of him. Eventually our forwards arrived on the scene and pushed them back. Thames then got their second wind and pushed our guys back. It went back and forth a few times and all the while beneath these thirty-two rampaging boots Griggy was being tossed around like a rag doll. The crowd went absolutely bananas and for everyone but Griggy it was pretty funny.'

It turned out to be a bad week for Grigg. He was dropped for the Test, and fullback Andrew Leeds made his Test debut, releasing David Campese to the wing.

On the morning of the match on 6 September, Greg Campbell, rugby writer for the *Australian* newspaper offered this opinion on who held the key for Australia. Under a heading 'Lynagh Approaches His Everest', Campbell began:

> Australia will be looking to Michael Lynagh for its finest hour in rugby union against New Zealand in the third and deciding Bledisloe Cup Test at Eden Park here today. Lynagh, the Australian five-eighth, faces the triple mission of landing the all-important goal kicks, of being the the linchpin as the backline plans to spin the ball wide, and also of keeping Frano Botica, the All Blacks most lethal attacking weapon, penned.

Campbell had read it accurately. Another mighty Australian forward effort was required to repel an All Blacks team hell-bent on attack, and the defence of the Wallabies was simply outstanding. But while Farr-Jones was once again the man of the match, it was Lynagh who paid the dues. He kicked five goals for a fourteen-point contribution in the 22–9 win. His penalty goal midway through the second half, which earned the Wallabies a winning nine-point break, was described by Jones as the most memorable moment of the tour. It was also one of the rare times Lynagh showed any emotion on the field after a successful kick. Usually, no matter how crucial the goal, Lynagh will turn, go back to his position and ready himself for the kick-off without a hint of a smile or any visible sign of his pleasure. This time though, there was a quick little air punch; it wasn't flamboyant in any way, but enough of a sign to his family, friends and team-mates that this was a significant moment in his rugby career. That goal had secured the Bledisloe Cup. He was a member of the first Australian team in thirty-seven years to wrest the symbol of trans-Tasman rugby supremacy from the All Blacks on their own soil.

The moment a team wins an important victory such as this one by the 1986 Wallabies is never the appropriate time for an individual to contemplate personal achievement. But the statisticians would have noted that Lynagh had notched 200 Test points in just fifteen matches. A measure of the magnitude of that record is that Paul McLean, previously Australia's highest points-scorer, had finished his thirty-one-match Test career with 263 points.

For Lynagh, the satisfaction at completing his task successfully was complemented by the delight of not having to think about rugby matters for a few months at least. It had been a hectic, if enjoyable schedule and now, for the first time in 1986, he was able to ponder on matters other than the game. He was a month away from his twenty-third birthday and had begun to contemplate what life after rugby might hold.

7
THE DEVIL'S NUMBER

Although Michael Lynagh realised the Human Movements course he had undertaken at the University of Queensland would not be all touch footy games and study of past sporting contests, he had hoped a fair percentage of it might centre around these activities. However, the academic reality was somewhat less appealing. It took only a couple of anatomy lectures for him to make that discovery.

When you are used to the sun, surf and the great outdoors, a laboratory can be a pretty cold place – particularly when it's full of corpses. Twice a week for three hours, Lynagh and 140 of his fellow 'Movers' – the label given to Human Movement students – descended into the university laboratory, headquarters for the compulsory subject of anatomy. Groups of six were allotted to each of the many stainless steel benches that were spread throughout the room, and as a mark of respect and for the more practical reason of hygiene, everyone was required to wear a white lab coat. At the end of the benches stood large bins, in which were stored various body parts. The morticians, the special few who worked full-time in the lab, were responsible for preparing the benches for the students and ensuring the correct parts were laid out and ready for study on a particular day – one day a torso, one day a shin bone, another, the whole body.

This was not the sort of environment anyone, let alone a particularly sensitive character like Michael Lynagh, steps into with any great gusto or enthusiasm. Not initially anyway. The saving grace was that if he was ever going to feel comfortable in the company of the deceased it would be beside those chosen to join him in his little group of six.

David Nucifora and Greg Martin, fellow University club rugby players and both later to play with Lynagh in the national team, were in his group, along with Michael O'Connor, a Queensland team-mate at the time. It was the misfortune of two young women straight out of school not only to have to get used to handling bits of cadavers, but to do it in the company of a male quartet whose behaviour wasn't always exemplary.

'It took a while to get used to walking into a room full of dead bodies,' recalls Nucifora. 'Some deal with it better than others, and some have a bit more respect than others. Our group wasn't short on the larrikin element and little things used to happen – livers in pencil cases, kidneys in purses, that sort of thing. It was a bit too much for the two girls. They quit midway through the semester. I guess it might have been us more than the course that turned them off.

'Noddy would always be a part of the shenanigans, but he was the silent partner in the business. He'd never be the lead man, but he'd have a good idea of what was going on. Somehow or other we all passed anatomy. Maybe the lecturer got us through because he was too scared we might repeat if we failed. Luckily, we got split up then and each of us headed off in different directions.'

Nucifora is now a licensed auctioneer, Martin, an apprentice carpenter, O'Connor, a media commentator and surf-shop proprietor, while Lynagh is involved in commercial real estate – so much for the impact of anatomy.

In the five years after Lynagh left school, the amount of time he spent on rugby pursuits was ever increasing, while the other facets of his life were pushed further into the background. In 1982 he was a full-time student, the following year he was part-time and by 1984 he completed just one semester part-time.

In 1986, when he discovered that the start of the second University semester coincided with the departure date for the Wallaby tour of New Zealand, he applied to continue his studies by correspondence. On return from that tour he found himself, for the first time in his adult life, with little to do. The local rugby had finished and there were no off-season tours. As an external student, there were no university lectures to attend and with most of his mates either working or completing their degrees, he was left to twiddle his thumbs – not an activity of which this action-oriented character was particularly fond.

'Rugby had become the number-one priority in my life and I was able to enjoy it due to the generosity of my parents. I was supported by them and accommodated at home, so life for me was basically rugby, touring and, when that wasn't happening, a bit of study. However, when I got back from New Zealand in 1986 I was at a loose end and figured it would be nice to actually earn some steady income and start to pay my way.'

Kim Weller, the Brisbane hotelier and Lynagh's University club-mate, was not only a close friend but also someone whose commercial contacts and advice were to prove of great assistance for a young man with a very high profile but limited business experience. It was at the opening of Weller's nightclub 'Fridays' that Lynagh met Ross Hewitt, the owner of a printing broking firm called Brisbane Business Forms.

Within a week of that meeting, Lynagh had secured his first job. He was now a printing-broker. Although 50 per cent of all the printing sold in the United States of America was done through brokers, it was a reasonably new concept in Australia. Brisbane Business Forms sub-contracts out to printing facilities and then resells. The shy, retiring, unobtrusive Michael Lynagh had become a salesman.

As he was employed on a profit-sharing basis, whereby the money he received depended on how hard he worked, he had to sell or sink. The fact he was still receiving payments late in 1988, some five months after he'd finished working for the company, indicated that however out of character the idea of the hard sell might be, Michael Lynagh was able to make a success of it. However, Wayne Maher, a workmate then, and still with the company today, saw that Lynagh was not a born salesman.

'He wasn't supposed to sell his name, but the fact he was Michael Lynagh naturally opened a lot of doors for him and he made plenty of contacts through it. To be honest though, I think he felt as if he was intruding when he called on people. There was no question he got us a lot of business, but he was not the sort of person who would go for the jugular.'

Nor was he the type who would betray confidences. 'As a workmate, he was fine,' remembers Maher, 'although he was shy to the point of being aloof. In 1987, when there was a fair bit of controversy in the press about a number of things including Alan Jones' coaching and rebel trips to South Africa, you wouldn't be able to get much out of him.'

For a man whose first sporting love was cricket, it was understandable that Lynagh might view the number eighty-seven with suspicion. Historically, Australian batsmen have considered it to be the devil's number and preferred not to land on it while batting, for fear of being dismissed. As a junior cricketer, Lynagh was conscious of eighty-seven's reputation, but when the 1987 rugby season arrived, he was full of optimism for the challenges ahead. The inaugural Rugby World Cup was at hand, and with Grand Slam and Bledisloe Cup victories still fresh in the minds of players, officials and supporters, the Wallabies began the tournament with heavy expectations resting on their shoulders.

Along with New Zealand, Australia had been the driving force behind the evolution of the World Cup. There was a world championship for just about every other sport – soccer, hockey, cricket and, rather farcically, rugby league. Rugby had been a part of the 1908 Olympics but since then there had been no official standard by which to judge the world's premier rugby nation. Wales, England, New Zealand, South Africa and more recently Australia had all achieved results that at one time or another indicated a claim to supremacy, but there was no definitive way to measure such claims.

Conservative administration and rigid tradition had, over a number of decades, frustrated those with visions of a rugby World Cup, but by the early 1980s there were enough modern thinkers who understood that the concept had to be realised. In February 1983 threats of a professional rugby tournament had also done their bit to accelerate discussion of the issue. Sydney media figure David Lord had conducted a number of meetings in Sydney and Brisbane with leading Australian players and mooted the idea of a professional world championship of rugby. Lynagh was one of a number of Queenslanders Lord invited to the Crest Hotel in Brisbane to discuss his feelings towards such an event. It was suggested that players should be contracted for three years for their involvement in an annual competition with the other leading rugby countries. For their efforts they would be paid $60 000 per season.

Despite the obvious uproar it would cause in traditional rugby circles, it was a concept that quite appealed to most of the players at the time. There were, however, too many unanswered questions and too much scepticism regarding Lord's ability to raise the capital involved in such a venture. One doubter suggested that if the predicted all-up cost of the exercise was to be $20 000 000, Lord would fall approximately $20 000 000 short.

Lynagh's first meeting with him was also his last; the idea never got past the discussion stage. It was an issue he was grateful he didn't really have to tackle. Although his gut feeling would have been not to rock the establishment boat, the temptation to bow to peer pressure would have been difficult for a nineteen-year-old rookie to resist.

The administrators took heed of the rumblings and at the annual meeting of the International Rugby Board in 1984, the Australian and New Zealand unions were given permission to pool their resources and ideas and return twelve months later with a feasibility study for a rugby World Cup. Both unions were certain the rugby public in general wanted it. The IRB included eight member countries – the four British Isles teams and France, Australia, New Zealand and South Africa – but it was felt the emergence and growing reputation of non-IRB nations such as Argentina, Fiji, Italy and Romania needed recognition, and there was only one way that could be given.

After the inevitable lobbying and behind-the-scenes manoeuvring, late in 1985 in Paris the World Cup concept was accepted by the IRB. Australia had wanted to stage the inaugural Cup as part of its bicentenary celebrations in 1988, but it was eventually decided that New Zealand and Australia should share the hosting duties in May and June of 1987.

The man who had begun it all was not forgotten. A superb sterling-silver cup was produced by Garrard, the British Crown jewellers. The first concrete symbol of world rugby supremacy was there to be won – the William Webb Ellis Trophy.

The twenty-six-man Australian World Cup squad assembled in Sydney in mid-May, with the Eden Park final in New Zealand scheduled for 20 June 1987 set firmly in its sights. Even outside the Wallaby camp, there were few objective observers who contemplated anything else but an Australia–New Zealand decider.

'This will be more difficult than any overseas tour we've ever undertaken,' warned Jones at the first team meeting. 'Away from home, we do not have the distractions of family, friends and work that we will inevitably have here. We must ignore the distractions and concentrate solely on the job at hand.' There was no argument from the players, who were prepared to do anything over the ensuing five weeks to ensure success.

The draw had been reasonably kind to the Australians with England, America and Japan in their pool. With victories over the last two countries a mere formality, qualification for the quarter-finals was a foregone conclusion. Defeating England in the opening game would ensure the Wallabies would not have to confront the All Blacks before the final. When that feat was accomplished courtesy of a conclusive, if rusty 19–6 win all looked in order.

Within team ranks though, not everything was calm. There was disquiet that Jones' call to sacrifice all in the quest for victory had been heard and adhered to by everyone but the man himself. Jones' profile in Sydney had increased enormously since the Grand Slam in 1984, and as a top-rating morning radio announcer on 2UE he was unable to put his work on the backburner during the World Cup. Training sessions were rostered to fit in with his radio schedule, and while there was no lack of overt enthusiasm from the players once training began, trying to kill time until mid-afternoon helped mix an unhealthy cocktail of boredom, impatience and frustration. The New South Wales players, who numbered half the squad, tended to go back to their jobs or families in the mornings, leaving the Queenslanders to while away the hours as best they could. There was no actual antagonism over this, because it was tacitly understood that the Brisbane people would have done exactly the same if the team had been based in Queensland, but as everyone had different agendas for the first half of the day, it hardly encouraged team unity or spirit. Although the Wallabies progressed with barely a hiccough to a semi-final meeting with France, there was a lethargy in their play that had not been recognisable in the preceding three years.

In later years, Bob Dwyer was to be given credit for the invention of the term the 'on–off' button, meaning that it should be made clear to players when they needed to give their full attention to the serious matter of winning games and when they could let their hair down, have a few drinks or do whatever else they needed to unwind. In fact, it had been Jones who coined that phrase in 1984, and the Wallabies' successes had been based on a fairly sensible use of the switch. Whether the personal or professional pressures that Jones felt as a very public personality in Sydney contributed or not, there was no question he had forgotten how to find the off button. As a consequence, the players were never able to fully relax and the tension trespassed into their football.

As is generally the case, the further back in time the event, the more exaggerated tales become. For example, Jones to some extent curtailed post-match festivities after the quarter-final against Ireland. There was, however, no total ban on alcohol – however much the coach may have approved – as one rumour had it.

Despite this uneasiness within the team, Australia was still only one win away from a berth in the final when they played France at Concord Oval (now the Waratah Stadium). The Wallabies believed the French were a better outfit than the one they had beaten at the Sydney Cricket Ground twelve months earlier. There was brilliance in the backline with Serge Blanco, Phillippe Sella, Denis Charvet and Pierre Berbizier, while the inclusion of locks Alain Lorieux and Jean Condom gave the forward pack a more formidable look. (When Condom was not chosen for that earlier game in 1986, it had given the Australians double reason to smile. First they believed he was one of the better French forwards and his non-selection would make it easier for the Wallaby pack, while the actual reporting of his ommission from the team also gave cause for mirth. After the French management announced the playing XV, a local newspaper ran the story under the headline 'French Go In Without Condom'.)

There was no protecting France from the brilliance of Campese and Lynagh, and just half an hour into the semi-final Campese touched down to become the leading try-scorer in Australian rugby history, while Lynagh once again etched his name in the record books, surpassing Paul McLean as Australia's top points-scorer. Australia lost two key players in the first twenty minutes when brilliant centre Brett Papworth and lineout wizard Bill Campbell were both replaced after injury, but the Wallabies looked to be on top as half-time approached.

However, with just seconds to go before the break, Troy Coker, the Australian number eight, a controversial choice ahead of David Codey, was dispossessed by Lorieux metres from the Australian line and the big French lock powered over for what was, considering the stakes, the softest of tries. There was no doubt that was the turning point. The French can get rattled when the pressure is on but that try gave them a sniff, and with the talent they had, the extra boost of confidence was all they needed.

Lynagh rates the match one of the finest in which he has played and it was without doubt the highlight of the tournament, but that was little consolation for the Wallabies who let in a late try and suffered a 30–24 defeat. The pressure Jones was feeling was obvious when the team returned to the dressing rooms. There was nothing that could be done to alter the result and, unlike a three-match series, there was no chance for revenge. It was do or die, and the World Cup Wallabies had died. The players wanted nothing but silence. Two years earlier, Jones might have recognised this need and left any comment until a more appropriate time. But he could not help himself and immediately pinpointed errors made by individuals, errors that had, in his eyes, contributed to the defeat. Some in the team viewed this public criticism at such a delicate time as a bad mistake on Jones' part. Others considered it unforgiveable.

Unlike a few of his team-mates, Lynagh had maintained a high standard of play throughout the tournament, and while he believed Jones was more on edge than in previous years, felt it was too easy to lay the blame for the failure at the feet of the coach.

'There was a lot of pressure on us all, and I don't think he helped ease it … But by the same token I think he became a convenient excuse for players who hadn't performed to expectation. Some reckoned that training in the afternoons was a big factor, but I'm damn sure the fact we had to train in the afternoon rather than the morning was not the reason we didn't win the World Cup. There were a couple of injuries, a few strange selections and, at the end of the day, we didn't have as much luck as we might have wished.'

There was nothing lucky about having to go to Rotorua for a meaningless play-off for third and fourth against Wales, and when English referee Fred Howard sent flanker David Codey off in the first ten minutes of the game, the tale of woe was complete. A try in the dying minutes by winger Adrian Hadley put the Welsh one point behind and gave fullback Paul Thorburn a chance to snatch the lead with his conversion attempt. Standing hopelessly behind the tryline, Lynagh realised the kick, although a difficult one, was bound to go over. He'd been in the situation himself enough times before to understand the pressure Thorburn was facing. He could see that the big Welshman had it under control. 'You get a sixth sense telling you how the kick will go,' says Lynagh. 'Even though it was a tough one, I knew as soon as he lined it up that it would be struck sweetly.'

Too sweet: fifteen Welshmen beat fourteen Australians 22–21 and the Wallabies exited the inaugural World Cup ingloriously. All the players wanted was to get home to their families as soon as possible, but they were required to remain in New Zealand for the tournament final between New Zealand and France. It was rugby's equivalent of slow torture. Everyone in the Wallaby squad felt they should be in the main event, and yet they'd twice taken knockout blows in the preliminaries. To add insult to pain, they were invited to take backrow seats at the championship fight.

The majority of the Australians opted to stay at their airport motel rather than make the trek into Eden Park and be forced to contemplate what might have been. Not good at sitting around doing nothing, Lynagh decided there was one way he could help ease the frustrations of his team-mates. He organised a game of rugby league on the field behind the motel and instead of vying for world rugby superiority on 20 June 1987, the cream of the game in Australia on that day was knocking the living daylights out of each other on a nondescript little mudheap in an outlying Auckland suburb.

When they had stayed at the same motel in Sydney as the state-of-origin league teams, most of the Wallabies had taken the opportunity to swap jerseys – the 'origin' jerseys had the players' names printed on the back – and so it was an impressive bunch of league players on show. Queensland took on New South Wales and within fifteen minutes, a healthy crowd had gathered. By full-time of the high-spirited clash the word had got around among the spectators: the Wallabies were so disenchanted with missing out on the World Cup, they were going to defect *en masse* to rugby league!

While that thought might have caused apoplexy among officials in Australia, something just as likely to do so was the subject of a possible Australian visit to South Africa. While in Rotorua, Jones held a series of supposedly confidential meetings with players, indicating that he felt confident a sanctioned tour of the Republic could be organised later that year. In the wake of the recent disappointment it gave the majority of the players something to look forward to.

It did not have the same effect on Lynagh. 'I thought the secret meetings before we were playing certainly didn't help our performance. It seemed a way of saying, okay, we haven't won the World Cup. This is the next thing on the agenda. It took us away from what we were supposed to do. In our minds we had been heading for the final, but there we were in Rotorua and I don't believe we approached the game as we should have. Sure, none of us wanted to be playing for third spot, but we were still representing our country and that should have been the only thing on our minds.'

The Jones push for South Africa withered, but as I had been to the country myself as a guest of sponsor Yellow Pages late in 1986, to watch the progress of the Kim Hughes-led Australian cricket team, the ball was still rolling. While there, I was approached by rugby administrators and the dialogue had continued over the ensuing months. It culminated when I made a rushed trip to South Africa with David Codey in August 1987, to sound out the possibility of an Australian rugby team, sanctioned or otherwise, making a tour of the Republic.

A number of high-ranking South African officials, including Danie Craven and Louis Luyt, affirmed their keenness for a tour to take place, but only if a near full-strength team was available. Codey and I knew that the three most important players needed in the side if we were to be given the go-ahead by the South Africans were Campese, Farr-Jones and Lynagh. If, as looked likely, a non-sanctioned tour went ahead the players knew they faced lengthy, if not lifetime bans from the game. A year earlier the New Zealand Cavalier players had received just a one-Test suspension for their unofficial tour. Australian rugby authorities were not going to be anywhere near as lenient if there was a repeat episode by its players.

There were three distinctly different reactions when we approached the star Wallaby trio. I was anxious not to put undue or unfair pressure on the players, hoping they would make the decision with which they felt most comfortable.

'Now, Campo, bear in mind you are only twenty-four and you have got plenty of years left in the game. You've got to consider the down-side should you be banned from the game.'

'Can't get there quick enough,' came the immediate reply. One down, two to go.

Farr-Jones was somewhat more circumspect and he didn't need to be told to consider all the pros and cons. He wanted to overcome certain moral concerns he felt personally, but after some weeks thinking about it he decided that if a tour went ahead, official or otherwise, he'd want to be a part of it.

Lynagh was never really keen. His sister Jane was married to Keith Connor, a black English Olympic athlete whom she had met at the 1982 Brisbane Commonwealth Games. Lynagh had always been conscious of his moral responsibilities, but the presence of Keith both as a friend and a family member made that awareness even more acute and personal. He had spoken with Keith and Jane about the rights and wrongs of contact with a society that promoted apartheid. He learned that while Connor had his own views on the subject, he also had respect for the right of the individual to make his or her own choice and whatever decision Michael took, it would in no way affect their relationship.

With time running short in which to give the South Africans a list of available players, I asked Lynagh for his answer and was astonished when he said he was prepared to go; I was less surprised twenty-four hours later when he rang to inform me he had changed his mind.

'I guess I initially succumbed to a bit of subtle pressure, but I soon realised it wasn't what I really felt comfortable with. Personally, I didn't think it was the right thing to do either morally or rugby-wise. I had views I wanted to stand up for and I thought if I went along with the group and did the easy thing I would be behaving unfaithfully to myself. So ethically I figured it was something I had to stand by. Also, I was still only twenty-three, and although the World Cup hadn't been what I'd hoped, it wasn't reason enough for me to get banned and go and do something else. Playing for Australia was important to me and if somebody tried to take that opportunity away from me I wouldn't have been very happy.'

No tour eventuated and an event that might temporarily have torn the heart out of Australian rugby was averted. Lynagh was satisfied with the way he had handled things through a testing period. He had been true to himself and he was more proud of that than of any pressure goal he had kicked in the heat of battle.

Yet another niggling injury due to further wear and tear on the knee cartilage caused him to miss the one-off clash with New Zealand in July. Against an All Black side that was deservedly the winner of the first World Cup there was no way an Australian team minus Lynagh could atone for the recent losses. The Wallabies performed manfully but were beaten 30–16 and the Bledisloe Cup returned to Wellington to sit alongside the William Webb Ellis Trophy.

A two-Test tour of Argentina in October was the final chance to extract some joy from the year. Poor form, dissatisfaction with some of

Jones' methods and the uncertainty created by the never-to-be South African tour had some of the more experienced players heartily sick of the whole rugby deal. Nick Farr-Jones considered opting out of the trip, before counsel from his father Max and fellow player Brett Papworth convinced him otherwise. Not for a second did Lynagh think about withdrawing. On the contrary he was looking forward to it. He had never been to South America and here at last was a rugby tour for which he didn't have to pack three jumpers, two lots of wet-weather gear, gloves and an overcoat. Buenos Aires under a blue sky beckoned.

Although he had been dropped for the most recent Test against the All Blacks, Simon Poidevin was named as captain of the touring party with Lynagh as his deputy. The World Cup and its associated difficulties were yesterday's news. Lynagh was ready to make the most of this trip. Argentinian rugby has many attractions. One is that when you tour with a national side, you are accommodated in Buenos Aires at the five-star Sheraton Hotel. With every possible facility, this was a long way from Thames Valley. But even the Sheraton looked like a hick, up-country pub compared with the Paraguay Golf and Yacht Club in Ascuncion, where the team stayed for their mid-week match against a Paraguayan invitation XV. However, in South America it is only a short walk from luxury to squalor and Lynagh retains vivid memories of the extremes of living conditions that could be seen on any bus ride from the team hotel to training. The poverty was a far cry from his own fortunate lifestyle, and brought home to him the relative unimportance of the result of a rugby match.

What really didn't seem to be helping the rugby cause was the coach. In previous years, one of Jones' strengths had been his ability as a selector. Not everyone had necessarily agreed with his choices, but he invariably had some acceptable logic to back up his choices. This was not so in a number of cases in 1987 and certainly not when the first Test team was named on the Wednesday morning of the match in Ascuncion.

Nick Farr-Jones, who had been injured in the opening tour match, was once again fit, but Jones chose to ignore the advice of physiotherapists, doctors, senior players, and Farr-Jones himself, declaring that although he may have recovered from the injury his preparation wasn't adequate. It made no sense to omit the man who was rightly acknowledged as the world's best halfback on the strength of a minor knee injury. He had missed only a fortnight of football, which for a man of his natural fitness was of no concern; the rest from what had been an almost non-stop year of rugby probably did him more good than harm.

Jones wasn't to be swayed and Brian Smith played halfback while Farr-Jones was on the bench. Only a couple of moments into the Test, it looked as if it wouldn't matter if Donald Duck was playing halfback for the Wallabies, so easily did they breach the Puma's defence. From the kick-off the Australians were awarded a scrum ten metres inside their own territory. With Stephen James at flyhalf and Lynagh playing inside centre the plan was to get the ball to Lynagh and let him make the choice to pass or kick. The speedy Ian Williams was making his Test debut on the wing, and Lynagh saw the opportunity for a long pass. It was fired with precision and the pace of Williams did the rest as he scored beside the corner post. Despite the boos and catcalls from the 50 000 spectators, Lynagh's kick was sweet.

However the ease and speed with which the first points came were misleading as the Pumas fought back, and riding confidently on the boot of Hugo Porta forced a 19–all draw. Farr-Jones' authority and skills had been missed.

'I remember before the first Test I'd had a meeting with Nick and assistant coach Alec Evans, when we expressed our concerns at the way the tour was heading,' says Lynagh. 'Every time four or five guys got together the talk was about Alan and what he'd done that was strange. I suggested we talk to him about it but Alec was as nervous as we were about broaching the subject. The tour was never going to be a success rugby-wise if things stayed as they were.'

Poidevin was injured in the first Test and subsequently would miss the second, allowing Lynagh to captain the side in a game that would make a success or failure of the tour. Lynagh wanted Farr-Jones in the team. He needed to make that clear. But the coach got in first.

'You don't like Brian Smith do you Michael?' said Jones.

'Yes I do. I think he is a very talented footballer … We get on pretty well.'

'Who do you think should be halfback?'

'Well, if Nick's fit, he should be halfback.'

'There you are. Why wouldn't you pick Smith?'

'I think Nick's a better footballer.'

At this stage, Lynagh was in uncharted waters. In the past there had been things that concerned him, but he'd decided against arguing the point. This time, however, he felt he had to speak his mind. In the interests of the team he had to say what he thought.

'Brian's pass is not as good as Nick's,' said Lynagh.

'That shouldn't matter,' replied Jones, who then referred to an exercise the players practised where they were required to catch poorly thrown passes. 'We've spent plenty of time on that shit-passing drill.'

At this, Lynagh threw in the towel. 'I thought then, I'm not going to win this. No matter what I said he'd have a counter. After that, we continued to function, but the team wasn't really happy.'

Jones clearly had inflated opinions of the playing abilities of certain members of the touring party and while Smith had special talents and was a worthy selection in the Wallaby squad, it was a living certainty that he was not a superior player to Farr-Jones. As Jones often proclaimed, Smith was an outstanding athlete, and it was this unfailing belief in his potential that meant Jones went beyond reasonable grounds to include him in the Test team. Unlike any other player in the side, Smith could be called on to play a Test match at halfback, fullback, centre or wing, and do the job admirably. He was arguably the finest all-round utility player Australian rugby had ever produced, but in terms of specialising there always seemed to be players better equipped for the individual positions. Jones struggled to accept that fact.

He finally did accept that Farr-Jones had to be returned to the Test lineup at halfback and when the team for the second Test was announced, Farr-Jones was back in his rightful position.

It didn't do the Wallabies any good. Eight years earlier, Hugo Porta had kicked three drop goals to condemn Mark Loane's tourists to a surprise defeat. In 1987 he was at it again. Five penalties, two drop goals and a conversion reaped him twenty-three points as the Pumas took out the Test 27–19 and so condemned the Wallabies to their first-ever series defeat to Argentina. It was a shattering end to a year full of disappointments.

Lynagh had captained his country in a Test for the first time and become Australian rugby's leading points-scorer, but despite his liking and desire to accumulate points and achieve personal goals, team success gave him the biggest thrill. In 1987 there had been precious little of that. His youthful suspicions about the devil's number had been well founded.

8
THE WORLD'S BEST RESERVE

As Bob Dwyer had felt the wrath of Australian rugby officialdom four years earlier, so Alan Jones was on the receiving end in February 1988. After building up such an impressive record in the first three seasons, Jones-coached Australian teams had failed to win a Test in their past five matches and the anti-Jones lobby had all the ammunition it required. Although disappointed with the way things had progressed in 1987, and particularly on the tour of Argentina, Lynagh believed that while Jones had flaws, he also had many strengths, which his detractors were never prepared to acknowledge.

'Alan occasionally failed to realise that not everyone was as driven as himself. This caused some friction within team ranks and while some might think it's the pot calling the kettle black, I feel he was overly sensitive to criticism,' claims Lynagh. 'None of us likes being criticised but he used to deal with it by getting on the front foot and counter-attacking. On the occasions where the criticism might be justified, it made him look bad. However anyone who underestimates his contribution to the game is only showing their ignorance. He had the ability to back up what he thought with very credible arguments. He certainly has the intelligence to sound convincing in just about any forum and he had a vision few coaches before him had shown.

'If he believed in something, he didn't mind putting himself up in front of the critics and running the risk of being shot down. He didn't lack courage and was all for the players. He used to say the administrators used the players as mobile banks and most of us felt that was pretty accurate.

'He was a vital part of the code's progression beyond the also-ran category and was responsible for pushing world rugby towards the professional level we now see. He turned it in that direction, and say whatever you want about him, if his worst enemy asked for help, I doubt he would ever refuse it.'

In his Sydney *Sun-Herald* newspaper column, Jones made little secret of the fact he felt victimised, but on 6 March 1988 was able to offer a generous parting comment:

> ... And above all, the time has offered lasting friendships and indelible memories.
>
> As I've said before, though the dogs may bark the caravan must move on. It now has a different driver, but its journey is just as important as ever.
>
> Let us all now forget the acrimony generated by a few (you can't forgive it), and join in the collective hope that 1988 will be a beneficial year for Australian rugby and those entrusted with its safekeeping.

'Waltzing Matilda, waltzing Matilda, you'll come a-waltzing Matilda with me ... ' That a crowd usually eager to boo Australian teams should burst into a spontaneous rendition of our best-known song was evidence enough that Dwyer's first task back at the helm of Australian rugby had been completed successfully.

Under the captaincy of Lynagh and with David Campese in vintage form, Australia beat New Zealand 13–12 in the final of the 1988 Hong Kong Sevens. When Lynagh received the silver symbol of sevens supremacy from Hong Kong bank taipan William Purves, the Royal Hong Kong Police band struck up 'Waltzing Matilda', but they might have stopped the drums and trumpets after a few bars. No one heard them anyway as all but the most rabid anti-Australians in the twenty-thousand-strong throng took up the singing. It was stirring stuff. In the *Australian* on 28 March Dwyer used the occasion to proclaim the start of a new era in Australian rugby.

New eras are usually equated with new leaders and Dwyer had to find himself a captain. In the last four Tests of 1987, four different captains had led the Wallabies. My own Australian career finished after the World Cup game against Wales, David Codey took over for the one-off Test with New Zealand and while Simon Poidevin had been named as captain for the tour of Argentina, injury had forced him out of the second Test allowing Lynagh to lead the team.

As the most recent Test captain, as captain of Queensland and as Dwyer's choice for skipper of Australia's victorious sevens squad, the odds of Lynagh getting the job were pretty short. If form was a criterion he hadn't let himself down on that count either. His first game as Queensland's official captain was his fiftieth for the state. It was against Wellington and despite an illness, which caused him to shed almost four kilograms in weight in the days preceding the match, not only did he play, but he played well enough in the 29–3 victory for former dual international John Brass to label him the world's best footballer. Wellington captain Neil Sorensen added this succinct post-match summation. 'If Michael Lynagh's got a virus, I'd hate to see the bastard when he's fully fit.'

Whether the 1987 World Cup had alerted people to the fact there was money to be made out of the game or whether it was a natural progression, increasingly commercialism was seeping through the very solid walls of amateurism that had protected rugby. In Queensland, Lynagh became the first recipient of the benefits that could be accrued. He was without a car and entered into an arrangement with Mazda Queensland. In exchange for the use of one of their vehicles he agreed to help conduct a series of coaching clinics and to use his name wherever possible to promote Mazda. Lynagh the businessman was emerging. Mazda became a sponsor of the Queensland Rugby Union, in a deal that benefitted both parties, while Lynagh was quite content driving around town in a smart new sedan. Lyangh and the QRU had their differences in the years to come, but at this time things were very amicable.

'I am very happy with the arrangement with Mazda and it has been approved by the QRU, which is probably the most progressive rugby body in the world,' said Lynagh in a press release, at the announcement of the scheme. He went on to moot the idea of a trust fund for players – something which is now an integral part of the game. 'I believe trust funds would be a sensible approach for the game,' he said. 'There is no way players are able to take advantage of their high profile, and as a result, many retire at about twenty-five or switch to rugby league because they are then starting to think about families and jobs and suddenly realise there is no commercial future for them in rugby. I don't see that the advent of trust funds would change rugby union for the worse. Indeed it would help bring it to the forefront again.'

He mightn't have been earning millions, but things were going along pretty nicely, thank you very much. Queensland had begun the season well, he was getting around in a flash new car and, although he was far from over-confident, if you could believe the papers there was a reasonably good chance he would get the Australian captaincy. Life doesn't get any better. Well, not unless a letter arrives in the mail inviting you on an all-expenses-paid jaunt to Monte Carlo and Switzerland.

The Warblers, a Dubai-based side, invited Lynagh and Nick Farr-Jones on the junket to end all junkets in the first weekend of May. There was just one problem. That same weekend, Queensland was scheduled to meet New South Wales in the first interstate game of the series. Commitment to the cause was one thing, but giving up the delights of the Riviera for just one more Queensland–New South Wales game was tough medicine to swallow. Lynagh, though, gulped it down, opting to stay at home while Farr-Jones and the New South Wales skipper Simon Poidevin, who happily took the plane ticket as Lynagh's replacement, left the Blues to their own devices. They must have known something Lynagh didn't, because even without two of their best and most experienced players, New South Wales was able to hand Queensland a convincing 37–15 beating.

Although Lynagh ultimately missed the game, due to more knee problems, his decision to remain at home for Australian rugby's most important domestic fixture was seen by observers as yet another tick in the captaincy box for the twenty-four-year-old Queenslander. However, Bob Dwyer and the selection panel had other ideas and, happy not to consult any of the long-serving team members, announced the Australian captain for the bicentennial celebration match against the World XV.

Nick Farr-Jones rests safe in the knowledge that he is the only Australian rugby captain ever to learn of his appointment while staying in a luxurious beachfront hotel in Monte Carlo. Although press reports at the time speculated that Lynagh was spared the burdens of captaincy because the selectors felt as flyhalf, goalkicker and the caller of back-line moves he had enough on his plate, in Dwyer's mind there was only ever going to be one man for the job.

'It seemed to me Nick was the obvious choice as captain,' says Dwyer. 'His leadership qualities were there for all to see. Nick has always been a commanding presence. I didn't necessarily think that about Noddy in 1988.'

Commanding presence or not, Farr-Jones was genuinely surprised. 'I thought, like everyone else, that Noddy would get the job,' he says.

Never afraid to show his annoyance when something has irritated him, Lynagh takes a different approach to genuine disappointment. He retreats, the camouflage comes out and he works through his disappointment on his own or with the help of his family. This was no different. He stuck out the chin, wished Nick well and stoically continued to ensure he would remain a valuable member of the Australian side. He acknowledges now that it mattered intensely to him that he had been bypassed for the top job, but no one then was allowed to see that. It was important that people saw him react to the disappointment in a dignified manner. Whining didn't equal dignity.

The knee injury, which forced him out of the interstate match, also caused his withdrawal from the game against the World XV. Brian Smith, his former Queensland team-mate, who had gone south in search of a permanent representative position, was called in as replacement flyhalf and promptly notched twenty-six points – a scoring bonanza not even Lynagh himself had been able to manage at international level. Writing in the *Australian* on 17 May, former Wallaby coach David Brockhoff called for Smith to be assigned the flyhalf duties ahead of Lynagh for the upcoming series with England. From a seemingly certain choice as Australian captain nine days earlier, Lynagh's very place in the Test team now seemed to be in jeopardy.

Ever appreciative of public shows of support, Lynagh's concerns were eased when Dwyer announced in the same newspaper that there was no doubt he would slot back into the side when fit. 'I would think Noddy would have to go in at this stage of proceedings,' said the coach. 'He showed great form before his knee problems and I don't think Smith necessarily handled flyhalf as a specialist would.'

So Lynagh wore the number ten in the first Ballymore match between the old enemies since 1975, when the infamous 'battle of Brisbane' saw local referee Bob Burnett send off England prop Mike Burton in the opening minutes of the game. In his book *Thanks to Rugby*, Bill Beaumont, England's successful Grand Slam captain of 1980 recalls that game.

> The Australian team had been psyched up way beyond the normal levels of acceptability and they began the match like caged

animals who had been starved for a week. It was as if their coach, Dave Brockhoff, had told them to go out and act as if each player was a bull in a china shop ... It would have been better for Australia and the game of rugby if some of the players had been encouraged to turn their attentions to some more suitable sport – perhaps head hunting in Borneo or some form of martial arts.

The 1988-vintage Australian team was confident they would have no need to resort to such tactics. However Lynagh and Farr-Jones felt like beheading themselves after each threw intercept passes that allowed England wingers Rory Underwood and John Bentley to score runaway tries. At 13–3 down, Lynagh recalled the words of Tony Shaw, his former Queensland captain. 'If you muck it up, fix it up.' His atonement came in the form of six crisply struck penalty goals – eighteen of the points in the Australians' 22–16 win.

Although Dwyer claimed the Wallabies would be a thirty-point better side by the end of that year, his first Test match back in charge had achieved the right result. Lynagh had seen to that. As is always the case after a win, the dressing rooms were packed with well-wishers and while Lynagh was willing to chat and share a drink or two with supporters, he was keen for the post-match formalities to be completed so he could head out to a restaurant with friends. With the concentration he puts into his performances he often takes a long time to wind down after a match and finds the best way to relax is to remove himself from the rugby scene. Occasionally he might 'kick on' at Ballymore but usually he prefers to choose his own company. As often as not, teammates such as David Wilson, Peter Slattery or Paul Carozza might join him, but rugby is rarely the topic of conversation.

Living quite close to the ground, he sometimes went home to change before going out and in the process would end up discussing the afternoon's proceedings with his father. The conversation invariably started with Michael asking the simple question 'What did you think?'

Ian's response was always positive, beginning with the good things Michael had done, and occasionally offering thoughts on how certain aspects might be improved. Michael still considers these post-match discussions with his father invaluable and regardless of where he might be in the world will nearly always endeavour to make contact with Ian.

'It's not just with football,' says Marie Lynagh. 'In everything from personal life to business matters, Michael has always waited to talk with Ian before making any big decisions.'

No disagreement from Noddy. 'In the early days of my career particularly, he was someone I looked to for guidance, but although some outsiders might think otherwise, he has not held me back in any way. He is a very prudent person and has given me a lot of advice. There have been plenty of people ready to give it, but Dad was one person whose guidance was well thought out and sound. He has helped me a lot and we have a fantastic relationship but that doesn't mean I agree with everything he says. There have been occasions when I've gone the opposite way. There have been times when we have had arguments.'

There have been times, too, when Ian's profession has left Michael's friends somewhat wary. 'In those early days, when sports psychology wasn't an accepted thing, I remember Damien Frawley used to have trouble coming over to our place. He always used to say, " … whenever I come over I always think your father is analysing me."

'Because he wasn't an accountant or a lawyer or a cab driver it used to throw people. "Oh – a psychologist! Will he read my mind or hypnotise me or something?"

'The fact is, despite the earlier antagonism with my sister Jane through our teenage years, we have always been a very close family. No way could I say that Dad has been in any way overbearing, although he has had the largest influence on me, not only as a sportsperson, but also as a person.'

Ian agrees that there has been the odd argument between father and son, but never over a rugby match. 'When it comes to football, I have always worked on the theory of "he asks first", especially concerning a particular game. There are lots of rugby players he has played with who would have got more help from me than he has, but he's obviously had more personal, emotional, ongoing support. Rather than try and give Michael advice directly, I used to tell stories about what I'd seen that was good, and he'd always listen. At times, I talked about things we both might have seen on television and when I'd noticed how well a particular athlete might have been concentrating. We'd talk about it and so I was giving Michael messages indirectly, whether he was aware of them or not. That was how not just values, but psychological or mental skills were communicated to him.'

Although Ian and Marie were keen for Michael to have his fun as he saw fit, they were always pleased when he skipped any post-match festivities early to come and discuss things with them. 'Michael is socially very competent when he wants to be,' says Ian, 'but he is probably a bit like me. I detest big parties. I'd much rather have dinner with a maximum of two or three others. I get anxious with any more than that.'

Of those involved in Lynagh's career, Alan Jones is one person not convinced Ian's obvious influence was always of benefit. 'One of the virtues of the British Isles tour in 1984,' he argues, 'was that Michael was able to cut his own destiny independent of influences close to him, positive or negative though they might be. His father obviously had a very profound influence, but it was not the influence but the persistence that I think created ambiguities in Michael's mind.' Michael himself says he has never felt conscious of any such ambiguities.

Dwyer's prediction that the Wallabies would be a thirty-point better team by the end of the 1988 season wasn't looking too inaccurate when they defeated the English 28–8 in the second Test of the series. They'd improved fourteen points in the space of six days so there was every chance that in six months they might just fulfil the coach's prophecy.

However the world champions had arrived on our shores and there is nothing the All Blacks like more than to knock down cocky Aussies a notch or three. The 32–7 walloping they delivered in the first of the three-Test series painted a more realistic picture of the state of Australian rugby. It was the biggest defeat New Zealand had inflicted on Australia since 1972. The Wallabies were handy, but they weren't in the same class as the big boys.

It was a bemused rugby public who read the headlines the morning after the Test. Despite the New Zealanders scoring five tries to one and winning all over the ground, Dwyer opted to fire a volley of shots at the display of English referee Fred Howard, labelling his performance an abomination. 'I thought he refereed like a novice,' barked Dwyer in the *Sunday Mail* on 3 July 1988. 'All the things he spoke about in the pre-match conference were entirely ignored. It was bad luck for him, because he wasn't up to the occasion.'

As an afterthought Dwyer added that the better team had won, but Lynagh and a number of his team-mates were embarrassed that the loss had not been taken with something akin to good grace. The referee was ordinary, and having sent flanker David Codey off in the opening minutes of the World Cup play-off twelve months earlier, he was hardly the Wallabies' pin-up boy, but when the team had been given a hiding like the one dished out at Concord Oval, whingeing should have been kept in-house. That's how it seemed to Lynagh, anyway.

Before the second Test, Queensland had its chance to salvage something from what had been a pretty dire season. After winning its first two games it had suffered six successive losses, including both games against New South Wales. It was the Maroons' worst year since the 1960s, when Queensland was considered little more than cannon-fodder for the New South Welshmen. Long-serving Queensland coach Bob Templeton, one of rugby's most enduring and popular characters, was stepping down after thirteen successive years at the helm and the team was anxious to send him off in appropriate style.

'Tempo has been a major influence on my career from day one,' says Lynagh, 'and I was disappointed that in the only year I had been captain under him, we had such a disjointed season. Inevitably, there is a selfishness in wanting to do well, but on this occasion everyone was just determined to give our all for Tempo.'

However sentiment has rarely won rugby games. In their previous 106 tour matches in Australia since 1945, the All Blacks had won ninety-seven. They were the current world champions, they were at the top of their form, and Queensland was in minor turmoil. All in all, a situation in which Lynagh performs best.

For an individual to dominate proceedings against the All Blacks is the toughest call in the game, but Lynagh did just that for the first forty minutes. His tactical kicking and his general play saw the Queenslanders enjoy a shock 6–3 lead at half-time, but when he was forced off the field with a badly corked thigh ten minutes into the second half, everyone realised there was to be no fairytale ending for Templeton. With Lynagh in the dressing room the Queenslanders succumbed, eventually going down in a 27–12 defeat.

Queensland's disappointment turned into Australia's concern. With only six days until the second Test, the Wallaby flyhalf and playmaker was struggling to walk, let alone run. Intense physiotherapy ensured a rapid recovery, but not rapid enough to leave Lynagh confident he would be able to perform at 100 per cent efficiency in the Saturday game. The Lynagh creed is that unless you can do it properly, don't do it at all. He applies it to himself as well as to others, and consequently withdrew from the Ballymore Test. Dwyer reshuffled the Australian backline, moving the creative Randwick back Lloyd Walker from inside centre into flyhalf to cover for Lynagh.

Against all odds the Australians rocketed to a 16–6 lead, before the New Zealanders fought back to claim a 19–all draw and in doing so retained the Bledisloe Cup. It had been a gallant effort by the Australians and one that promised much for the third and final Test a fortnight later. With Lynagh, Australian rugby's leading points-scorer, back for that match, the Wallabies had good cause to think they could square the series. Incredibly however, the Australian selectors felt they could get by without him. Although available, Lynagh was named on the reserve bench. Walker, who had played impressively at Ballymore, was retained at flyhalf, and Lynagh's old Terrace mate Michael Cook was chosen at inside centre.

'It has been terribly difficult,' said Dwyer in the *Courier-Mail* on 11 July. 'Lloyd was always going to be the flyhalf because we feel he is the man for the occasion. He has the type of game we want for the All Blacks.' Many felt that with an average of 13.1 points every time he turned out in a Test match, Lynagh had very much the type of game needed for the All Blacks. Dwyer continued:

> We recognise Noddy's talents. I had planned to use his running game in the second Test at Ballymore had he been fit. When he was forced to withdraw another man came along and made the most of it. It's as simple as that. So it came down to a decision between Noddy and Cookie for inside centre. We chose Cook because of his defence. Not that Noddy can't tackle but Michael is so aggressive.

The unassuming Cook would have laughed had anyone suggested he'd make a Test team in preference to Lynagh, but he was only too happy to take the opportunity offered. He admits that had he been a selector the first person chosen would have been Lynagh. He may have found a position for himself somewhere, but not at Noddy's expense.

Other observers were astonished that an Australian team could afford to leave Lynagh out of its starting lineup. Former Australian captain David Codey wrote in the *Daily Sun* on 14 July that the selectors had made a monumental blunder. 'The ommission of Lynagh was a mistake of the magnitude that Dwyer had made in 1982 when he selected Glen Ella ahead of Roger Gould for the Test against Scotland.'

Des Connor, another ex-Test captain and coach said in the *Courier-Mail* on 18 July that with no Lynagh playing he had to lean toward an All Black victory. And although a fan of Walker's play at flyhalf, David Brockhoff argued in the same newspaper that possessing a quality goal-kicker was of such importance he would have picked Lynagh on the wing. If that seemed outlandish, it fitted quite nicely with Brockhoff's reputation for unorthodoxy. After a bad loss to Argentina in 1983, journalists had asked him his remedy for the next Test. He suggested that coach Dwyer would have to spend morning and night working with his forward pack to get them up to speed for the game. When asked what should be done with the backs, Brockhoff replied, 'Give 'em a bottle of beer and a sheila and make sure they show up on Saturday!'

His non-selection as captain two months earlier had been a big blow for Lynagh but again he won admiration for the way he accepted his disappointment. There were many who felt he had every right this time to give full vent to his anger. Those expecting a big blow-up in the press are still waiting.

'Naturally I'm disappointed,' said Lynagh in the *Courier-Mail* on 11 July, 'but it's something I have to accept. I'll live to fight another day and I'll give the team my full support.'

The hurt was far deeper this time. There was anger too, but it stayed inside. It was a depressing time but he realised he could not afford to drag people down with him.

'I was shattered really, but selections are a subjective thing and everyone is entitled to their opinion. I'm not the sort of person who will pretend that it's not a big deal and laugh it off. Nor am I the type who'll go to the pub and drown my sorrows. I generally stick to myself at times like that because I find it hard to mask the disappointment, but at the same time I don't want anyone having to feel sorry for me.'

With the advantage of hindsight, it could be said that Lynagh's presence would have made little difference to the result of the Test. The All

Blacks were, without question, the better team and they proved it by taking out the series in style with a 30–9 victory. By the time Lynagh came on, as a replacement for fullback Andrew Leeds in the dying moments, there was nothing he could do to alter the outcome. However, it was not said publicly but the lesson learned from that match was that while Michael Lynagh was fit and available, no Australian team would ever again enter the Test match arena without him.

That was the intention anyway, but Lynagh himself appeared to put the kibosh on it when he announced his unavailability for the Wallabies' next commitment, a tour of England, Scotland, Wales and Italy. The rugby fraternity was stunned, but Lynagh stuck to his guns. He'd been playing almost non-stop for the best part of six years, he had a few niggling injuries, his form had been mildly inconsistent during 1988 and he felt stale. He did not, however, feel any animosity towards those responsible for the disappointments he had suffered during the season.

'There was no conflict of personalities or anything like that. I just felt a break would freshen me up and my rugby in the future would be better for it.'

Always formal and correct about such matters he wrote to John Bain, the chairman of selectors, to inform him of his decision and he explained his reasoning to Dwyer and Templeton. None of them was delighted at the thought of a Wallaby tour without him and tried more than gentle persuasion to change his mind. The mind was made up though, and he would not budge. Other respected Wallaby watchers believed he was doing the right thing. Mark Oberhardt, rugby columnist at the now-defunct *Sunday Sun* and a former GPS player, sensed in Lynagh's play the signs of fatigue and wrote on 18 September:

> One of the great tragedies of the 1988 rugby season was the dropping of Michael Lynagh from the Australian team.

Lynagh's instinctive talent puts him in the champion class, but it was hard to equate that player with the bloke wearing the University number ten against Brothers in a recent club game.

Putting it simply, Lynagh slaughtered a try which last year he would have set up easily.

Lynagh would still be the first player I would pick in an Australian team. He isn't playing bad football by normal standards – it's just he is below the champion class we know he can attain.

Lynagh at half ability is better than 95 per cent of the opposition. Nevertheless, I would love to see him have a couple of months rest and get himself right for next year.

A couple of months of surfing and mucking around with his mates should have him freshened up for a big 1989, when he should grab the Australian captaincy.

That would mean missing the trip to England and Scotland – but Lynagh still has five or six years to go at the top.

A break now could only do him good.

Despite the hiccoughs in between, Lynagh finished the season as he had begun it – in triumph. After three previous grand final appearances for University had all ended in defeat, the 1988 University team claimed Brisbane's club premiership. Souths had entered the match as favourites and it was no secret they felt that if Lynagh was controlled, the University challenge would fizzle. Lynagh was only too aware that opposition teams would often focus on him, but he also appreciated the talent around him. Peter Slattery, Greg Martin, Jeff Miller, Andy McIntyre and Brendan Nasser were all internationals who played with Uni, and in this match Lynagh underplayed his hand beautifully. While Souths waited to pounce on him, all manner of havoc was being wreaked by his team-mates. University won 18–10, capturing its first premiership in nine years, and Lynagh headed happily into a few months uninterrupted R and R. Or so he thought.

There was now the chance to give a bit of time to his new employers. Just a month earlier he had left the printing business to join commercial real estate company Richard Ellis. A reasonable amount of time away from rugby would at least give him some chance to get into this new caper, to learn something worthwhile and really begin to earn his keep, not just open doors through his rugby fame. He was looking forward to that and, of course, there was the beach. On Friday afternoons he would head straight up to his parents' beach house at Point Cartwright on Queensland's Sunshine Coast. He'd leave the office at five o'clock and by six he would be on his board, thinking only occasionally of what he might be missing in the north of England.

His twenty-fifth birthday was coming up and, as he had spent five of his previous seven birthdays on tour, he figured it was time for a party. A barbecue at Point Cartwright with a few guests on a warm summer's afternoon would do the trick.

'Happy birthday to you, happy birthday to you, happy birthday dear Michael … ' Michael excused himself from the three cheers and went to answer the phone.

'Hello, Michael Lynagh speaking.'

'Templeton here, Noddy. Knoxy's broken his finger. We need you.'

'Ring me again in the morning Tempo. I'll think about it overnight and give you an answer then.'

The Wallabies had lost three of their first four games in England and it was painfully obvious that Lynagh was being sorely missed. In truth, they could have covered David Knox's injury, but it was a convenient excuse to call for Lynagh. Although he told Templeton he would sleep on it, Lynagh knew immediately he would say yes. Less than twenty-four hours after opening his presents, Lynagh was on a jumbo jet *en route* to Heathrow.

'I couldn't say no a second time. I'd had a month off and had enjoyed my break from the game. Like everyone else at home I was concerned about the losses and I felt if I could help I would.'

There was nobody more delighted at Lynagh's decision than Nick Farr-Jones, his captain and halfback partner. '1988 was a very tough year for Michael with his injuries and then being left out of the third Test. Although he tried to hide it, I could tell he was down, but as soon as he knew he was needed, he changed. He felt wanted and it altered his attitude. We'd had a bad start and everyone knew that without Lynagh something was missing. He was bouncing around and obviously happy when he got to England and although the results weren't immediate, his arrival gave everyone a lift.'

Lynagh arrived on Thursday to learn he would be playing against the tough Midlands outfit in Leicester on Saturday. The Test against England was only nine days away and there was no time to worry about insignificant little matters like jet lag. He could probably have performed in his sleep if asked, but he looked wide awake as he contributed thirteen points to the 25–18 win.

Outside the rugby, the team's most important engagement on the tour was a trip to Buckingham Palace to meet the Queen. Lynagh was in a particularly jovial mood on the bus trip to the palace and decided to share his latest joke with the lads. As he'd heard it only five days before on Queensland's north coast, he was confident it had not travelled to Britain ahead of him. It concerned a meeting of apprentice kamikaze pilots in Japan during the war. Addressing the young flyers, the squadron leader explains the importance of their role. He waxes lyrical about the honour it is to die for your country and goes into some more sordid detail of just how these young men should end their lives, suggesting that the greater the pain they suffer in death the greater the hero they would become. At the end of the lecture he asks the assembled class if there are any questions. One wide-eyed innocent, obviously not too keen on this kamikaze idea, immediately calls out from the back of the room, 'Are there any bloody questions?'

The joke went over well with the boys and Lynagh was feeling pretty pleased with himself when the bus arrived at Buckingham

Palace. As is always the case, there was a quick lesson on the correct etiquette for addressing the Queen or any other passing royal. A very official, pukka-looking palace official led the Wallaby party into a special ante-room, where in very solemn tones and with an appropriately cultured accent, he explained the dos and don'ts. His final words were, 'Are there any questions?', to which, as one, the thirty Wallabies replied, 'Are there any f...ing questions?'

Understandably it caused much mirth among the players themselves and when Lynagh explained the background to the gentleman concerned, he too was able to see the funny side.

Lynagh's selection in the Test XV for Twickenham was a formality but the match turned out to be a disappointment. With Will Carling leading England for the first time, the English won comfortably to leave the Wallabies with an unsatisfactory record of four losses from their seven matches in England. The critics back home in Australia were in full cry and a loss to the Scots at Murrayfield would necessitate the rolling of heads. Murrayfield, though, had been the happiest of hunting grounds for Lynagh, and after the successes he had tasted there with the Schoolboys in 1981 and with the 1984 Wallabies, he could see no reason why his love affair with the ground shouldn't continue. After a tentative performance at Twickenham, returning to Murrayfield was like coming home. It was territory which had been kind to him before and he expected the same again. It was as if his playing personality was changed and he was again in control.

Australia won 32–13 and although Lynagh was successful with only five kicks from eleven attempts, two delicate chip kicks provided tries for David Campese and ensured the restoration of Australia's rugby reputation. And although 1988 was arguably the least memorable of Lynagh's own years in international rugby, Scottish coach Ian McGeechan pinpoints the Murrayfield Test as the return of the class act that every other international side feared.

Midway through the second half, Lynagh gathered a ball from the kick-off, executed a little jink and ran right through the Scottish pack, setting in chain a seventy-metre movement. No try resulted but an ensuing penalty, which he kicked, put Australia 28–7 ahead.

'When he took that kick-off,' says McGeechan, 'I thought to myself: there he is. Welcome back to international rugby Michael Lynagh – unfortunately!'

Campese had been the undoubted star of the tour, and that was made clear by the four youngsters who ran up and down the Murrayfield pitch after the game waving a large banner reading 'David Campese Walks on Water'. But if the form of Campese had been the highlight, the best news to come out of the tour was the resurrection of Michael Lynagh.

He was back to his best and by way of confirmation scored forty-three points in his last two matches of the tour – against the Barbarians in Cardiff and Italy in Rome. The match against the Barbarians featured one of Campese's greatest-ever performances and the Welsh crowd afforded him the rare honour of a standing ovation as he left the field. The Australian players were similarly impressed and held back after the full-time whistle to allow Campese the chance to walk off first, much as cricketers let the star bowler lead the fielders from the field after the completion of an innings.

Lynagh and Campese are vastly different personalities and in later years they had some serious differences of opinon but Lynagh, more than most, recognises genius, and he admitted the performances of Campese throughout that tour were certainly in that class.

The 1988 tour ended in Rome and little did the owner of the café adjacent to the Trevi fountain realise the quality of the trio of rugby stars among his customers on one unique afternoon. They might combine like clockwork on the field but rarely did Farr-Jones, Lynagh and Campese socialise together. Farr-Jones and Lynagh occasionally, Farr-Jones and Campese reasonably often, Lynagh and Campese very rarely. The three out together – this was a oncer.

And just as it usually does on the field, on this occasion everything came together. There was no skylarking or acting like bullet-proof tourists, just a bit of shopping, a look at some of the landmarks of one of the world's most beautiful cities and a few hours' drinking short blacks.

Lynagh had some Wallaby pins, which are given to the players to distribute among the fans after games or at training sessions. No sooner was the first passing child handed one by Lynagh than thirty or forty people descended. The delighted owner soon had a full café, and the 'famosi Wallabies' were given free drinks all afternoon.

'For no particular reason, it was a great day,' recalls Farr-Jones. 'Noddy was really relaxed, so was Campo, and it was great to see the two of them getting on so well, with none of us thinking about rugby problems. I've been on a lot of tours with Noddy, but we'd spent more time than usual together on that one and I felt really close to him. I know he's the sort of bloke who doesn't immediately let the words flow if you haven't seen him for a while; you almost have to break the barriers down again, but when you do, it is worth it. What we did that day was nothing more, I guess, than any normal tourists might do with a free day in Rome, but I cherish it as one of the best times I've had on any tour.'

9
'KNUCKLES' KNUCKLES NODDY

If you play rugby and are known as 'Knuckles', it is a fair chance you are not the type likely to shy away from confrontation. Very few Brisbane club rugby players of the 1970s and 1980s will argue that John Connolly earned this nickname without cause.

Connolly was a sporting star at Ashgrove's Marist Brothers College in Brisbane, playing flyhalf, flanker and frontrow for the first XV, as well as opening the batting and keeping wickets for the first XI. Like Lynagh he earned elevation to the élite school teams well before the usual age. He was an unlucky omission from the Australian Schoolboys rugby team that toured South Africa in 1969.

When he graduated to senior rugby ranks, injuries wrecked any aspirations of playing glory – a badly broken leg robbed him of pace, and condemned him to life in the forward pack. A converted hooker, he did enough damage to be selected as a reserve for one Queensland game in 1973, but most of his playing days were spent alternating between first and second grade, occasionally terrorising young pretenders who might have their rugby education completed in a friendly joust with 'Knuckles'.

While still playing, Connolly began his coaching career. A stint with the Casuarina club in Darwin was followed by success in the lower grades at Brothers, some under-age representative teams, and eventual nomination as Brothers first-grade coach in 1987. He took that team from fifth at the end of the premiership rounds, through the minefield of do-or-die semi-final football, and on to a grand-final victory over the highly fancied Souths. It was the only time a fifth-placed team had won a Brisbane premiership.

After the retirement of Bob Templeton as Queensland coach the following season, Connolly stood for the position and defeated a quality field, which included respected Brisbane coach Gary Bird as well as Alec Evans, assistant to Alan Jones during his time with the Wallabies.

Connolly stepped into the breach after the worst season Queensland had endured since the Maroons' representative commitments had been expanded in the mid-1970s. To try and stem the bleeding of seven successive losses, and to expose some new talent to the rigours of first-class football, the Queensland Rugby Union organised a pre-season tour of Argentina in March 1989. Connolly's first role as state coach, even before choosing the twenty-six-man team, was to select a captain.

Despite the poor record in 1988, no blame had been apportioned to Michael Lynagh, the skipper. He had done what he could, but the turnover of talent due to retirement, injury or unavailability had made for a disjointed team. Some forty-odd players had worn the Queensland jersey in 1988 and any consistency or pattern had been impossible to attain.

Apart from the few players he coached at Brothers Connolly knew very few of the Queensland squad personally, and like a player entering the representative arena for the first time, a new coach can also suffer from nerves. It seems more likely that at first he will err on the conservative side rather than attempt any radical changes, so when Connolly invited Lynagh to have breakfast at the Crest Hotel with himself and John Brass, the assistant coach, Lynagh could have been forgiven for expecting the get-together to be a strategy meeting: nothing more than a chat to iron-out the thinking and approach for the season to follow. Outside the Brisbane club scene, Connolly was a little-known figure; Lynagh was one of the biggest names in world rugby. It was perfectly understandable that Connolly would want to bounce the odd idea or two off such a respected figure, and the team captain to boot.

'Michael, I have no doubt you are the best player in the team by a street, and the role I want you to play in 1989 is the most significant in the team,' said Connolly. 'You have to run the show on the field. I am going to put restrictions on Slatts (halfback Peter Slattery). We'll aim to win as much ball as possible and then all he need do is deliver it to you. There'll be no backrow moves, no rolling mauls. We just win the ball, Slatts passes it to you and you do what you think is best. Oh, and by the way, Bill Campbell will be captain.'

If ever a player was entitled to choke on his cereal, this was the time. The new coach had begun his stint with a bombshell.

'I remember being pretty nervous about it beforehand,' recalls Connolly. 'Here we had a player who is pretty close to being the best in the world, if not the best, and another bloke, who had never set foot in the senior representative arena in any capacity, suddenly appeared and took something he valued away from him. I had no doubt though, it was the best thing to do. I needed the forwards to be led in a particular way if we were going to win the ball, and Bill was the man to do it. Noddy had enough to worry about and I felt it would be best for the team and for him if he didn't have to worry about captaincy.'

The previous season Lynagh had completed an apprenticeship in how to cope with slaps in the face, and having distinguished himself in the class of 1988, he was again able to mask his disappointment. Knowing how some might have reacted, Connolly has always been grateful to Lynagh for the manner in which he took the news.

'I was aware of the frustrations he suffered in 1988. I have a vivid picture in my mind of the television camera showing a close-up of him sitting on the bench for the third Test against the All Blacks. I thought to myself how ridiculous it was that the best footballer in Australia was unable to get a place in the starting team. I ranked it as one of the worst selection decisions ever made but then, in my first act as state coach, I sacked him from the captaincy. He handled it better than me though. I know he didn't agree and he gave his reasons, but he accepted mine and promised it would not affect his attitude in any way.'

It is all very well and proper to mouth words of understanding and give pledges of loyalty in such circumstances. The proof of the sincerity of these claims comes when the games and tours begin. Connolly quickly learned Lynagh was a man of his word. 'Not once during the tour of Argentina could you detect any sense of annoyance. He was the vice-captain and he went about that job as thoroughly as you could wish without ever giving the impression he had any ill-feeling towards Bill or me.'

Indeed, he didn't. Although always happy to bear the responsibilities that captaincy brought with it, Lynagh believes it was others who made more of an issue of his demotion than he did. 'When people miss out on a job they feel they might be capable both of doing well and enjoying, there is a degree of disappointment. I'm no different, but as with being overlooked for the Australian captaincy six months earlier, my attitude was one of, hey, life goes on. I'd rather be captain than not, but I understood that coaches had certain agendas. Journalists and people around me seemed to be more upset than I was. I didn't live up to their expectations.'

Although Lynagh not only enjoys, but seeks the accumulation of individual achievements and milestones, and is happy to acknowledge they are important to him, his main motivation has always been team-oriented.

'The crucial thing for me is to be in the team, to be playing well and to be winning. That really is my belief. That's why I get annoyed if anyone within the team publicly criticises the way individuals might have played a particular game. After some Australian games, Campo [David Campese] has occasionally had a crack at me in the press saying how little he enjoyed those matches because he didn't get all the ball he wanted. The first thing I think about is wanting to score tries, but sometimes games don't work out that way. It frustrates me because I know how hard I try to be a cog in the team. Decisions are made, not with my own best interests at heart, but for the benefit of the fourteen other people in the side. Captain or not, that is always the way I've approached my rugby.'

Doctor Bill Campbell was yet another Gregory Terrace old boy. A member of the second XV, his school sporting record was not quite the same glittering array of achievement as Lynagh's, but the pair made their Test debuts together against Fiji in 1984. After four years in the Australian and Queensland squads, Campbell spent a year in England studying at Oxford University, and subsequently missed the entire 1988 rugby season at home. With the horror record Queensland endured in that year it was as good a season as any to be absent, and when Connolly's coming-home present at the beginning of 1989 was the Queensland captaincy, he envisaged a frosty greeting from the man he'd replaced.

'I'd read the year before that Michael had been bitterly disappointed at missing out on the Australian captaincy in favour of Nick. I figured that if this was accurate he was going to be bloody annoyed at losing the Queensland job to me.'

There was however no personal animosity, although the pair's ideas on how the game should be played varied. 'In a couple of trial matches, he'd want to tap the ball, and run, and do all the crowd-pleasing stuff,' remembers Campbell, 'while Connolly and I were trying to work together to create a pattern of play. There was a little bit of friction over that, but it wasn't from pique at losing the captaincy.'

One of the most intelligent players to grace Wallaby teams over the past decade, Campbell was aware that to get the best out of his team, a lot would depend on how its best player performed. He saw Lynagh as a complex character, who needed to be handled differently if he was to produce his best. Most teams live with the adage that what is good for one is good for all. Campbell didn't believe any of that.

'Noddy was left to his own devices. Connolly and I agreed that we'd let him be a free agent. It worked far better than laying down the law. If you told him he had to do what everyone else did, it probably would not have worked. I expected him to respect the position I'd been given and if he wanted to change something he could say so. Although he may not like to be seen as getting star treatment, that is exactly what I wanted to give him. We never put the pressure on him to toe the line like the other players, and I think he responded positively to that.'

Such treatment led to the birth of the term 'Lynagh-time'. When it comes to training, Connolly has always been a stickler for punctuality. The training runs at Ballymore before the tour were invariably scheduled for 6 pm and woe betide the man who turned up one minute late. Short of being knocked over by a runaway semi-trailer, there were few excuses Connolly would accept as valid enough to pardon tardiness – unless the excuse came from Noddy.

As the player with the highest profile in the Queensland side and busy with his commercial real estate work, Lynagh would occasionally struggle to make the deadline. Not a word was said. On seeing him drive through the Ballymore gates, assistant coach John Brass would announce it was six o'clock Lynagh-time, even if his watch told him twenty past. Time to train. In recent years Horan-time and Little-time have been introduced, to accommodate the youthful superstars.

Had Lynagh and Campbell got their way, the Queensland touring party that departed for South America in early March would have included two promising eighteen-year-olds. Asked for their opinions at the team selection meeting, Campbell plumped for the up-and-coming, goalkicking lock John Eales, from Brothers, while Lynagh had heard and seen enough of the Souths colts player Tim Horan to believe he was worth a punt. The subsequent deeds of Eales and Horan suggest those opinions should have been heeded. As it was, seven new caps were included in the first Queensland team to be known officially by a different name.

The Brisbane public had been bombarded by local sporting teams with easily recognisable and identifiable names. There were the Bullets basketballers, the Bears Australian Rules club and the heavily publicised Broncos league team. The Queensland Rugby Union's flagship needed a new hook on which to hang its hat in the marketing contest and although the jersey remained maroon, the Queensland team was dubbed the Reds. For a game with the conservative traditions of rugby such a move was not taken lightly.

Jason Little, son of a Dalby pig-farmer, did not expect to be making his Queensland rugby debut at the foot of the Andes mountains in South America. But just six months after his eighteenth birthday there he was, named in the Reds XV to play Cuyo in the quaint Argentinian city of Mendoza. Not since Lynagh's debut seven years before had a young player generated so much anticipation or excitement among rugby followers. To their mutual benefit, Lynagh recognised that Little was about to be subjected to pressures similar to those he had experienced all those years ago. He enjoyed having Jason around because his situation reminded him so much of his own. As a teenager fresh out of school he'd gone on tour to New Zealand in 1982 with grown men, some of whom seemed old enough to be his father, and now it was Jason's turn to cope. Although by nature the laid-back Little was very much a country boy, and nowhere near as intense as Lynagh could be, the two hit it off immediately. Lynagh enjoyed being able to provide guidance for Little, while Little was delighted to be shown such unconditional friendship from one of the greats of the game. Lynagh's openness did not surprise assistant coach John Brass. He had seen his attitude in the pre-season camps where the whole Queensland training squad of sixty hopefuls assembled for weekends of daytime exertion and night-time relaxation. Ten players were grouped together

– the combination always comprised three senior team-members, a couple who had been on the scene a short time, and youngsters straight out of school or colts teams.

'Noddy was always terrific with the new guys,' recalls Brass. 'He related so well to their situation and in turn they looked up to him and had enormous respect for him. Often I think he can be pretty difficult to talk to, but in those situations when a young bloke is stepping into the big unforgiving world of senior football, he is fantastic.'

In Argentina, Lynagh's relaxed frame of mind was aided by the presence of Greg Martin. His former schoolboy opponent, and a University club-mate and fellow reveller in the Human Movements anatomy lectures, Martin's zany sense of humour and his apparent total lack of concern for what people thought of him appealed to Lynagh. Lynagh couldn't help caring what people might think – Marto didn't give two hoots. Both had been to Argentina with the Wallabies eighteen months earlier, when Little was still at school, so the new kid on the block was pretty impressed when they took it on themselves to make him feel comfortable.

'Noddy helped me a lot on the field and made sure I was involved in social events. Marto was sensational and his relaxed personality rubbed off on Noddy a bit as well. We had a terrific time together.'

No better time was had than after the game in Santiago, Chile. The tour had been tossed into semi-controversy in the lead-up to the match against the Chilean national side. To make a better contest, the Chilean XV was to be bolstered by the inclusion of some South African players. Queensland had agreed to five guest players, but on arriving in Santiago the Reds discovered seven South Africans on the scene, all expecting to get a game. At the time, sporting contact with South Africa was still a very sensitive issue and the Australian government, in its wisdom, ruled that seven players constituted a Springbok representative team. Queensland faced a brawl, either with the Chileans and the South Africans or with their own government; manager John

Breen stuck firmly to his guns and insisted that if any more than five South Africans turned out, the match would be abandoned.

Not the types who relish being told what to do, the South Africans turned heel and departed. If there was any boycotting to be done, they decided they would get in first. As a result the game was a mismatch and Queensland thrashed an unstacked Chilean team in a 60–12 rout. The pre-match tensions and the anti-climactic game didn't make for the most jovial atmosphere at the after-match function. The team escaped as soon as was politely possible, figuring a full frontal assault on the nightclubs of Santiago was the best way to vent their frustrations. However the suspicion a Connolly training special might be called some time after breakfast caused them to retreat shortly before dawn, with the idea of grabbing a modicum of rest before the torture began.

A five-man posse, which included Lynagh and Martin, commandeered a taxi to take them back to the team hotel. The cab driver didn't speak English but he could count, and as four passengers were the legal limit, he refused to make any exceptions for a bunch of under-the-weather *gringos* from Australia. With teamwork temporarily put to one side, it was each man for himself and Martin was left on the footpath as his four colleagues clambered into the taxi. Always quick to seize an opportunity, he realised the roofrack would be a more comfortable alternative to a two-hour walk. Up he sprang as the cab took off, the man at the wheel none the wiser for the non-paying passenger atop.

Varying between the Chilean speeds of fast and really fast, the cab careered through the streets of Santiago, while Martin wondered why he'd ever paid good money to ride the roller-coaster at the Brisbane Show, when this was twice as much fun. On the cab's arrival at the hotel, he promptly slid down the front windscreen, gave the driver a quick wink and walked inside. A quicker sign of the cross was never made as the driver reached for the rosary beads hanging from the rear-vision mirror.

On the field, Lynagh was in magical touch. He played five games and made a personal contribution of eighty-three points. He then dropped in on the Hong Kong Sevens on the way home, and was the tournament's top scorer with fifty-six points. It was a promising preparation for the next few months, in which a three-Test tour by the British Lions was the highlight. The Lions represent the best of British rugby and the side brings together the cream of the English, Irish, Scottish and Welsh teams. In earlier decades they had rarely bothered to visit Australia, confining themselves to contests against the big two – the All Blacks and the Springboks. Before the 1980s, the Wallabies were respected, but in the world rugby scene, considered as little more than small fry. In 1989, with South Africa out of the picture for almost a decade and the consistency of Australia's performances increasing, the powers-that-be in Britain finally consented to a full tour of Australia.

Even to the most experienced players in the Wallaby outfit, a berth against the Lions was an enticing carrot. Lynagh, Campese and Farr-Jones were certain selections for the series opener at the Sydney Football Stadium, but for fringe candidates the two scheduled interstate matches would be of crucial importance. The Red wave that had begun to gather momentum in Argentina was looking to swamp the Blues and ensure a liberal sprinkling of Queenslanders in that first Test team.

Since 1976, when Queensland turned Australian rugby on its head by thrashing New South Wales 42–4, the animosity between the two unions had been clear for all to see. On the 1982 Scottish tour of Australia, Scotland captain Andy Irvine warned that the Wallabies would never reach their potential until New South Wales and Queensland forgot their differences. No one listened too closely. New South Wales behaved like a bossy big brother while Queensland seemed evenly balanced – it had a chip on both shoulders! The arrogance of New South Wales emanated from years of dominance on the field; Queensland's dissatisfaction stemmed from the almost complete control New South Wales had of the game's organisation in Australia. For many years the voting on all major decisions to do with Australian rugby was made by a committee which so flagrantly favoured New South Wales that power could never shift out of Sydney. Western Australia, Tasmania and the other minor unions each had one vote, Queensland had two, while New South Wales enjoyed a five-man voting team. As those five would invariably vote as a block, it was only a matter of securing one or two votes from the other states to achieve any desired aim. Consequently, all the major coaching and selection appointments favoured New South Wales. Whether those positions were always awarded on merit is open to debate, but only two Queensland-based coaches, Des Connor and Bob Templeton, have taken charge of Wallaby preparations in the past four decades.

In 1988, Queensland lost its first interstate series in thirteen years. Coach Connolly and the players realised that a loss to the Blues in 1989 would not only mar a promising start to the season, but would virtually assure New South Wales' domination of the Test team. There was only one place to mount a definitive case for the Reds and that was on the field. Experience told them that even then it might not be enough.

New South Wales came to Ballymore with the intention of both putting the Queenslanders in their place and also taking out the South Pacific Championship, a prestigious early-season competition between the leading provinces of New Zealand and Australia. Just seven days earlier the Blues had beaten Auckland, a team touted at that time as the strongest provincial outfit in the world. A win over Queensland would give New South Wales the championship, so their officials organised to have the trophy on hand at Ballymore for a post-match presentation. Queensland doesn't need any extra motivation when playing New South Wales but this classic example of Blues arrogance was just the sort of thing Connolly loved to use to motivate his players. Every word written in the press in praise of New South Wales after the Auckland game simply fuelled the fire that Connolly and Campbell were building under the Queensland team. 'Such talk,' remembers Campbell, 'of building them up and putting us down, was simply meat and drink to us.'

The marauding Maroons, as the Queensland teams of the 1970s were popularly referred to, had become the rampaging Reds. They made a mockery of the pre-match claims by spanking New South Wales 31–3: a four-try-to-nil shellacking, in which the forward pack dominated the play and Michael Lynagh had been the solo lead. Greg Martin had enhanced his Test claims with a trade-mark defensive performance but also, more importantly, a brilliant effort in attack. He scored a try as well as setting up another for centre Anthony Herbert – both the result of his simple game plan: 'I just made a point of following Noddy all day. He's the one who puts you through the gaps.' New South Wales skipper Nick Farr-Jones didn't hide from the facts. 'We were beaten in every facet of play. Queensland played astonishingly well.'

The Australian selection debate, which simmers constantly throughout every interstate series, was given further heat by Campbell's somewhat inflammatory post-match comment. His suggestion that the fifteen Queensland players would all look good in gold jerseys raised hackles in the south prior to the return match in Sydney a month later. The New South Welshmen were shattered by the magnitude of the defeat at Ballymore and, in a clear indication that panic was afoot, there was a concerted campaign to lure Mark Ella out of representative retirement. Ella, whose last first-class match was in 1984, had earlier that season returned to grade football with Randwick. The Reds were on the Argentinian tour when they had first heard of Ella's comeback plans and there was a strong suspicion among them that the mercurial flyhalf had been promised a crack at the British Lions by some high-ranking Wallaby official.

Dick Laffan, the New South Wales coach, confirmed that he would approach Ella to determine his availability for the return interstate match, while Ella himself suggested in the *Sun-Herald* on 27 May that if he did feel up to a representative return, the ideal match would be the scheduled Australia B fixture against the Lions, rather than the interstate game.

To Lynagh, who at this stage had a weekly column of his own in the *Courier-Mail*, it was like a red rag to a bull. Normally a sensitive, measured media commentator, particularly when he is referring to his former or present colleagues, there was plenty of spirit in his response to Ella's plans. On 3 June 1989, under the heading 'Who Is Ella To Select Himself?', Lynagh let fly in a most uncharacteristic fashion.

'Who, if I may be so impertinent to ask, does Mark Ella think he is?', he began. 'His column in a Sydney newspaper this week bordered on the arrogant, not to mention the ridiculous.' Reading this, just twenty-four hours before the return interstate match, Connolly was beside himself with excitement. Lynagh continued. 'Who is this guy, who is taking it upon himself to tell the selectors when he is ready to play the British Lions? What gives him the right to nominate the match that would best suit his comeback plans?'

Lynagh went on to describe Ella as one of the greats of Australian rugby, but argued that this didn't give him the right to dictate his own terms. 'He is giving the impression that he is doing the Australian selectors, and Australia in general, a big favour by coming back and helping them out of a hole at flyhalf. You can just imagine how that makes me feel. I feel like I've been dismissed as a second-rater. At the risk of being immodest, I feel the football I'm playing this season is some of the best I've ever produced.' This was a very annoyed Noddy. He may have thought those sorts of things before, but there was no way he had expressed them publicly. He then followed up with as rough a punch as he is ever likely to throw.

If Ella is serious about this comeback why isn't he ready by now, so this could have been settled on the football field in the interstate match? Ella's prediction before the interstate match that the Blues would thrash us at Ballymore was a big motivational boost for us. The 31–3 was Queensland's response. I don't know whether his latest column has stirred the other Queensland players to the same degree, but he certainly has helped me get fully motivated for tomorrow's game.

Lynagh now admits to a certain embarrassment when reading his handiwork. 'Mark and I have always got on well and he is a pretty laidback bloke, so there were no dramas after I wrote the article, but it's not really my style.' However, by the time Connolly had finished reading the column, he was air-punching, absolutely over the moon with joy. He figured he hardly needed to show up the next day.

And so the final 31–0 tally proved. It was the first time the Blues had been kept scoreless since 1900 and the *Sydney Morning Herald* headline told the story. 'Lynagh's Tactics Savage the Blues'. In another mud bath and once more behind a dominant pack, Lynagh controlled proceedings. Despite the heavy ball, his kicking, running and choices of moves were on a different plane. He had toyed with some of the country's best rugby players.

The combined match score of 62–3 gave Queensland its biggest series-winning margin in more than a century of interstate competition and it provided Connolly with another chance to let the Australian selectors know his thoughts. Not surprisingly he believed most, if not all of his players deserved promotion, but when he suggested halfback Peter Slattery should replace skipper Nick Farr-Jones, his credibility with the southern press plummetted. Even some parochial Queenslanders raised their eyebrows.

Those players on the fringe of the national team who wished to rubber-stamp their selection had the ideal opportunity when the Reds played the Lions a fortnight before the first Test. There was a rousing pre-match speech, reminding the team of the last Queensland–Lions game in 1971 when Queensland caused the boilover of the century with a 15–11 win. The Lions had been expected to win that game by thirty points or more, and indeed they later confirmed their quality by going on to lose only one match on their twenty-four-game tour of New Zealand. It was one of Queensland's most memorable victories, and even if the 1989 team weren't big readers of rugby history, they were convinced they could repeat it.

That some of his team-mates' hopes for a gold jersey rested on the performance of Lynagh was something that he couldn't afford to think about. An average performance in a winning side can often be of far greater selection value than a good performance in a losing side. Lynagh was Queensland's match-winner and no one from either team had any doubts about that. Lions captain Finlay Calder rated Lynagh the best flyhalf in the world and described him as the complete general. On 17 June, the *Courier-Mail*'s rugby writer Wayne Smith didn't underestimate the Lynagh factor.

> Today's battle in the appropriately colosseum-like setting of Ballymore is the psychological watershed of the Lions twelve-match Australian campaign. If they contain Lynagh on their way to their third victory of the tour, their confidence for the three-Test series will soar. Lose, with Lynagh dominating as he has in most of the Reds' fourteen games this season, and the bogeys will grow in their minds.

'It's Gonna Be A Jungle Out There', was the slogan the Queensland Rugby Union publicity machine had invented to promote the Lions tour, and spot on it was too. The Lions beat Queensland 19–15 in a brutal encounter, one which underlined that only the fittest would survive the upcoming series.

Whenever someone mentions the term 'over-vigorous rucking' you can be sure they believe there has been some kicking going on, and not the type that sends the ball downfield. After the match, Lions coach Ian McGeechan was unapologetic about his team's 'over-vigorous rucking'. 'We came here to win good tight ball,' he said. 'If that means rucking bodies out of the way, we will do it.' Queensland's pack, so dominant against New South Wales, was outplayed, and despite scoring all of Queensland's points, it had not been one of Lynagh's more fluent performances.

The writing was on the wall for the Test series. This was one of the most physically intimidating sides to ever tour Australia. Lynagh recalls that one glance at the personnel told you they played the game seriously. With his prematurely grey hair, it was said about Finlay Calder by the Wallaby players that it wasn't actually hair growing on his head, but rather, iron filings. 'Their backrowers, Calder, John Jeffrey, Mike Teague and Dean Richards all looked really mean,' says Lynagh, 'and they played in a very uncompromising fashion to match. They called Richards "Magilla Gorilla", and he wasn't a very pretty sight running at you with hate in his eyes.'

The loss to the Lions was Queensland's last match for the year. In his first season as coach, Connolly had exorcised the demons of 1988. Lynagh describes the 1989 team as one of the happiest he had been associated with, and he had a good relationship with the man who had stripped him of the captaincy duties. Now his immediate concerns were with Magilla Gorilla and his cronies.

The opening Test against the Lions was the first played in the newly constructed Sydney Football Stadium. After the final Test had been played at the Sydney Cricket Ground in 1986, the Australian Rugby Union shifted all international games to Concord Oval in Sydney's west. While rugby has grown enormously in popularity in that area, geographically it was a move that suited only a minority of the code's followers. The return to Paddington, where supporters could again indulge in the pre- and post-match tradition of congregating at the many pubs in the Moore Park area, was warmly welcomed. With Test rugby back in the vicinity, one local publican predicted his Saturday take would triple. There were other advantages for the hotels. 'I'd have to say the rugby supporters make a better class of drunk,' one experienced barman pronounced.

While the New South Wales–Queensland bickering continued, the Australian selectors settled on a team of fifteen for the first Test. It included eight Reds and seven Blues. What could be fairer than that? And no one but Lions supporters had cause for complaint after Australia humbled the Brits 30–12 in a performance that left the Lions skipper with no option but to philosophise. 'It's like life,' remarked Calder. 'It has a habit of kicking you in the groin from time to time. But the fifteen of us are better people for it.' Lynagh felt a better person for his fourteen-point contribution and his role in setting up two of the four Australian tries.

The huge haul had taken his Test match tally in thirty-one appearances to 399, and his confidence received a boost when, in the lead-up to the second Test at Ballymore, Farr-Jones paid a hefty compliment to his halfback partner. 'Noddy can run, he can set up players, he can step and he can kick. I'm not saying he is the best player I've seen, but the most complete. I put him up there with Mark Ella.'

While Farr-Jones chose to laud his colleagues, Bill Campbell focussed his attention on the second Test. 'They'll be desperate men, but if they go in for the kicking and the punching they'll be falling into our hands,' he said in the *Courier-Mail* on 4 July. 'Don't think the first Test was an easy task, because we had to do plenty of ducking and weaving when the boots started flying in the tight stuff.'

What eventuated at Ballymore was little more than bitter mayhem. There was plenty of the above-mentioned kicking and punching, but if the scoreboard was a reflection, Campbell's prediction that 'they would be falling into our hands' was off the mark. Two late tries gave the Lions a 19–12 victory in one of the most spiteful Test matches since the Welsh tour of Australia eleven years earlier. By half-time, Lynagh,

Campbell and Farr-Jones were all bleeding from head wounds while Steven Cutler was lucky to survive a ferocious first forty minutes with his senses intact. Pinned at the bottom of a ruck, Cutler's head was the target for some kicking practice by Lions prop David Young.

The niggle had started at the very first scrum when Lions halfback Robert Jones stood on Farr-Jones' foot in an act of pure provocation. When the Australian skipper responded, Finlay Calder flew off the side of the scrum and hit him. The result was a first half of brawling, vengeful football, which did little credit to the code. There were suggestions that the Lions had resorted to the infamous 'ninety-nine' tactic used during the tour of South Africa in 1974. Whenever fighting broke out in matches on that tour, a call of 'ninety-nine' was the signal for all the British to wade in. The one-in all-in theory worked on the basis a referee was less likely to send a player off if everyone was involved in the melee. Coach Ian McGeechan dismissed the suggestion as fanciful, but Lynagh was certain there had been a premeditated plan to take the Wallaby players' minds off the game. 'I feel they sat down as an opposition and worked out where our centre was. Nick Farr-Jones was the captain and the link between the brilliant backs and the ball-winning forwards. They figured if they could disrupt us at half-back they might be in with a chance.'

After the match Farr-Jones' swollen and bruised face was visible proof that he had indeed been a marked man, and while Calder categorised the Lions' tactics under the label of commitment, there were plenty of commentators who believed thuggery was the more applicable term. The Fitzgerald inquiry into police corruption was in process at the time, and the *Sunday-Mail*'s rugby writer, Wayne Smith made his feelings clear in a post-match report on 9 July 1989.

> With three policemen in the Lions pack, it seemed the tourists themselves were in need of a Fitzgerald Inquiry, so blatant was the general disregard for law and order.

John Moulton, the Australian team doctor, was a busy man in the rooms after the game as five Wallaby players required stitches in the head. That not one Lions player required treatment suggested they had won the fight as well as the match.

It is a fact of rugby life that no matter how talented a team's backline might be, without a forward pack that can dominate its opponents, there is little hope of the backline stars shining. Prior to the series-deciding third Test, Lynagh reminded his team-mates of a story which illustrated this quite clearly. In 1978 when the Wallabies toured New Zealand, former All Black coach J. J. Stewart was invited to supervise a training session. He asked who was the fastest man in the squad and on being told winger Brendan Moon, the middle-aged, somewhat overweight Stewart immediately challenged him to a race over twenty-five metres. The one condition was that on the word 'go', Moon had to take two steps backwards before setting off. Stewart won the race comfortably and the moral was there for all to see. If the forwards present the backs with the ball as the pack is going backwards there is no chance of success. Little quality ball had come the way of the Wallaby backs at Ballymore, and even in those circumstances Australia was only beaten in the closing minutes. If the forwards could dominate at the Sydney Football Stadium, the Wallaby backs would do the rest.

Easier said than done. The Lions forwards, that bunch of mean-looking bovver-boys, had improved immensely since their meek efforts in the first Test. They weren't only tough and uncompromising they were highly skilful in the bread-and-butter work of scrums and line-outs. In the first half of the decider, the Lions dominated all phases of play, but like a terrier unprepared to let go its grip, Australia defended tenaciously. When Lynagh set up Ian Williams for the only try prior to half-time, it was 9-all and the Lions had nothing to show for their territorial superiority. The Australian players were aware that if they could break clear early in the second half, frustration might slow the

British down, and the Wallabies could at last get in front. A Lynagh penalty straight after the resumption was the ideal tonic, and it seemed the Bulldog spirit finally had been cracked. Five minutes later, disaster struck.

Lions flyhalf Rob Andrew's attempted field goal had gone wide and was gathered by winger David Campese, a player renowned for his attacking genius. Although running the ball from behind your own tryline is one of the most exciting things in rugby, there are times when the only sensible option is to dot the ball down and return for a dropout from the twenty-two-metre line. With the physical mauling the Australian forwards were taking it was certainly what they wanted: take the rest, slow play down, remain in control.

Not for Campo though. He ran with the ball and when confronted by Welsh winger Ieuan Evans threw a wild pass to fullback Greg Martin. Martin was unable to handle it and Evans fell on the ball to score the Lions' only try and wrest back the initiative that the Australians had worked so hard to get. Some thirty metres away, Lynagh clasped his head in his hands in total disbelief while the despair was clearly evident in the body language of his team-mates.

'I will never forget how I felt,' says Lynagh. 'It had been a really tough struggle but we were finally in front and feeling we were about to go over the edge. We could sense their last breath when all of a sudden we resuscitated them. I just felt my shoulders sag. It was deflating and depressing – we'd worked so hard.'

Despite two late Lynagh goals the Lions went on to win 19–18. Campese became the target for a virulent press and the blunder has become one of the most notorious incidents in the recent history of the game. Although accepting the blame, Campese reacted poorly to the criticism that followed. Captain Farr-Jones wrote an open letter to the *Sydney Morning Herald* trying to absolve his team-mate. It was a noble and understandable act of unity but within team ranks there was no doubt where the finger of blame was pointed. Sure, other players may not have performed at their best at some stages of the game, but one incident lost them the contest and that was Campese's error.

Lynagh believes the mistake has haunted Campese because he complained for so long about being criticised over it. Campo himself was prepared to say he made a mistake but he wasn't happy about other people agreeing!

'While he kept making it an issue, people would keep writing about it,' says Lynagh, adding that the irony was that had Campese decided to dummy-pass to Martin and then run himself, he probably would have been able to make twenty metres or more and then unleash one of his powerful punt kicks. Instead of being under the posts in the middle of a nightmare, the Australians would have been in Lions territory and back on top.

Amid the upsets of a squandered series, Lynagh had changed jobs, moving from Richard Ellis to Lewis and Partners, another commercial real estate firm in Brisbane. Former Queensland centre Peter Lewis was the managing director and Paul McLean joined soon after, so there was a heavy rugby influence. The Lynagh name was again seen as a marketable tool and he hoped his own business experience would be broadened while it opened some doors for the company.

He arrived at the office early one August morning with the depression of the loss to the Lions and defeat in a one-off Test against the All Blacks still lingering. Work, he thought, might take his mind off those disappointments. Instead a phone call from the other side of the world had that effect.

'Hello Michael, my name's Joe Pickavance from St Helens Rugby League Club in England. Have you heard of us?'

'Yes Joe, I certainly have.'

'We'd like to make you an offer to come and play for us. Are you interested?'

'Yes, I am.'

Within fifteen minutes Lynagh had a contract in his hands. Bewildered by the magnitude of the offer, the twenty-five-year-old realised he was a mere signature away from securing his financial future.

10
THERE'S ONLY ONE MICHAEL LYNAGH

There it was in plain English.

Offer of playing contract to Michael Lynagh

1 Fifty thousand pounds sterling, tax paid per playing season, i.e. August to May inclusive.

2 One hundred and fifty pounds sterling per week tax paid throughout the playing season.

3 Suitable accommodation in residential area for duration of the contract.

4 Provision of a new car for the duration of the contract.

5 Air fare from Australia to the United Kingdom for yourself and girlfriend, plus return airfare from the United Kingdom to Australia at the end of each English season if required, i.e. from mid-May to return by 7 August.

This offer of contract would be for a period of four years.

Alex Murphy, a legend in British rugby league, was the St Helens coach and he didn't try to camouflage his admiration for Lynagh. 'He is the best standoff in the world,' he said in the *Courier-Mail* on 31 July 1989. 'He is quick, has a tremendous pair of hands and a good footballing brain. His goal and tactical kicking are bonuses. Rugby league is made for him.'

Looking beyond the praise, it didn't take Lynagh long to work out that the offer was worth approximately $100 000 more per year than he was currently earning from his rugby pursuits. While the sceptics outside the game believed stars like Lynagh were looked after financially by the Australian Rugby Union, he emphatically denies that this was ever the case. All he had previously received over, under or to the side of the table were the legitimate expenses paid to all Wallaby players on tour. By 1989, that amounted to about $80 a day and there were no exceptions. If you'd played dozens of Tests and scored hundreds of points, you still got the same amount as a rookie making his first tour.

Like all his colleagues, Lynagh loved the game of rugby and the things it had to offer – the tours to exotic destinations, the camaraderie, the world-wide contacts that could be made. However, he was only too aware that used airline tickets weren't much use as a deposit for a house. The cold, hard stuff tends to be more useful in those situations, and this piece of paper he was staring at was the golden key to the bank manager's door.

A fortnight later however, Lynagh faxed his reply to St Helens.

Dear Joe,
I would like to thank you for your generous offer to play with St Helens Football Club.

I regret to inform you that I decline the offer to join your club.

Once again thank you for your patience. It has been a pleasure to deal with you and I am sorry I cannot bring you better news.

Yours sincerely,

Michael Lynagh

One of the bird-in-the-hand-is-worth-two-in-the-bush school of thinking, Lynagh decided the positive attributes of his current lifestyle weren't worth sacrificing for the discomforts of life in the north of

England. That he could be getting £50 000 a year for the next four years was certain, but he failed to convince himself that the money would compensate for the other things he already enjoyed.

'The offer had one major factor going for it – money. But in the end that didn't stack up against what I already had,' says Lynagh. 'My lifestyle was important to me, and the fact I was playing a game I enjoyed at the top level, and was considered to be pretty good at. I was enjoying my work, I lived in a good place and the thought of four winters in the north of England didn't particularly appeal to me.'

Despite Murphy's words, Lynagh was unsure also how good he would be at league – a game with a heavier emphasis on defence. As a tackler in rugby, Lynagh sometimes suffered from his habit of trying to strip the ball from runners, rather than make a full-blooded tackle. In recent years, he has altered his style so that he has become quite a punishing tackler and the change underlines the fact he would indeed have made a fine league player. Nevertheless, at that time, this uncertainty helped him decide the whole venture would have been too big a risk.

It had been one of the toughest decisions of his life and he was delighted to know his loyalty had not gone unnoticed among the ordinary supporters of the code. Within hours of the newspapers proclaiming the news that Lynagh had rejected the offer, a telegram arrived for him at work.

> It's news like this that makes my world go around, Michael. A great decision that you will never regret. Congratulations.
>
> Tom Nutley

Lynagh knew he had made the right choice but such an affirmation made him feel even better about it. He was disappointed however, that despite the widespread coverage the league offer had received in the media, not once did he get a call from a rugby official offering any sort of advice or guidance. Nor, when he knocked it back, was there a response from Ballymore or the ARFU indicating they were grateful for his loyalty.

'I'd have thought it wasn't expecting too much for one of the administrators to phone and acknowledge that they were pleased I had stuck with rugby,' says Lynagh. 'Thankfully, things have changed and nowadays, if a player gets a league offer, the officials are on to them in a flash trying to help out.'

There was no doubt Lynagh was the man the world wanted. While he was making his decision about the St Helens offer, he received an invitation to make a five-match tour of South Africa with a World XV. He wasted no time with his reply this time. Not only did he refuse the offer, he also declined to publicly elaborate on his reasons for doing so. He considered himself a sportsman and nothing else. Although toeing the diplomatic line by saying he was honoured to be invited, he made no other comment, fearing that anything he said might be used by people for political or social purposes. When television sporting personality, Mike Gibson condemned him for not speaking out, Lynagh used his column in the *Courier-Mail* to respond on 12 August 1989.

> Simply turning down South Africa wasn't good enough for Mike Gibson ... The simple fact is that the South Africans invited me as Michael Lynagh, rugby player, not Michael Lynagh, politician or moral activist. And I responded simply as a sportsman. My politics and moral views on South Africa are personal and I choose to keep them private. If that creates problems for Gibson, or anyone else, then so be it.

With University in the 1989 Brisbane grand final, it was sheer relief for Lynagh to become once more the target of rampaging flankers rather than persistent media men chasing a scoop. There was no question he was happier under physical pressure than the sort exerted by the press. Souths discovered this as Lynagh produced what was described by some as the most clinically perfect performance of his career. Two field goals, one from fifty metres, and a try helped University to a 34–9 disposal of the Magpies. It was an ideal climax to a domestic season in which Lynagh had displayed the best form of his career. Recognition came in the form of just about every rugby award that was handed out. Within the space of a fortnight he was named the Australian Society of Rugby Writers' Player of the Year, and received the same honour from the *Australian* newspaper and his home state.

He had three weeks to reflect on such honours before again packing his bags and heading for France with the Wallabies, fully aware of the old rugby adage, 'You're only as good as your last game!'

Peter FitzSimons, Nick Farr-Jones' biographer, Australian team-mate of Lynagh and a conscientious student of human character, made his first Wallaby tour with Lynagh to Fiji in 1984. In the intervening five years, while Lynagh was amassing hundreds of Test points and earning a reputation as one of the world's finest players, FitzSimons was busy making the most of his rugby passport. He chose to depart the Australian rugby scene and played with various teams overseas, including three years with the Brieve club in France. He returned to Sydney in time to impress the selectors enough to make his way into the 1989 touring party and was selected for his Test debut in the opening international in Strasbourg.

The Australian team was a gamble – four new caps including FitzSimons and nineteen-year-old centre Jason Little, as well as tyros Phil Kearns, Tony Daly and Tim Horan, each with only one Test appearance to their name. The Wallabies' lead-up games to the Test match had all the elements of a French farce – three losses from four games; the Australians' play was characterised by ineptitude and indiscipline. In short, things didn't look good.

However, the success of tours is never judged by what happens in the provincial games. It is the Test matches that matter and the

Wallabies knew the memory of their woeful start could be wiped away with eighty minutes of commitment. Dwyer worked hard to ensure the newspapers were proclaiming a French win as a *fait accompli* and he laid on a heavy diet of back-to-the-wall thinking among his players. He was near tears in his pre-match address, as he urged the players to dig deep into their reservoirs of personal pride and courage. It was the old- fashioned, love-of-flag-and-country motivation. Take no prisoners. Lay your body on the line. Every cliché got a run. And what's more they worked – the Wallabies surged to a 32–15 victory. But they worked only because control and composure were not lost amid fury and aggression. For that, the Wallabies owed much to Lynagh.

'I was just about weeping adrenalin,' remembers FitzSimons. 'But Nick Farr-Jones and Noddy were in such control, so seemingly laid-back and comfortable it was incredible.' At one stage late in the match, when the game was as good as won, Lynagh released a booming fifty-metre punt. As it spiralled towards French fullback Serge Blanco, golf enthusiasts Lynagh and Farr-Jones urged the ball to bounce correctly, just as they might do to a well-struck one-wood off the first tee. 'Get left!' they called simultaneously. 'Get left!' The ball landed five metres in front of Blanco and broke left before rolling into touch and gaining Australia valuable ground. 'I just remember both of them running down towards the lineout laughing about it,' says FitzSimons. 'It has stuck in my mind for two reasons. I thought that having a big giggle in the middle of a vital match like that was one, very odd in a Test match and two, very un-Noddy-like.'

As a fellow member of the Australian under-twenty-one team in 1982, FitzSimons recalls telling Lynagh the news that Paul McLean had announced his retirement. As that opened the door for Lynagh into the Test squad, FitzSimons had expected some sign of glee. 'I'd have been doing cartwheels,' says FitzSimons, 'but he just took it on board in a sober fashion. There was certainly no overt expressiveness and that was symbolic of the man. It was therefore pretty surprising to see him burst out laughing in the middle of a Test.'

It also surprised Farr-Jones, whose on-field communication with Lynagh was usually non-verbal. 'There was never a lot to be said,' says Farr-Jones. 'We always had a quick handshake before we ran on and there was always a nice, warm feeling but there was never a lot of talk … Often with other flyhalves, I'd find myself saying to them, talk to me, talk to me, tell me which way you're going, but there was never that necessity with Noddy.'

One problem Farr-Jones did have, according to FitzSimons, was working out the best way to treat Lynagh and Campese, the side's two biggest stars, so as to ensure their optimum performance. 'Campo and Noddy were both just a little removed from the centre of the side and Nick used to spend half his time building bridges to Campo. Noddy liked being on his own a bit more than most but there was no hard feeling towards him because of that. He enjoyed the company of most of the blokes but wasn't in the middle of the social action. Nor was Campo, but while Nick was always trying to bring him back into it, he didn't have to do that with Noddy. He was generally quite happy on his own or with just one or two of the guys.'

FitzSimons believes that while not all the players got close to Lynagh, they were more appreciative of his attitude than that of Campese. 'There was active resentment towards Campo because he would get all the publicity, all the glory … but with other things, such as unloading bags from the bus, he was never there, and that was where the resentment came. With Noddy it was just neutrality. If you got out of the shower you'd flick everybody with the towel. If you saw Noddy, you'd hesitate and then not do it. Noddy was just there. He won you the game. Good on him!'

Not even Lynagh could win the Wallabies the second Test. The team had moved to Lille for an Armistice Day appointment with a re-vamped French side. Never afraid to press the panic button after a loss, the French selectors dropped nine of their fifteen players after Strasbourg. Six forwards were axed, while Captain Pierre Berbizier and Serge Blanco, one of France's most admired players, were also omitted.

The new-look team had a flyhalf playing in the centre, and the centre at fullback, the prop was hooking and the hooker propped while the flanker shifted to lock and the lock was at number eight. Australia had never won a Test series in France, and with the confidence gained from the first match as well as the upheaval within the French side, there would never be a better opportunity.

But as often as not logical assessment is of little relevance in French rugby, and that was obvious in Lille. An Australian team, together for the past month and buoyed with confidence after the first Test, were beaten 25–19 by a side cobbled together at the last minute and littered with men playing out of their normal position.

With a shared Test series and a poor record in the provincial matches to show for their five weeks away, the tour had been only moderately successful, but it was to prove a gilt-edged investment in the future. The centre partnership of Tim Horan and Jason Little, which was to blossom into one of the greatest midfield combinations of all time, was seen for the first time in Wallaby colours. While their arrival on the scene caused much excitement for Australian rugby followers, they were a double bonus for Lynagh. Not only did he have a couple of world-class performers outside him to help alleviate the on-field pressures, he also enjoyed their company away from the rugby. Coach Bob Dwyer considered that a major plus.

'Noddy is basically a very withdrawn character and he needs to relax. That seemed to happen more often than not when he was with Tim and Jason. He really is just one of the boys when he's with that pair, while in the big group he tends to feel much more serious about things. The formality comes out of him when he's around Tim and Jason and he can be quite impish.'

He can be quite canny as well. Rooming with the first-time tourist Horan in France, Lynagh was able to boost his bank balance by a few francs thanks to the naïveté of the new boy. Before the teams were being chosen for each of the matches on tour, Lynagh and Horan would have a bet on who could come closest to picking the side. Invariably Lynagh was the more accurate with his predictions. It was not until the final week of the tour that Horan realised that as vice-captain of the touring party, Lynagh sat in on all the selection meetings with Dwyer and Farr-Jones, and knew the teams before they were announced to the players.

As head of the Australian Broadcasting Corporation and president of North Sydney Rugby League Club, David Hill was a man of not inconsiderable influence. When he rang Lynagh in January 1990 there was no chance his request to meet would be refused. Although he did not divulge what he wished to discuss, Lynagh had a fair idea. 'I didn't think he was about to offer me a job as the ABC newsreader.' Less than a week after that brief phone conversation, Hill was sitting in Lynagh's Brisbane office. He went straight to the point. 'We want you to come and play for North Sydney this season. As our goalkicking five-eighth you'll be one of the highest-paid rugby league players in Sydney.'

In quantitative terms, Lynagh didn't know exactly what that meant, but he realised it had the makings of a very lucrative deal. Hill added a sweetener. 'The ABC is one of the biggest property users in Australia and, as you are in that line of work, we could help to find something appropriate for you to continue your business career. If you are keen to do any media work, we should be able to work something out there as well.'

The meeting went amicably and, although Hill had not given a figure nor had Lynagh asked for one, the temptation that had been resisted only six months earlier was offered even more strongly. 'I thought more seriously about this offer than the English one,' says Lynagh. 'I liked Sydney as a place to live, it was nearer to home, and as well as the money and challenge factors, there also seemed to be professional opportunities that might be difficult to pass up.'

Hill closed their meeting by informing Lynagh that the last thing he wanted was for news of his approach to be getting out. Not one to breach confidences Lynagh told no one, preferring in any case to toss the options around in his own mind. The place he could do that best was at the beach, and it was after a long surf the next weekend that he returned to his parents' beach house to be told an ABC news reporter had been constantly ringing trying to contact him. 'Mum said this guy had heard I'd had a rugby league offer and he wanted to come and interview me. I rang him back and told him I wasn't going to say anything, and I then asked him where he'd heard the rumour. He told me the story was doing the rounds of his office.'

As no other station but the ABC had picked it up, Lynagh put two and two together and got Hill. Whether or not his maths were correct, it didn't sit very well. 'Here was a guy who had asked me to keep quiet and as there were only two of us in the office, and I knew I hadn't said anything, I could only assume he hadn't been prepared to do what he'd asked me to.' Although it was not a major issue, Lynagh felt a slight sense of betrayal. As one always keen to toe the line, he is intolerant of those who expect behaviour of him that they themselves cannot display. When Hill rang again the following week, it didn't take long for Lynagh to gauge the secrecy factor was now totally forgotten. 'Michael, the Bears are playing a trial match in Bundaberg on Sunday. I'm going to fly up for the match. Would you like to come along and watch us play?' inquired Hill.

'For me to fly with the president of Norths to watch the club play a trial match in a country centre is hardly keeping things under our hat is it?' Lynagh responded.

'Come along anyway, Michael, who cares?'

'No thanks.' Lynagh far preferred to go surfing.

He also preferred to stay put, so after a fortnight of consideration he rejected the offer. The newspapers put their own prices on the contract. Lynagh told the journalistic fraternity that they could speculate on the figure which, of course, they did. The world was told that Lynagh had knocked back a three-year, million-dollar deal. No was becoming the most commonly used word in his vocabulary as he also told the Brisbane Broncos he would be staying in rugby.

'I went and had a chat with the directors of the Broncos, but they were never a chance. I'd knocked back a lot of money from St Helens and yet the Broncos weren't prepared to offer any real financial inducement. It was all maybes and perhaps. We'll be a good team and if you play A grade you'll be well paid was their line. What they wanted to pay me up front was a joke. I could see where they were coming from business wise, but if they thought they could lure me away from what I had for about $20 000 they were kidding themselves. I asked them about the last five years where I'd established my reputation. Didn't I get anything for that? The meeting was amicable but pretty short.'

The attempts by rugby league to tempt union players over the years has seen no shortage of animosity between followers and officials of the two codes. Some of the diehards have been known to suggest that once a rugby player defects to league, he should never again be allowed to take part in a game of union. Although he has never taken the opportunity to play the professional game, Lynagh is an unabashed fan. 'I have never liked the war of words that develops between league and union people. I enjoy both games as I do soccer and Australian Rules. They are different sports and have their own strengths and weaknesses. In the two rugby codes there are different objectives. In league, it is an advantage to be short, stocky and fast. If you're short, stocky and fast and want to be a second rower in union, you are not going to get too far. In rugby, there is a position for every build of player. People are always asking how this rugby player or that might go in league, but you could just as well ask the question in reverse. I believe rugby has more subtle skills than league but good games of both codes are great while both can be deadly boring if not played well.

Nearly every player in the Wallabies enjoys and appreciates the league. I think good sportsmen know how difficult it is to excel, whatever the game.'

Rugby league's money men might have been desperate to get the Lynagh name on a contract but that didn't get him special treatment at rugby headquarters. After being chosen to captain Australia for the 1990 Hong Kong Sevens on his seventh consecutive trip to the tournament, Lynagh rang ARFU chief executive Bob Fordham to try and alter some details of his travel arrangements. 'Michael Lynagh speaking,' he said to the receptionist. 'I'd like to speak to Bob Fordham.'

'He's not available,' came the reply. 'What's it about?'

'I want to talk to him about the Hong Kong Sevens.'

'Sorry sir,' she said. 'We don't handle ticket sales here.'

Despite that lack of co-operation, he soon found himself at the Hong Kong Hilton enjoying the special atmosphere created by this unique event. All the teams stayed at the Hilton and on his first trip Lynagh had remarked in the foyer to a Papuan opponent how luxurious and comfortable the rooms were. The Papuan nodded but mentioned that he had never slept on a bed before and so was playing it safe and lying on the floor.

Although the top teams had begun to take the competition more seriously than in Lynagh's early days, there was still plenty of fun to be had by the more eccentric teams and individuals. In 1988 inventive Frenchman Eric Blondeau had used the Australian players, among others, to help him in his proposal of marriage. 'NATHALIE, WILL YOU MARRY ME?' was spelled out on one-metre-high cardboard letters held by twenty-seven players in the grandstand of the Hong Kong Government Stadium. Nathalie obviously thought about it overnight. At the other end of the stadium on the following day three girls held up cards of their own: 'OUI' was the response.

With more than 20 000 jugs of Carlsberg and San Miguel beer swilled during the two days of competition there is always as much action off the field as on, and the many Australians who visit for the weekend are never far from the play-makers. Perth businessman and West Coast Eagles supporter Neil Hamilton and a group of cronies are regular pilgrims who leave the worries of the financial world behind to enjoy some relaxation and frivolity at the Hong Kong Sevens. They formed the There's Only One Michael Lynagh Club, which involves a number of rules that are strictly adhered to. The first requirement is to wear the club uniform – a T-shirt with the words 'There's Only One Michael Lynagh' emblazoned across it. Those words also provide the sum total of the lyrics of the club song, as first rendered by Max Farr-Jones, father of Nick, at an airport bar, and now part of an annual ritual. Sung to the tune of 'Guantanamera', 'There's only one Michael Lynagh' rings out constantly across the stadium from the forty-strong choir any time the Australians are playing. Not confining their excursions strictly to the rugby, Hamilton and his merry men also frequent the bars of Hong Kong and no new establishment is entered without the pilgrims first singing the club song. The unsuspecting patrons quickly discover there is a Michael Lynagh songbook, which each member of the club carries with him, and should the occasion warrant it, the full repertoire is delivered. Lynagh and a few of his team-mates will often join the 'club' at the ground when playing commitments allow. 'I think Noddy and the boys sit in amazement watching us playing up … and wonder what the world is coming to,' says Hamilton.

One Michael Lynagh was one too many for Wellington to cope with. Boasting a powerful lineup, which included All Blacks John Gallagher and John Schuster, the proud New Zealand provincial team was thrashed 59–10 by the Reds in the South Pacific Championship match at Ballymore. Lynagh, who had a sluggish start to the Queensland season after returning from Hong Kong, was back to his best. His contribution of twenty-seven points helped bury the Wellingtonians and led assistant coach John Brass again to state his belief that Lynagh was the best footballer in the world. When his confidence was high it was difficult to argue with that assessment and his record haul against Wellington was the boost he needed as a heavy international season beckoned. The interstate wrangles again provided a touch of internal bitterness. Queensland enjoyed another two-nil series win, and the post-match comments from the coaches indicated the ill-feeling that continued to simmer. In the *Courier-Mail* on 28 April 1990, New South Wales coach Dick Laffan described the refereeing of Kerry Fitzgerald, Australia's leading whistle-blower at the time, as a 'sham, an absolute sham', while Queensland's John Connolly suggested the Blues should learn to take defeat on the chin.

Despite the rancour that develops during the course of almost every interstate contest, no ill-feeling ever seeps into the Australian team. 'Everyone has their own opinions on who should or should not be chosen,' says Lynagh, 'and while there is plenty of so-called hate dredged up during the interstate matches, the players have it all in perspective. On occasions the media don't mind suggesting the Queensland–New South Wales rivalry affects Wallaby team harmony but that has never been the case in any Australian team I've been involved in.' Lynagh's good friend Peter Slattery spoke on behalf of most players at a press conference preceding the 1994 interstate match at Ballymore. Questioned on whether there was still plenty of hate left in the series, Slattery responded simply. 'Mate, I don't hate anybody!'

Internal bickering was certainly not appropriate in the months ahead, with full series to be played against France and New Zealand. Coach Jacques Fouroux, or 'Jackie Fourex' as the Wallabies dubbed him, arrived in Sydney with a French team intent on building on the Armistice Day triumph seven months earlier. France's reputation for flair was second to none in the rugby world, but after recent inconsistent results, Fouroux had moved slightly away from the crowd-pleasing style that had been the Gallic trademark. He wanted to build a side based on enormous power and physical presence in the forwards, capable of wearing down opposing packs. Perhaps France needed little less *joie de vivre* and *laissez-faire*, a bit more of the heavy stuff.

Peter FitzSimons, the Wallabies' French connection, warned his team-mates that he could sense the tourists were on edge and ready to explode. He was right. The match began with a vicious brawl and with only thirteen minutes gone the French were already one man down – Moroccan-born flanker Abdel Benazzi was banished by English referee Tony Spreadbury for stomping. Australia went on to win a dour victory with Lynagh again in wonderful scoring form, kicking six goals from six attempts to notch seventeen of the Wallabies twenty-one points. Colleague David Campese though, was less than impressed by the Australian efforts. Campese had not been selected for the Test due to his late return from his Italian commitments, and was obviously not pleased by the performances of Lynagh and FitzSimons. In his book *On a Wing And a Prayer* Campese offered this appraisal.

> During that match, Michael Lynagh must have kicked away 95 per cent of the possession the Wallabies won. And, perhaps for the first time in my entire life, I felt glad I was not wearing a Wallaby shirt that day.

Lynagh was not the only one to stop some Campese bullets. Referring to the brawl in the opening moments of that first Test, he laid the blame fairly at the feet of FitzSimons.

> … all I could have done that day was to hang around on the wing and get cold. Or I could have been caught up in the middle of a brawl started by Peter FitzSimons, which was a disgrace to the good name of rugby. It was quite obvious that Peter had played countless matches against some of the French players while playing for Brieve and had a grudge to settle.

It was somewhat ironic that in the same book, Campese indicated how disappointed he was that former team-mates could be critical of him in the press. 'I hope I never get myself into a position where I start publicly slagging off guys I have just finished playing alongside,' he wrote. The subtle difference must have been that Campese hadn't just finished playing with the men he was criticising.

It was perhaps just as well that the book was still some twelve months away from publication, as neither Lynagh nor FitzSimons might have been quite so welcoming when Campese returned to the Australian team for the second Test in Brisbane. Between the first two Tests, Lynagh had calmly scored all Queensland's points in the Reds' 15–3 win over the French, and his name was creeping into rugby league newspaper columns in the lead-up to the Test. Brisbane Broncos halfback Allan Langer had no doubts about the Wallabies trump card when he wrote in the *Sunday-Mail* on 24 June 1990:

> With a win under their belts, the Aussies look the goods to wrap
> up the series, especially with Michael Lynagh in peak form.
> Make no mistake, this bloke is a champion footballer. I reckon
> he could be the difference between the two sides today.

In terms of pure statistics, Langer's prediction was accurate. In a breathtaking game, described by the ARFU president Joe French as the greatest Test match he had seen, the Wallabies broke a host of records as they took an unbeatable two-nil lead in the series. In the 48–31 win, almost a point a minute, Australia registered their highest score against an International Rugby Board country while Lynagh's ten goals from eleven attempts gave him a personal total of twenty-four, breaking by one the record he had set twice before. In the first two Tests Lynagh had accumulated forty-one points, more than the French team's combined score.

After the dreadfully desultory affair at the Sydney Football Stadium a fortnight before, the ten-try bonanza turned on by the two sides at Ballymore was a timely reminder that running rugby, with the emphasis on the players and not the whistle, was what the public wanted. Welsh referee Clive Norling had given only thirteen penalties, ensuring the continuity needed by sides with the attacking flair of France and Australia. A close study of the video replay shows that Norling made at least six major mistakes, five of which led to points being scored. Nevertheless he was hailed as a hero for his willingness to let the players be the stars.

Norling, though, is quite an eccentric and by no means looks a streamlined sportsman. A tall man with thin white legs, which hold up a belly of ample proportions, he pranced around the field at Ballymore looking more like a proud rooster than an international rugby referee. His concentration technique included giving himself a running commentary on how each try was scored. That was all very well for him, but somewhat disconcerting for the goalkickers. As Lynagh lined up for goal, there was Norling nattering away in the background. 'Great swerve by Campese. Good advantage played there, boyo.'

Norling awarded a penalty try after French forward Olivier Roumat dived into an Australian scrum and justified the decision to himself as Lynagh prepared to kick for goal. 'I have no doubt it was a professional foul. It was the right decision,' muttered Norling. Down on one knee, lining up the shot, Lynagh turned to the gregarious Welshman. 'And a pretty amateur professional foul it was too.' Behind the goal line, the French must have guessed at a conspiracy as the referee and the Wallaby sharpshooter enjoyed a laugh.

Six minutes into the third and final Test in Sydney Australia was awarded a penalty goal within kicking distance. As he had done count-less times before Lynagh stepped forward to take the attempt. He knelt down in a pose similar to a six-year-old in front of the television, his left leg folded beneath him, his right knee looking to all intents and purposes like a resting place for his chin. Considering the variables of distance and wind strength, he adjusted the ball on the mound, ensur-ing a perfect strike. He rose and took one step back, pausing a moment to satisfy himself that his initial alignment was accurate then slowly, but with an even rhythm, took a further five steps backwards before he wheeled to his left another three paces. He stopped and regathered, took a couple of deep breaths before wiping the sweat from his brow with his sleeves, a slight stutter of the feet and he moved in, eyes focussed on one spot on the ball … Thwack!

The ball never deviated and in his thirty-ninth international Lynagh had become the first person in the history of the game to reach 500 Test points. 'If you are in the field in cricket, you are expected to take the catches,' reckoned Lynagh afterwards. 'If you are the goalkicker in rugby you are expected to kick the goals.' Despite this typically under-stated public comment, Lynagh was thrilled to have reached the mile-stone. Statistical achievement has never been his primary aim in rugby but it was good motivation and this is something of which he is excep-tionally proud. As for the goalkicking style that had brought him the majority of his points, he has had plenty of advice on it from all quar-ters. 'I wipe my brow because I don't like the sweat trickling down my face and it has become a habit. But I've had people ring me up and tell me that I missed a kick because I didn't wipe my brow with both sleeves!' Not everyone however, understands the need for the routine. Lynagh received a letter from one anonymous observer suggesting these particular quirks were both stupid and juvenile. An average of more than twelve points per Test match was obviously not good enough for that hard marker.

Although the third Test brought personal triumphs for both Lynagh and Campese, who was playing his fiftieth Test, it was another case of Australia failing to hammer home the advantage. A lacklustre perfor-mance against a French side a man short after one of their forwards was sent off allowed the Tricolours to salvage their pride. France won 28–19, and the Australian players had hardly showered by the time the critics were questioning the Wallabies' ability to compete in the upcoming three-Test series against the All Blacks in New Zealand.

Lynagh's professional career continued to be moulded around rugby, and on the eve of his departure for the six-week tour he was appointed Queensland State Manager of Robt. Jones Investments Pty Ltd, a New

Zealand company which had stakes in Brisbane central business district property. He looked forward to the new role but his concern at what people might think again preyed on his mind. 'I liked working for Peter Lewis a lot and I learned a hell of a lot from him. When I went to see him about resigning I was very nervous because I thought it would disappoint him. However he told me it sounded like a great opportunity and to go for it.' Paul McLean, Lewis' fellow director and Lynagh's former team-mate, had always been of the opinion that Lynagh wouldn't last long in the firm. 'He was hungry and keen to learn, and his time with us helped him along, but he was never going to stay in an organisation where he wasn't the boss. He wasn't a normal staff member. He needed to run his own show ...'

The careful preparation that was important for him in his rugby endeavours also stood him in good stead in business. Although aware of his responsibilities as state manager, Lynagh wasn't fully *au fait* with the workings of the company when he set off on the tour. He understood there was every chance he may be asked about his involvement once he arrived in New Zealand, and so he studied the annual reports and paid careful attention to the thoughts of chairman Sir Robert Jones before he left. As he'd expected, a New Zealand financial newspaper had picked up on the story and was keen to interview him. 'I did the interview and basically just rehashed what I'd read from the annual reports. If I hadn't have read them, I might have looked a bit silly.'

New Zealand was once described as the University of Rugby and with three very stiff exams coming up, there was a lot of cramming to be done if the Wallabies were to return home with a pass. Injuries and work commitments had robbed the squad of top-class players Simon Poidevin, David Wilson, Jeff Miller and Jason Little, while the All Blacks were in a healthy enough state to omit captain Buck Shelford from their first Test squad.

Although Shelford's omission dominated the front pages like no other sporting incident since Trevor Chappell's underarm delivery, the All Black selectors soon could point to results as justification for their decision. With Auckland lock Gary Whetton at the helm, New Zealand easily accounted for Australia in the first two Test matches. As in the previous year, when the Lions had targetted Nick Farr-Jones, the All Blacks too gave much of their attention to the Australian skipper while also applying plenty of pressure to Lynagh. With the two Wallaby linchpins in a temporary rut, Australia could not match the Kiwis.

Lynagh was feeling pressure also from sections of the media who believed he was guilty of playing negative rugby. ABC television commentator Gary Pearse raised Lynagh's hackles by accusing him of 'irresponsible' play. Across the Tasman the disappointment of a lost series was already having repercussions. David Codey, former Wallaby colleague of Lynagh and Farr-Jones, suggested both players should be replaced for the final Test, with Peter Slattery and Tim Horan brought in as the new halves combination. The coach too was feeling the pinch. The prospect of a whitewash just fourteen months before the World Cup would not make good reading in Bob Dwyer's curriculum vitae.

It was time for the flyhalf to have a chat with the coach. Nothing confrontational, just a friendly meeting in which he could get his point across. 'Bob, I don't know that the training we are doing is overly beneficial.'

'Is that so Noddy? What's the problem?'

'The backs and the forwards spend all this time apart when we train, yet I thought it was supposed to be a team game. We concentrate too much on our scrum and lineout at practice, with the backs working alone on another part of the field. The forwards and backs have got to link more and that means including more actual game situations in our sessions. The backrow and the midfield have to develop a better under-standing. We are leaving too much to chance.'

Lynagh had never considered Dwyer a particularly good listener and was slightly concerned his appeal might be taken the wrong way but, to his pleasant surprise, Dwyer not only listened but acted on it. The training in the lead-up to the final Test included far more team-oriented work and, although the war had already been lost, there was a bit more spark in the Wallaby step as the Wellington battle approached.

The day before the game, Lynagh, Farr-Jones and FitzSimons lunched with Sir Robert Jones, Lynagh's new boss, and another New Zealand knight, cricketer Richard Hadlee. During the afternoon, Hadlee recounted how New Zealand had scored a famous victory over the West Indies a decade or so earlier. In a seemingly impossible position the Kiwis had agreed to say the word 'Win' to each other at every opportunity. The idea appealed to Farr-Jones and he decided to use it as a weapon for the following day's encounter.

So armed with pre-match training geared to the realities of the game, a motivational catchcry that would appeal to individuals who liked that kind of thing, and a singlemindedness of purpose to ensure that the tour would not be a total disaster, the Wallabies ran on to Athletic Park. Eighty minutes later they had restored their credibility, kept their coach in a job and given Australian rugby fans the hope that the following year's World Cup might not be too big a mountain to climb.

As for the weapons behind the 21–9 win, Lynagh wasn't prepared to dismiss any possible reasons for the improvement in form. 'I'm not sure everyone knew what Nick was on about with the "Win, win, win" business, and it's not really something I thought I needed to ensure my concentration and commitment ... but there are a lot of things that go into winning and maybe it kept us focussed on the task.'

Regardless of the factors behind it, Lynagh views that match as the first piece in the World Cup jigsaw puzzle. 'The match was a real turning point for us. We hadn't beaten the All Blacks for four years and the New Zealand teams throughout that era were the strongest sides I had played against. It was life or death for them every time they ran on the field. They had an attitude that any time they walked on to a field they deserved to win. It was something we needed to learn and that win was the perfect lesson.'

No rest for the gifted. After another arduous representative season, Lynagh was back in University colours for the club grand final. Now the Brisbane rugby grand final is a reasonably big occasion, but it is not in quite the same class as the Australian Football League equivalent or the New South Wales Rugby League's season closer, and pre-match entertainment is hardly the same Hollywood-style production that is the norm in Melbourne and Sydney. Nevertheless the Queensland Rugby Union marketing people were doing their best, and organised a few army parachutists to land on the ground just prior to kick-off. Well, that was the plan. Unfortunately the intrepid air traffic controller at Eagle Farm Airport decided that the parachutists could not jump at the scheduled time and thus ensured this grand final a place in rugby history. Unaware of the altered decision above, referee Kerry Fitzgerald blew the whistle to begin the game. Three minutes into the premiership decider, when opponents are expected to be at their most motivated and committed, down floated four parachutists who landed almost on top of the sixteen bodies engaged in the second scrum of the match. Apart from a few embarrassed officials there was hardly a spectator or player who could contain their laughter.

Undeterred by the unexpected drop-ins, Lynagh went on to control the game, scoring two tries in University's 19–10 win and in doing so notching the club's third successive premiership. His dominance is best summed-up by Brothers Test forward Rod McCall. 'If Michael Lynagh hadn't played, Uni might not have scored a point.'

As if he hadn't had enough rugby, Lynagh then figured in an Australian clubs championship win over Randwick before a quick jaunt to London, where he'd been invited to represent the British Barbarians in their centenary match against England. Finally he was back in his Brisbane office, at last able to give some time to Robt. Jones Investments. It was 2 November and he was pondering ways to lift the company profile when Bob Dwyer rang.

'Mate, I'm just sitting here having a glass of Champagne.'

'That's nice Bob. Any special reason?'

'Exactly one year from today, we'll be winning the World Cup.'

'Terrific mate, have one for me.'

11
POWER STRUGGLE AND THE PINNACLE

In terms of public interest and media attention, the sport of rugby in Japan is only outshone in popularity by sumo and baseball. The national team has qualified for every World Cup, and although lack of size in the forwards means the Japanese will always struggle against the figurative and literal rugby giants like Australia, South Africa and New Zealand, they set a fine example as generous hosts.

Lynagh's first experience of Japanese hospitality came at the beginning of the 1991 season. After the retirement of Bill Campbell, Lynagh was reinstated as Queensland captain and he led the side on a two-match pre-season tour of the Land of the Rising Sun. There was no shortage of official duties, but unlike other countries where such tasks can become tiresome chores, in Japan there was always the feeling that a little extra effort might be worth it. John Brass, the Reds' assistant coach, who had been to Japan a couple of years earlier, hinted at this prior to one of the assigned coaching clinics at a local school in Kumagaya.

'Noddy, I'd suggest you don't wear your watch when we go to the school.'

'Why not?'

'Well mate, the Japanese are pretty heavily into giving presents, and there's every chance that if they don't think you own a watch, they'll give you one.'

'Sounds a great idea to me!'

Lynagh duly attended the coaching clinic with Peter Slattery, David Wilson and Fijian-born prop Peni Volavola. After the session, the headmaster hosted the Queensland quartet for dinner. Educated in the Brass school, and watchless, Lynagh decided he wasn't going to let the chance go by and constantly asked if anyone had the time. Eventually the hint was taken and the host removed his own watch and gave it to the visitor. Not really cut out for clever subterfuge, Lynagh's sting counted for little – it was a long way from the smart-looking Seiko piece he'd bargained on. 'It looked like a sundial. You'd have to do weights to wear it,' says Lynagh. After training the next day, he slipped it into one of Volavola's boots. 'All my useless planning was worth it just to see the smile on Peni's face,' says Lynagh. 'He actually didn't have a watch and absolutely loved it. I think he still wears it to this day.'

But the electronic equipment Lynagh really needed was a calculator. When the team arrived in Japan, his points tally stood at 992 for Queensland. On paper, the game against the Japan All Stars looked certain to provide him with ample opportunity not only to pass the 1000 mark but also to become the state's leading points-scorer ahead of Paul McLean. As a game against the New Zealand province of Canterbury was scheduled at Ballymore for the following Sunday, management and Lynagh decided it would be more fitting and appropriate if the milestone was reached on home turf. That meant that unless it was absolutely necessary to win the game, Lynagh would be rested from goalkicking duties.

But while it's simple enough not to take the kicks for goal, it's a little harder not to score tries if you happen to be in the right place at the right time. Lynagh had scored an early try, and against the home side's flimsy defence he realised there was every chance another four-pointer might come his way. With minutes to go in the match he found himself in the clear with the tryline beckoning. Going against every natural instinct in his body, he applied the brakes, waiting for the defence to catch him.

'Luckily one of my team-mates got there before the tacklers so I was able to pass the ball and present him with the simplest try he was ever likely to score. We won 41–6 so it wasn't as if I was letting the team down. I was really pretty keen to set the record at Ballymore.'

Before returning home to complete that unfinished business, there was another official function to attend – this time at the Ministry of Education and it was a formal, do-and-say-the-right-thing kind of occasion. As with Lynagh's visits to Buckingham Palace, there was a brief lecture before on how to act, when and when not to speak, and enough instructions were given to leave a couple of the Queensland contingent wondering whether or not they should blink. As much as was possible between one group that speaks exclusively English and the other Japanese, niceties were exchanged before lunch. All the Queenslanders, including some of the more hard-to-impress team-members like Anthony Herbert and David Nucifora, were on their best behaviour. Lunch was served. The first course was soup.

'Slurp.' The guests' heads swivelled in amazement while their hith-erto beautifully mannered hosts emitted a chorus of noise as they dived into their soup with unfettered gusto. It was too good an invitation to refuse for Nucifora. He joined in and Herbert, Lynagh and the other Queenslanders then took up the challenge. Not an eyebrow was raised among the locals as the soup disappeared amidst a cacophony of sound. Having moved quite comfortably into the swing of things, Nucifora decided a post-prandial belch might be the order of the day. His Queensland colleagues cowered in embarrassment until some moments later the Japanese official sitting nearby put Nucifora's belch in the shade with one of quite thunderous proportions. They hadn't taught this sort of behaviour at Gregory Terrace.

In the presence of the Duke of Edinburgh, Paul McLean had scored his one thousandth and final point for Queensland against the Australian Barbarians at Ballymore, in a celebration match to mark the beginning of the 1982 Brisbane Commonwealth Games. When asked after the game how long he felt the record might last, McLean replied, 'As long as it takes Michael Lynagh.' Less than nine years later, Lynagh was on the verge. He woke early on the morning of the match against Canterbury and went straight to the television to view the third round of the United States Masters golf tournament. Ballymore was a long way from Augusta National but if anything could help get the rythmn right, watching the likes of Greg Norman, Nick Faldo and company would do it.

For Lynagh and millions of other golf fanatics, it appears the world's finest golfers are totally nerveless as they line up those two-metre putts that can make the difference between champion and also-ran. When Queensland was awarded an eleventh-minute penalty against Canterbury thirty-five metres out, Lynagh had his equivalent of a two-metre putt. Rugby fans saw no sign of the jitters, but they were there. 'I must admit I was very nervous before that kick,' says Lynagh. 'It wasn't just another kick.'

First-class goalkickers have a habit of turning away as soon as they strike a kick well. They know it is heading in the right direction, there's no need for confirmation. Lynagh is no different. By the time a truly struck kick crosses the crossbar, he is usually on his way back for the restart of play. This time though was different. From the moment it left the boot, he knew where it was heading but rather than turn away he savoured every millimetre of its flight as it sailed unerringly between the uprights. It was a moment that mattered, not just another kick – rather a part of rugby history. In the grandstand, the crowd rose to its feet in acclamation. Watching with the Queensland reserves and coaching staff, McLean applauded loudest.

Lynagh didn't need to follow his other seven kicks at goal in the match nor the drop goal – they weren't special. He was just doing his job. Eight out of eight and a drop goal – it was a great way to celebrate a record. 'There is no doubt, someone will eventually go past me,' says

Lynagh. 'But as the great English fast bowler Fred Trueman once said, "Whoever breaks the record will be bloody tired!"'

From the penthouse to the outhouse: three weeks after his record-breaking performance against Canterbury, Lynagh faced lifelong expulsion from the game. The rugby administrators who had lauded his footballing feats were now spitting out his name with a vehemence usually reserved for a sworn enemy. It was all about loyalty or the lack of it, money or lack of it, having a say or lack of it, and it was also about beer. The Queensland Rugby Union was involved in a sponsorship deal worth $7 000 000 with Castlemaine Perkins, the brewer of XXXX beer, and understandably was anxious to ensure the major sponsor was supported in every possible way. At the time in Queensland there had been a number of quite public disputes over advertising rights between Castlemaine and rival brewer Powers. The Brisbane Broncos league club, which now ironically enjoys XXXX sponsorship, was the main flagship for Powers and there were numerous well-publicised brawls between the two brewers, in which marketing strategy and business advantage left no room for any restraint.

At about nine in the evening of Thursday 2 May 1991 shockwaves were sent through the upper echelons of the Queensland Rugby Union when a commercial appeared on television espousing the virtues of Powers Light Bitter, and starring none other than Michael Lynagh, the captain of the XXXX-sponsored Queensland rugby team. The headlines the following morning indicated how quickly the administrators had responded. 'Lynagh in Strife', 'Ads Threaten Rugby Career', 'Lynagh Faces Expulsion Over Beer Ad'. That night, another advertisement was screened, involving Lynagh and Queensland rugby league captain, Wally Lewis.

The QRU was highly embarrassed, and extremely nervous that the commercials would threaten their multi-million dollar association with Castlemaine Perkins. In QRU eyes it was the end of Michael Lynagh,

Mr Nice Guy. The man who so often had been the beacon for the game in Queensland, who had always shown such responsibility and concern that the correct image be portrayed seemed to have suddenly, inexplicably, turned on his own. There had been no consultation. He had acted on impulse, out of greed, and rugby be damned. That was how it was perceived by some, anyway. The QRU was prepared to rub him out for life and what is more, it looked to have the firepower to take such drastic action.

International Rugby Board regulations govern the running of the game in Australia and there were two counts on which Lynagh was in trouble. Regulation 4.1, which had been adopted in March 1991 stated:

> A person may receive material benefit from any form of appear-
> ance or communication (written, oral or visual) provided always
> that the material benefit, subject to the exceptions hereinafter
> mentioned, does not derive from the game and that the accep-
> tance of the material benefit would not prejudice or interfere
> with any actual or anticipated financial arrangements of an
> union or club ...

It might be legalspeak, but it wasn't too difficult to pick out the key element – 'prejudice or interfere with any actual or anticipated financial arrangements ...' The code's golden boy advertising the major sponsor's chief rival might certainly prejudice financial arrangements.

The second noose that was hung around Lynagh's neck concerned an Australian Rugby Football Union by-law, which forced players to seek permission with the union before entering into advertising contracts. No such permission had been sought. What Lynagh had sought some weeks earlier was the documentation concerning players' rights in regard to such matters. 'I had rung, written and asked personally for a copy of all the rules and regulations,' says Lynagh. 'I was told it wasn't available but I would receive it once it was. It never arrived.'

Lynagh was at the Hong Kong Sevens in March when he and Powers chief executive Bernard Power first discussed the idea of doing a commercial. 'Bernie and I were talking about how XXXX monopolised Ballymore and the QRU to the extent where no other beer could be sold,' says Lynagh, 'and the idea of me doing something for Powers sprung from that conversation.' Lynagh had tired of being a pawn in the sponsorship game. He figured he had given enough of himself to the game to be allowed to earn some financial reward through his own initiative and profile. 'My disappointment with XXXX was that the company had a multi-million-dollar contract that allowed it access to the players, and although the players were central figures in the negotiations they were not privy to them,' says Lynagh. 'XXXX had basically unrestricted access to all the Queensland players.'

Along with Mark McBain, Bill Campbell and Cameron Lillicrap, Lynagh had been used in a XXXX commercial in 1990. 'The ad took two days to complete because of certain technical problems and we ended up receiving $400 each. It was about 3000 per cent below market value for the involvement of sportsmen of our stature in such a campaign. We were told we were lucky to get that!'

In the week the Powers commercial was to go to air, Lynagh and Greg Martin were at a coaching clinic in the Queensland country town of Warwick. On the drive back to Brisbane, Lynagh confided in his old mate. 'Noddy told me that there were a few feathers about to be ruffled,' recalls Martin. 'He told me all about the ad and asked my opinion. At that stage, nobody was making any money out of anything. It was before any of the trust funds that are in place today had been set up and so I told him to go for it. It was too good a chance to knock back when you could see players from other codes doing the same thing … '

Michael Blucher, the QRU media director had enjoyed a long lunch on the day the commercial first graced the screen. Any possible lack of sobriety was jolted out of him when he saw it. 'There was absolute panic within ten minutes of it going to air,' he recalls. 'It spread like wildfire around Brisbane. Noddy couldn't have targetted a more sensitive area. XXXX and Powers were at absolute loggerheads. Eye-gouging, ball-grabbing marketing tactics were the order of the day.' In hindsight, Blucher believes he should have realised the volcano was about to explode. 'Noddy always had a big thing about the influence of sponsors. He was very touchy about the size of logos on playing gear. We might have a team photograph and I'd ask him to turn a particular way so the logo would be more visible and he'd always have some sarcastic comment up his sleeve. "Oh sorry Blooch, yeah I'd forgotten. The advertising logo is far more important than the Queensland badge isn't it? Yeah, that's right, sorry."'

In no way was Lynagh trying to belittle the contribution of Castlemaine Perkins or, for that matter, any sponsor. He understood and appreciated the role they played in ensuring rugby would benefit not only at the élite level but also the grass roots. 'I accept XXXX's contribution to the code has been magnificent,' says Lynagh. 'But my argument all along was that players would have been much happier and been more available to promote the product if they were receiving some direct financial benefit. There were indirect advantages – we were never short of a drink on tour – but there was nothing there to pay the mortgage or ease the burden at home.'

Lynagh wasn't chasing sympathy and he certainly didn't get it from the more hard-nosed traditionalist elements within the game but he sincerely believed the majority of the rugby public could look behind the emotion and understand his position. Many took time to make their stance clear. One letter to the editor of the *Courier-Mail*, published on 7 May 1991, spoke for many others. Under the headline, 'Lay Off Lynagh', it read:

> If the rugby union hierarchy carries out its threat to expel Michael Lynagh from the code, I will never see Ballymore again.

He is a skilful and outstanding player – one who plays the game in the right spirit. The fact that he has resisted approaches from the professional game should prove that his interests lie solely with rugby. As an ex-player and an enthusiastic follower of rugby since the early 1930s, I am disgusted that Lynagh should be treated in such a way.

Such support encouraged Lynagh, emphasising that he had done the right thing. He had stated throughout that neither he nor Powers objected to him continuing to wear the XXXX logo on his jersey or being involved in any team promotion. Where he did draw the line was at the calls on him personally to play the XXXX tune. As far as he was concerned he was a private individual, who had made a commercial decision to advertise a company in which he was a shareholder and in which he believed.

The fallout reached Sydney in no time and a paper war developed between Ballymore, Sydney, the offices of Castlemaine Perkins, the Powers company and Lynagh's solicitor. In a letter to Lynagh, Bob Fordham, the ARFU's executive officer, stated the union's view.

… Regarding the claimed difference between what a person does as a 'private individual' and a 'rugby player', we take the view that it is not simply a matter of players asserting that what they have done, or propose to do … is done by them as private individuals and has no relation to the game. In most cases the player has no status or value for marketing purposes other than as a result of representative rugby honours. Whilst there may be exceptions, we contend that at best it would be naïve and at worst disingenuous for players to take refuge in the 'private individual' argument.

As the furore erupted on a Thursday evening, the earliest a QRU management committee meeting could be arranged to discuss the issue was the following Tuesday night. In the meantime Lynagh was available to play. University was playing Brothers on the Sunday and running on to Ballymore, he was unsure if this was his last game of rugby. Indeed, he performed as if there was no tomorrow. Wearing the University club shorts, which sported a XXXX badge, he shut the off-field worries out of his mind to set up four tries and scored a fifth himself in his team's 37–9 victory. Jim Tucker's match report in the *Daily Sun* on 6 May 1991 told the tale.

> Ballymore fans yesterday were not certain if they were watching Michael Lynagh's testimonial rugby union match or the reason Australia can win the World Cup.

Lynagh was adamant he was innocent of the two rule breaches of which he stood accused. He refuted the notion that his action had prejudiced the financial arrangement between the QRU and Castlemaine Perkins, arguing that like all other players he had not been a party to the sponsorship discussions and could not therefore be bound or affected by those arrangements. As for asking permission to make the commercial, he had not received the new, but unpublished ARFU by-laws. He was aware the union had drafted a regulation concerning players' obligation to seek consent, but as he had no official notification he was not prepared to abide by it.

The two beer company chiefs entered the fray. XXXX's Frank Burnett assured the QRU of his company's ongoing support, while Bernard Power was made to realise the gravity of the situation during a discussion with management committee chairman, Dick McGruther. Pushing the 'Michael Lynagh is a private individual' argument, Power was taken aback when warned that Michael Lynagh the individual, who appears in the ads, could well be Michael Lynagh the footballer, who doesn't play in the World Cup.

However, both Power and Lynagh had prepared for the worst and, although they did not inform the union, they had created a loophole to use if absolutely necessary. In the contract proper there were several special conditions, the last of which was crucial. It read:

> The Company also wishes to see you continue to play rugby union football for the Queensland and Australian teams and, if requested by you, the Company will cancel this agreement with you and release you from any further obligations if that is what is required to enable you to continue to play for Queensland and Australia.

Lynagh wrote to the QRU stating his strong desire to keep the matter out of the courts. However, he felt so strongly he was the innocent party that he admitted he was prepared to take whatever steps necessary to 'protect my rights and legitimate expectations'. Lynagh had never been seen as the shop steward, and by self-admission was looking after number one, but suddenly, there he was talking about players' rights and trade practices, matters that could have ramifications throughout the sport.

Ballymore's Murrayfield Room is situated above the QRU offices at the back of the McLean Stand. A walk up the winding steps to the entrance takes you past a cabinet of rugby paraphernalia, historical mementos and photos of teams long gone but not forgotten. After each representative match, the two competing teams, officials, friends and families gather to enjoy the QRU's hospitality and go through the various traditions of tie-swapping and the like. In countless post-match speeches delivered in that room, Lynagh had been the subject of much praise and adulation. This first Tuesday night in May 1991, he was again the main talking point but the QRU management committee, that body of men who run the game in Queensland, were speaking of the Reds' captain in far graver tones. What they decided was going to determine whether one of rugby's icons had any future in the game.

Lynagh loves being in control. On the field or away from it, he wants to dictate his own destiny. Here was a situation where everything was out of his hands. He could only sit and wait. It was a long wait, the meeting lasting two-and-a-half hours before McGruther emerged with the news that Lynagh would be allowed to continue playing rugby for Queensland.

The lifeline thrown by Castlemaine chief Frank Burnett had been a crucial factor. On the alleged breach of the IRB regulation concerning the prejudice of current sponsorship arrangements, the committee found that in light of Burnett's confirmation of ongoing support for the Queensland sponsorship, the question of financial prejudice did not arise. On the second point, it was accepted Lynagh had not been in possession of the new by-laws and, on legal advice, the committee accepted such by-laws could not therefore be considered binding.

McGruther argues that many people misinterpreted what the dispute was about. 'It had nothing to do with any crusty ideals of amateurism,' he says. 'Nor was it about the capacity of Lynagh or any other player to earn money outside the game. The real issue was avoiding situations of conflicting sponsorship interests.'

As it happened, all sides had a win. Lynagh got to keep playing the game he loved, while also receiving a healthy reward from the offending commercial. The QRU kept their star player and were perceived to have treated the matter with a common sense not always evident among sports administrators. Castlemaine, through the actions of chief executive Frank Burnett, was seen as very much the selfless white knight, while Powers got an untold amount of air time and newspaper space.

The battle was won but the war continued. While he was cleared to play for Queensland, there were Test matches coming up in July against Wales and England. When chosen to play for Australia, each player is sent a letter of invitation that requires acceptance of certain terms and conditions as set by the Australian Rugby Football Union. In 1991 that invitation included both regulations that had caused the initial stand-off. Having been through the process with the QRU,

Lynagh could not plead ignorance. He had meetings with ARFU president, the late Joe French, and with Norber Byrne, the International Rugby Board's amateurism regulation officer in Australia. The writing was on the wall – unless Powers gave him a partial release from his contract until after the World Cup, Lynagh could not sign the player's agreement and, as a consequence, would be ineligible for the Wallabies. Through to the bitter end, Lynagh never informed rugby officials of the special condition in the contract that permitted his release. The final chapter came when French rang on Friday 12 July and told Lynagh if the player's agreement was not signed by four pm that afternoon he would not be chosen for the Test against Wales the following week. He suppressed his anger long enough to put pen to paper. Australian rugby supporters breathed a sigh of relief.

'All along I believed I was quite within my rights to do what I did,' says Lynagh, 'and I still feel that way. The ARFU hadn't furnished me with any relevant regulations stating what I could or couldn't do and even as late as 1994, the regulations weren't distributed until we met as an Australian squad. So the forty-odd players got these things and were expected to sign them after flicking through a hundred-page document virtually on the spot, with no legal advice.'

Lynagh describes the episode as one of the most harrowing periods of his life but was buoyed throughout by the support of many players at state and national level. It seemed they were tired of the disproportionate ratio of time and effort spent to financial return, and although inevitably there were the odd pockets of suspicion that Lynagh might get something others might not, the vast majority were only too pleased for the issue to be brought out in the open. There would have been a fair amount of tension in the higher offices of the game had they been aware that Nick Farr-Jones contacted Lynagh and told him if a ban was applied, he too would withdraw his availability for selection. And he wasn't the only one. That Australian players now receive a percentage of all the union's sponsorships through the Wallabies' trust fund is in no small way attributable to the Powers saga. It may have happened eventually anyway, but it is unlikely it would have happened as quickly. Lynagh does not deny that self-interest was a principal motivator throughout, but at the same time he was aware the ramifications could be beneficial to all concerned. 'I loved rugby and I badly wanted to keep playing,' he says. 'I had no desire to disrupt the game but when I dug my feet in I was pretty sure that in the long run it would have a spinoff for the other players and I think it is fair to say it has.'

At the same time that Lynagh was having his board-room scuffles, the touring Welsh team was embarrassing itself both on and off the field. Wales is one of the proudest rugby nations and for many years had been one of the best. During the 1970s it boasted players like J. P. R. Williams, Barry John and Gareth Edwards, who provided some of the most scintillating rugby ever witnessed. Regrettably, those days were long gone. New South Wales beat the 1991 tourists 71–8, with David Campese scoring five tries. The ensuing Test match at Ballymore followed a similar pattern. Australia registered its highest score against an International Rugby Board country with the 63–6 win. Lynagh, now cleared to play after the Powers drama, had a golden opportunity to break his own individual points record of twenty-four, but missed eight of his fifteen kicks at goal. With an afternoon's work that reaped two tries and seven goals he could only scrape together a measly twenty-three!

The Welsh were plunged further into disgrace at the post-Test dinner when a scuffle broke out between members of the touring party. The Wallaby players, guests, and sponsors were stunned as several of the Welshmen began pushing and shouting at each other. At the height of the drama, a glass was smashed and Test centre Mike Hall had to be treated for a cut hand. As a witness to the fiasco, Lynagh was saddened to think that spirit within a national team could ever sink so low.

Things had not always been sweetness and light in the Wallaby squads he'd played with – twenty-five men away together in a competitive situation for up to three months are not going to get on perfectly with each other every minute of every day, but they had always managed to keep things in perspective. Had the Australian team ever suffered the disharmony that afflicted the Welsh, Lynagh's signature would have been on a league contract in a trice.

After the Welsh Test there was some potential for disagreement in Wallaby ranks however, when popular Queensland flanker Jeff Miller was dropped in favour of Simon Poidevin for the following week's match against England in Sydney. Players are always at the mercy of selectors' whims, but after his universal choice as man of the match against the Welsh, Miller must have felt pretty confident that if the axe was to fall it wouldn't be on his neck. Lynagh felt compelled to speak publicly about the decision, believing that any discontent over the matter within the team was potentially more damaging if kept camouflaged. He was not afraid to tell Peter Jenkins, the *Australian*'s rugby writer, that he was concerned about the effect Miller's sacking might have on his team-mates.

'I'm not the only one thinking this way,' he told Jenkins on 22 July 1991. 'A guy plays so well and gets dropped. Other players say, "What's this about?" Normally you get rewarded for playing well.' After making his point he was quick to add that the issue would not lead to division with the team. 'At the end of the day, you go out and do your best for Australia,' he said. 'And that fact will rise above all this. Once we get into camp on Wednesday, away we'll go.'

And away they went. As if to prove those words had not been uttered purely for the sake of diplomacy, Australia whipped a fine England team by twenty-five points in a performance Lynagh described as the benchmark for their World Cup assault later that year. It also earned the Wallabies favouritism for the first of two Bledisloe Cup matches against New Zealand, to be played at the Sydney Football Stadium a fortnight later. The World Cup has become so much the focus of rugby that intervening international series are often reduced to little more than preparation for the upcoming tournament. This is not so with Australia–New Zealand matches, they're always crucial in their own right and the Australians were primed to recapture the cup that had been in New Zealand hands for four years. The William Webb Ellis Trophy might be first on the Wallabies' wish list, but Lord Bledisloe's silverware is a close second.

Captain Farr-Jones and Vice-captain Lynagh stood side by side as more than 40 000 supporters joined the Wallabies in the rendition of 'Advance Australia Fair'. The traditional reticence of Australian crowds to sing has been slowly eroded in recent years and even for the most sceptical of observers, it is hard now not to be moved by the atmosphere in those emotion-charged minutes preceding kick-off. It was a special moment for the skipper and his offsider, not only because any match against the All Blacks is special, but also because it marked the thirty-fifth time they had played beside one another in a Test match, thereby equalling the world record set by Scottish halfback combination Roy Laidlaw and John Rutherford.

The result fitted the occasion. As Lynagh had suggested after the third Test victory in Wellington almost twelve months before, the Wallabies were no longer overawed by the All Blacks' reputation. It was Australia's turn to show a touch of arrogance, and combining that with large doses of class and courage the Wallabies sent the All Blacks packing. For the highly respected New Zealand flanker Michael Jones, it was his first taste of defeat in eighteen Tests.

The only downside for the Australians was that the Bledisloe Cup itself had not been at stake. The cup is traditionally presented at the end of a three-Test series in either country but the practice in recent years had seen it also awarded at the one-off matches scheduled for non-tour years. With two Tests programmed in the build-up to the World Cup, the ARFU had requested the trophy be on offer at both the Sydney and Auckland games. New Zealand had declined and after the Sydney win Farr-Jones expressed his annoyance at the Australian officials for not putting further pressure on the Kiwis. 'The majority of the guys had never won the cup,' he says. 'At that stage I had won it only once in eight seasons in the Australian side. It is a very special thing to say that you were a part of the team that won it.' But it didn't really matter. The Wallabies still had their chance at Eden Park in Auckland.

Just prior to the start of the match, a few former Wallaby and All Black stars kicked footballs into the crowd. That was close to the most interesting part of the day. Slippery conditions, wind and a pedantic referee made this game of rugby look like slow-moving chess. Nevertheless, the Bledisloe Cup still hung in the balance. The thousands of supporters who had crossed the Tasman wanted the Wallabies to win it in style, but if solid drudgery was to be the course of action, then so be it.

At the Sydney Football Stadium two weeks earlier, Lynagh had steered home five kicks from five attempts. At Eden Park, he had succeeded with just one out of six when Australia was awarded a penalty with fifty-seven seconds of the match left. All Black Grant Fox's percentages weren't much better, but his two true kicks gave New Zealand a 6–3 lead. Lynagh was two metres outside the quarter line and eight metres in from touch. Success would level the scores at 6–all. With the win in Sydney behind them, a draw would be good enough to snare the cup.

He felt no noticeable increase in his heart rate as he made his preparations. The boos of a small section of the Auckland crowd were blocked out as he approached the kick. It was just the opportunity goalkickers enjoyed. This was his chance. The game, the series, the trophy – all depended on his skill and composure. Lynagh had kicked goals from this position countless times before. On the other side of the field the indefatigable David Campese took time to chat with a radio commentator on the sideline. 'It's been a hell of a struggle,' he said. 'But if this goes over it will be all worthwhile.' As the ball left his boot, Lynagh was confident it was heading between the posts. But the breeze was being blown by a New Zealand god. It veered to the right and with it went the Bledisloe Cup.

Not suprisingly the team rallied around Lynagh in the aftermath. Dwyer was ropable, but not with his kicker. 'I feel so sorry for Noddy that the team played so badly, and then put all the pressure on him to win the game,' he said in the *Sunday Sun* on 25 August 1991. 'We lost because we played badly, not because Noddy missed that kick.' Had he been successful there would not have been much overt expression of delight – inside though he'd have been bursting with joy. In failure he also kept his real feelings well bottled. Here was a man who enjoyed responsibility, indeed thrived on it, and who was dismissive of those who couldn't carry it. Now in his moment of greatest responsibility he had failed the test.

Official functions aren't cancelled because someone is disappointed with a result but Lynagh would have been excused if he'd sought permission to miss the post-match festivities. He didn't need every second person telling him how sorry they felt for him and he could certainly do without the odd inflammatory comment offered by the smart alecs whose courage through the day had increased with every sip of the local lager. He knew it wasn't going to make him feel better but Lynagh took his medicine. He went to the function – as a member of the Wallaby team it was his responsibility to do so. The support he received from his opposite number was some consolation. The brotherhood of goalkicking flyhalves was alive and well; Grant Fox sought him out and offered a word of support. Fox, more than any other in the room, might know how Lynagh was feeling and the Australian appreciated his great rival's words. However, not one to drown his sorrows, he returned to the team hotel after he had fulfilled his duties to contemplate the worst day of his career.

He awoke on Sunday morning to the realisation it had been no bad dream. Checking out of the team hotel, the receptionist was pleasant. 'Thank you, Mr Lynagh. Bad luck yesterday.' The guests in the foyer were also sympathetic. 'You're Michael Lynagh aren't you? Better luck next time.' The customs official at Auckland Airport wasn't quite as refined. 'We did you blokes again, hey? And to think we're just warming up for the World Cup.' The pilot made mention of the match on the flight home. Through the customs again in Brisbane. 'Bad luck mate. I've seen you kick those before. Guess you can't get 'em all.' Every comment, positive or otherwise was a reminder of his failure. He couldn't wait to reach the sanctuary of his home. When he finally did, the pent-up frustration and disappointment was released. 'As soon as I walked through the door that Sunday afternoon,' he recalls, 'I just let it all flow out of me. I lay on my bed and cried. It took me a while to realise nothing was going to change what had happened the day before and that I had to get on with life.'

Messages of support from both Australians and New Zealanders in the following days provided great solace. Although Lynagh himself wasn't searching for excuses for his goalkicking woes at Eden Park, the booing sections of the Auckland crowd obviously made an impression on others. Numerous letters arrived from across the Tasman. They all echoed similar sentiments.

Dear Michael,

It is rare for me to be moved to the point of needing to write to a young and much admired player like yourself, but my indignation dictates to me that I should do so. You see, I was at the Bledisloe Cup match on Saturday and am still feeling enraged, embarrassed and ashamed of the public who created such a needless din each time you attempted a kick in those difficult conditions ... So to soothe my soul, will you please accept deepest apologies for such ignorance displayed ...

And Lloyd Coombs, a former Australian Barbarians player from country New South Wales wrote:

> ... anyone that has the temerity to say that it was your fault is
> not a true Australian, not a true rugby follower and certainly has
> never ever felt the pressure of a game such as a Test match ...
> You gave it your best shot, and you missed. You cannot be
> blamed for that. There are certain other members of the
> Australian team who must answer for their actions, but certain-
> ly not yourself.

As always, Lynagh answered every letter. His reply to Coombs, written ten days after the match, suggested he had by then begun to look forwards not backwards.

> ... The fact that I kicked one out of seven on that day is some-
> thing that I have to accept responsibility for, learn from, and get
> on with the business of winning the World Cup for Australia
> over the next two months ... It is certainly nice to know that the
> Australian Wallabies have supporters such as yourself, and I
> hope that we can perform well in the World Cup for people such
> as you.

Pontypool Park in Wales sits in the middle of a grassy amphitheatre, surrounded by an imposing array of vibrantly green and healthy oak trees. When it is not packed with Pontypool supporters, a village-green atmosphere prevails and for those twenty-five minutes in the winter when the sun is shining, it is indeed a glorious venue. For the rest of the season, when the rain is falling, and the wind blowing at a strength somewhere between strong and gale-force, it can be a most forbidding place. Australia played Western Samoa in its second pool match of the 1991 World Cup at Pontypool and constant downpours, driving wind and a fiercely competitive Samoan side jolted the

Wallabies into the realisation that if the William Webb Ellis Trophy was to be theirs, they'd have to pay their dues. The Samoans' tackling style showed they had no respect for their own bodies, let alone those of others, and the ferocity of their commitment stunned an Australian XV which was not at full strength. Captain Nick Farr-Jones was forced out of the game with a knee injury that was to bother him for the rest of the tournament, and Wallaby leadership was left in the hands of Lynagh. Centre Anthony Herbert was in no doubt he was the one who steered the Wallaby ship to shore. 'Had Noddy not played, we would have lost. It was that simple,' he says. 'After Nick was replaced ... Noddy was the one who kept a cool head. He realised that in those conditions we had to play the game in their half and he had the talent to ensure we could do that.' For a long period, the game was poised at 6–3, until Lynagh kicked a penalty in the last five minutes to give the Australians a 9–3 victory and assured them a place in the quarter-finals. The demon of Eden Park was about to be exorcised.

As Farr-Jones was unavailable for the final pool match against Wales at Cardiff Arms Park, Lynagh led the side in what was his fiftieth Test-match appearance and, as had almost become the norm whenever he played, it was a record-breaking day. Australia's 38–3 win was Wales' worst home defeat and in an astonishing statistic, the Wallaby team won twenty-eight lineouts to two. The acting Australian captain became the first player to score 650 points in international rugby but his try two minutes before full-time was his personal highlight. He'd captained the side, he was heading to Ireland, one of his favourite places, for the next couple of weeks and all was on track for the capture of the big prize. Yes indeed, Eden Park was very much yesterday's news.

Although a fine player, Anthony Herbert went to the World Cup resigned to the fact that unless one of the star midfield duo of Tim Horan and Jason Little was injured he would be, at best, on the reserve bench for the big matches and at worst, a dirty-dirty – the term given to those players in the touring party who fail to make the playing team or the reserves. Not one to let personal disappointment stand in the way of a good time, Herbert did all he could to maintain team spirit. He organised 'Herbie's Happy Hour' (quickly abbreviated to HHH), which meant each team-member had a standing invitation to join Herbert, reserve halfback Peter Slattery and a few other regulars in Herbert's hotel room at six o'clock each evening for a quiet drink before dinner. Lynagh very much enjoyed the company of Herbert and Slattery and was, during the early part of the tour, an occasional visitor to HHH. However, after the narrow quarter-final win against Ireland, in which Lynagh rescued the Wallabies from oblivion, Herbert noticed a dramatic falling-off in the numbers attending HHH. 'We didn't see anything much of Noddy or anyone else in the playing XV after that,' recalls Herbert. 'Some of the non-players would still attend but as far as the Test guys were concerned everything suddenly became very serious. Even those who'd normally go out up until two or three days before the game weren't socialising at all. Everybody was super-focussed and super-intense … It was a great sign that they meant business.'

They certainly did the business against the All Blacks in the semi-final in Dublin, a match that Lynagh admits was seen by all the Australians as the final. New Zealand was without dynamic flanker Michael Jones, whose religious beliefs precluded playing on a Sunday. Team management had tried to convince him that 2.30 on Sunday afternoon Dublin time was in fact early Monday morning Auckland time, but all to no avail. So without Jones, the All Blacks confronted a Wallaby outfit able to reproduce the form that had brought them victories earlier that year against both England and the All Blacks themselves. The game produced a piece of rugby magic that has become perhaps the most enduring memory of the whole unforgettable tournament. Appropriately, it involved the holy trinity – Farr-Jones, Lynagh and Campese.

It began with a short side foray from Farr-Jones and Lynagh. Searching for that no-man's land between the New Zealand full-back and the fast-following Campese, Lynagh weighted his kick to perfection. As if controlled by radar the bounce found Campese, who then fooled the approaching defence with a slight feint. With the extra-sensory perception that belongs only to a genius, Campese threw an outrageous blind pass over his head, straight into the hands of centre Tim Horan who scored the try. A Lynagh conversion gave Australia a 13–0 half-time lead and no side, not even New Zealand, could bridge that gap in forty minutes against this Australian team. As a rookie observing proceedings from the reserve bench at Ballymore over seven years earlier, Lynagh had seen the All Blacks rise from the dead. But Lazarus was nowhere to be seen this time. The Wallaby tackling in the second half was inspirational. New Zealand's only response was two penalty goals scored by Grant Fox, as they tumbled out of the tournament with a 16–6 defeat. It was their first loss in a World Cup fixture and only their third since 1987, in which time they had won thirty-one and drawn one of thirty-five Test matches.

For Lynagh, the victory was not the catalyst for exuberant celebration, and only the following day did the sweetness of success truly hit home. The Wallabies and the All Blacks arrived at Dublin airport simultaneously on Monday morning – the All Blacks destined for Cardiff and the ignominy of the third and fourth play-off to which Lynagh had been subjected four years earlier, and the Wallabies for London and a World Cup final.

'Most of the time I have got on with the majority of the All Blacks pretty well. I'd class John Kirwan, Grant Fox and a couple of others as good friends,' says Lynagh. 'But that doesn't change the fact that the highlight of the World Cup for most of the Wallabies came when we arrived at Dublin airport and saw the All Blacks looking so depressed. No one said anything publicly at the time. In fairness, the New Zealanders took it very well and I know most were supporting us in the final, but it was just so good to send them packing after they'd done it to us so often before.'

In London, the Wallabies were housed at a hotel in the stockbroker belt, at Weybridge, just outside London. It was what Lynagh imagined a nineteenth-century manor house might be like, and the pitch-and-putt golf course in the grounds provided both himself and room-mate Jason Little with as much excitement as they were seeking in the days leading up to the game. On Friday there was an early-morning call for the Australian squad. A photograph of the World Cup winning team was required, and as the Australians were flying out of Heathrow first thing on the Sunday morning after the match, there would be no other opportunity. Certainly the Australians hadn't yet won the cup, but on the other side of town the English side were going through the same process, to keep all bases covered. The weather was cold and miserable, which was a fair reflection of the Australians' moods. The William Webb Ellis Trophy has since been superimposed on that photo taken at Weybridge the day before the final and if you've ever wondered why the Wallabies should look so grumpy after winning the spoils, there's the reason.

When the photo session was over, some of the players went back to bed. Others set out for Twickenham on an expedition of familiarisation. For some it was a way to kill the time and expend some nervous energy. For Lynagh it was a necessity. Whenever possible he visits the ground the day before any important match and checks the lie of the land, the length of the dead-ball area, the likely position of the sun at game time and the peculiarities of the prevailing wind. He has a few practice kicks from different angles, a couple of high balls and some long, raking touch-finders to test the ground's slope. It's thorough preparation – no more, no less.

There is no more uncomfortable time for an international rugby player than the morning of a Test. The hours drag and when you're playing for the championship of the world, the minutes move like months. For an early riser like Lynagh, there is extra time to kill. On Saturday 2 November 1991, he read the papers from cover to cover and browsed through some of the 7000 faxes the team had received from home. As he does before most games, he had a couple of baths to aid the relaxation process and, in the knowledge there was an early flight the next day, began to pack for the journey back to Australia.

The bus set off for Twickenham. There was no talk – everyone was left to their own thoughts and to focus, focus, focus. Before the team alighted, Anthony Herbert spoke on behalf of the non-playing members of the touring party in one final reminder of support. From then, they were on their own.

It turned out to be not so much a game as a struggle. Australia scored the only try and was leading 9–3 halfway through the second half when Welsh referee Derek Bevan awarded a penalty following an English infringement. Psychologically it was a crucial kick. The English were winning copious amounts of possession and applying heavy pressure, but should the Australians be able to get their lead to nine points it would be a great boost. The English would need to score twice to win, and the Wallabies knew they had the defence to prevent that. Irish flanker Gordon Hamilton had scored the only try against them since the opening match against Argentina. Not Western Samoa, Wales nor the All Blacks had breached the Wallaby line. England surely couldn't do it twice in twenty minutes.

When Lynagh was at Twickenham the day before, he had made a vital discovery. The wind, it seemed, was deceptive. 'At ground level it came one way,' he recalls, 'but once the ball got up into the air, it appeared to blow from the other direction.' Having got his bearings on Friday, he felt less anxious as he lined up the attempt, some forty-five metres from the goals and ten metres from the touchline. The previous day's investigation paid its dividend: 12–3 in Australia's favour. According to Dwyer it was a pivotal moment. 'That goal was just a gem,' he says. 'It was on the right-hand side of the field, which is the more difficult side for him, and the wind was blowing in all sorts of directions. It was just a super, super kick and very important at that stage of the game.'

England managed another penalty to ensure nine tension-packed closing minutes but when Bevan finally blew the whistle to announce full-time, the Wallabies were world champions. There was an element in the players' reactions that signalled the obvious joy and elation at such an achievement, but the body language of most hinted at one overwhelming feeling – relief. Lynagh was numb. The build-up of stress and pressure, which had multiplied as the game came nearer, disappeared with the sound of the whistle. At that moment, nothing else mattered. He was almost oblivious to the well-wishers as instinct alone took him up the Twickenham steps to stand beside Nick Farr-Jones as Her Majesty presented the William Webb Ellis Trophy. This was rugby's equivalent of winning the Olympic 100 metres. It was the greatest moment – the pinnacle.

The players' families were herded into the Rose Room underneath the Twickenham grandstand to wait for their loved ones. In the confusion that followed the match, Lynagh had been unable to talk with his parents. Via an understandably boisterous dressing room he eventually made his way into the reception and spotted Ian and Marie. There wasn't a lot that needed to be said. The three of them embraced before Michael withdrew and reached into his blazer pocket. He pulled out the winner's medal he had been presented by the Queen an hour earlier and showed it to his parents. 'Isn't it wonderful?' they said. 'Yes, it is wonderful,' he replied as he handed it to them. 'And it's also yours. Thanks for everything.'

Outside in the darkness, the touts were trying to squeeze the last drops out of what had been a profitable day. One cockney lad had been selling supporters' caps since eight o'clock in the morning. He was ready to call it quits. 'Git yer Ingland caps 'ere. They was six quid on the in –

I'm takin' two quid on the out.' There weren't any buyers, but one Wallaby follower inquired if there were any Australian caps available. 'Sorry cobber,' came the reply. 'I've only got three left and them's collectors' items. They ain't for sale.'

12
NEW DIRECTIONS

In Treviso, a charming fifteenth-century Italian township, thirty kilo-metres north of Venice, the Franchin family – father Giuliano, mother Daniela and daughter Isabella, were glued to the television set. *Bravo* Australia! The Wallabies were world champions. Giuliano, a former committee member of the Benetton rugby club, based in Treviso like the Benetton company itself, was especially pleased. 'Isabella,' he said. 'You see the number ten for the Wallabies – Michael Lynagh. He is coming to play for Benetton this season. He arrives next week.' As an exchange student in the United States four years earlier, Isabella had become fluent in English and was anxious to keep it that way. '*Bene*, Papa,' she replied. 'He looks nice. I'd like to meet him and practise my English.'

At the Royal Lancaster Hotel in London, that is exactly what Lynagh was doing. Whether it was a germ, exhaustion or sheer let-down, Nick Farr-Jones felt ill prior to the 1500-strong all-male World Cup celebratory dinner after the game. He went to his vice-captain. 'Noddy, I'm crook mate. You'll have to make the speech.' So much for relaxing. Although he rises to the occasion, Lynagh never really likes the prospect of public speaking. Thankfully he had downed a beer or three by the time Farr-Jones hit him with the bad news, so the butter-flies weren't quite as severe as they might have been. Following Tony

O'Reilly, a former Ireland and British Lions player, chairman of the Heinz Corporation and one of the most eloquent, humorous and thought-provoking after-dinner speakers in the world, didn't make the task any easier. But when Lynagh was called to the microphone to respond on behalf of Australia, he surprised himself at how easily the words came. He began, 'As you can see gentlemen, I'm not Nick Farr-Jones ... When Nick told me he was sick and I had to do the talking tonight, I can assure you I wasn't all that thrilled. However it didn't take me very long to realise how privileged I really am, because I think every single person in this room would like to be in my shoes right now ... '

Thirty-six hours later, he was again standing in for the skipper. Farr-Jones and family had not returned with the team, and it was Lynagh who emerged first from the customs hall at Sydney's international airport carrying 'Bill' – as the Wallabies had come to refer to the William Webb Ellis Trophy. The enormous crowd of supporters that had gathered burst into spontaneous applause. The smile on Lynagh's face seemed to have become a permanent fixture. A civic reception was organised in Brisbane the following day and twenty-four hours after that, Lynagh was on another aeroplane, this time Rome-bound. Flights were a blessing – they gave him the chance to sleep! He was in Treviso just long enough to check out his accommodation and meet a few of his new team-mates, before the head-spinning travel schedule contin-ued, now back to Australia for an official ticker-tape parade through the streets of Sydney. Like most of his team-mates he was caught unawares at the extent of the public interest created by the cup success. 'I was just hoping someone would turn up at the parade,' says Lynagh, 'to save us from being embarrassed.'

There were no red faces, as tens of thousands of people lined Sydney's central city streets, scores of others hanging out office windows to shower the Wallabies with streamers, confetti and adula-tion. Rugby was now big-time.

Offers to play Italian club rugby had been coming Lynagh's way since his first year in senior ranks. At that time, Mark Loane had counselled wisely, advising the youngster there would be plenty of opportunity in the future for such adventures. By 1991, the future had arrived. At the Hong Kong Sevens, Fabrizio Gaetaniello, a former Italian fullback and Benetton's full-time rugby manager, spoke to Lynagh and received a commitment that he would play the 1991–92 season with the club. It had been no cut-and-dried matter for the self-confessed conservative.

He'd broached the subject with Robt. Jones Investments executives Ian Crichton and Sir Robert Jones, and received the same advice from them as he had from Peter Lewis a couple of years earlier. 'Go for it while you can.' Six months' leave of absence was granted. 'It was a big decision for me to make,' says Lynagh. 'I like being around people I know and am close to and once I am out of that environment I can get very nervous. To go there on my own, to a place where I couldn't speak the language and didn't know anyone was really scary.'

To many in rugby circles, Italy means one thing – lire. For years, the rugby establishment has been frustrated by the traffic of players to Italy and France. There were well-substantiated claims that the top players received enormous financial inducements to join clubs. Like most of the other overseas stars, Lynagh carefully guards his financial arrangements, but points out that his contract with the Benetton clothing company, which happens to sponsor the rugby team, is based on the same principles as those used by major sponsors of rugby in Australia to employ various Wallaby players.

Would Castlemaine Perkins have employed a player if he hadn't been a damn good footballer? Would Benetton have employed Michael Lynagh if he hadn't been a damn good footballer? Didn't Castlemaine Perkins give players as much time off as needed for rugby? Doesn't Benetton give Michael Lynagh as much time off as he needed for rugby? Only the countries and the companies were different and Lynagh had no pangs of conscience at grasping the chance that had been presented.

The facilities at the Benetton club are impressive enough – a fully appointed modern gymnasium, basketball courts, golf driving range, tennis courts, restaurant and six rugby ovals – while the township itself is travel brochure material. Situated on a fertile plain between the Botteniga and Sile rivers, Treviso's original reason for existence was as an agricultural support system for Venice. World War Two bombing had reduced parts of the township to rubble before rebuilding took place in the early 1950s. Today the cobblestone streets and the moat that circles the old quarter are quaint reminders of its history.

Lynagh's first game for Benetton was at L'Aquila, where eight years earlier he had made his Australian debut against Italy B. What he'd have given for the company of his Wallaby team-mates on this day. 'It was an eight-hour bus trip from Treviso to the game, and once on the field I couldn't pronounce our halfback's name, let alone talk to him. On the bus trip back to Treviso, I was feeling very much the outsider and I kept saying to myself, what am I doing here?'

The presence in the club of Mark Giacheri and John Manenti, two Australian residents with Italian passports, made communication a little easier but in those first months Lynagh was frustrated not so much by his inability to speak the language, as by the sense that he didn't belong. Often his mind switched to the coast north of Brisbane, and he'd daydream about the warmth of the sun and the roll of the surf. In the dressing room before the second match, he was left wondering if he'd misunderstood the nature of the game completely. '*Die, die, die,*' screamed his team-mates at each other before running on to the pitch. 'Hang on fellas,' thought Lynagh. 'I'm as committed to winning as much as the next bloke, but let's not get too serious about things.' One of his compatriots noticed the nervous look in his eye and taking him to one side explained quietly that '*Dai*' was Italian for 'Come on'.

Although in those uncomfortable first few weeks, Lynagh would have jumped at the chance of having a familiar face with him, he slowly came to the realisation that this would have been counter-productive. 'I was fortunate to be on my own. Otherwise I would have retreated back to the company of the person I knew, and ensured we kept pretty well to ourselves. As it was I purposely put myself in situations I wasn't used to and that wasn't something I liked doing. The people were very friendly and I was asked out every night. No matter how tired I might have been or how much I didn't really feel like it, I forced myself to go every time. It was easier for them to accept me because they could see I was making the effort. I was the visitor and I was the one who had to change.'

He attended Italian classes and slowly began to pick up snatches of the language. He'd started work at the Benetton company headquarters in the marketing department, monitoring the media's perception of Benetton world-wide. Although his rugby ability was the primary concern, his employment was not a mere cosmetic addition. Benetton was hopeful of getting good value out of him in the office as well as on the field.

It was a slow and at times painful assimilation process and the rugby itself took some getting used to. Although he didn't particularly enjoy training in the below-zero temperatures or in the fog that sometimes meant he was practising his goalkicking unable to see the posts, he accepted such hardships as the lot of any rugby player. In the games, it was obvious he was in a class of his own and he learned to accept that while his team-mates were high on passion, discipline was not their strong suit. The fans too were a law unto themselves. Despite Italians' love for soccer, Treviso is very much a rugby town and a lot is expected of its team. In close matches, everyone looks to the international stars to save the day. If they do the job, they are the toast of the town. If not, the greetings in the piazza during the next week are not nearly so numerous nor as warm. Benetton also owns the town's basketball and volleyball teams and in Lynagh's first season, the Benetton basketball fans went on strike. The team wasn't playing well, so although the fans still attended the games they refused to cheer. They just sat there before walking out halfway through the game.

As every second match was an away game, Lynagh quickly learned to cope with the hostility of home-town supporters throughout the length and breadth of Italy. But not even the repeated warnings of team-mates prepared him for his first game in Catania, Sicily, home of the Mafia. The ball-boys who bring sand onto the ground for goal-kickers had occasionally caused Lynagh a bit of *angst* in the past. In 1987, during the World Cup semi-final match in Sydney against France, Lynagh was about to line up an acutely angled kick which, if successful, would give Australia the lead at a vital stage of the game. The ball-boy ran on to the field, promptly emptied the bucket of sand at Lynagh's feet and calmly announced, 'You'd better slot this one Noddy or we're in strife.'

'Yeah mate. Thanks for the advice!'

In Catania, he had another difficult penalty facing him when a young Sicilian lad ambled on to the pitch. He poured out about three grains of sand, on which Lynagh was expected to lie the ball. 'More, please,' Lynagh asked. 'No,' came the curt reply. Lynagh decided to dig up the turf to make his own mound. The boy pushed him. 'You cannot do that here. Leave the ground alone.' Lynagh appealed to the referee. The man with the whistle had officiated in Catania enough to know where his bread was buttered, but nevertheless ordered the ball-boy to pour out some more sand. Another four or five grains and that was that. Lynagh made do and as he prepared his kick, the boy, who was standing only three metres away, swore constantly, in an unsuccessful attempt to distract him.

John Kirwan, the All Black winger and Lynagh's Benetton team-mate, also found the going tough in Catania. After tackling one of the local players over the sideline, a scuffle devloped between the two and

Kirwan was pushed onto one of the crowd-control fences, which are fixtures at all Italian grounds. In most places they are a good idea, in Catania they're an absolute necessity. With Kirwan preoccupied with his opposite number the crowd rushed to the fence, and one supporter put his hand through the wire mesh and grabbed Kirwan's hair. Thus pinned to the fence, he was an easy target for the Catanians. In no time a brawl involving both teams had erupted within a metre or two of a very excited crowd. While the fight went on, an umbrella pierced the reserves' dug-out, which backs on to the fence. Had anyone been sitting there at the time, a murder investigation might have been the main post-match activity.

Embarrassed by the afternoon's events, the Italian federation ordered an inquiry into the violence and in what amounted to the lightest of reprimands, the Catania team was docked two competition points. 'It's always pretty frightening down there,' according to Lynagh. 'Shotgun pellets have been fired during games and legend has it that there's a contract out on Knoxy [Wallaby team-mate David Knox] after he broke one of the local player's jaws in an accidental head-high tackle. The ground is adjacent to the airport so if we win we go straight from the dressing rooms to the airport and out of there!'

'Michael, you must meet our daughter Isabella.'

Lynagh wasn't convinced. As the months progressed he grew accustomed to the Italian culture and lifestyle and had made some firm friends, among them Giuliano and Daniela Franchin. Giuliano never missed a match, and while Michael enjoyed his company he was wary of anyone trying to play Cupid with a girl he had never laid eyes upon, and Cupid's daughter to boot! 'I wondered what kind of daughter she was if she needed her parents to come along after each match and insist that we meet. It didn't augur particularly well ...'

In May 1992, with Lynagh in control, Benetton won the Italian national championship final against northern neighbour Rovigo.

Lynagh kicked the goals that mattered and scored a couple of tries, the second of which came right on full-time to seal the match. In a list of favourite memories, it measures up with grand slams, world cups and the like. 'The emotion throughout the whole day was incredible,' says Lynagh. 'Before the game, all the players were in the dressing rooms crying openly. I was swept up in it and tears were streaming down my face too. Then after we won, everyone went beserk. I was on the touchline trying to convert my second try, but I didn't have a chance. One of our reserves wouldn't stop hugging me.'

Most things in rugby are relative. It might have been a long way from London, but there was as much joy in those Treviso dressing rooms as there had been at Twickenham on 2 November the previous year. It was the perfect, if unforeseeable climax to an uncertain begin-ning, and as Lynagh emerged from the excitement and warmth of the rooms into a warm spring evening, he was reflecting on his good fortune and the surprises life can provide. 'Ciao, Michael. At last you two can meet. Isabella, this is Michael Lynagh. Michael, Isabella.'

The figure in front of him was not the picture Michael had painted in his head. Certainly he had not envisaged a slim, blue-eyed blonde with striking features, who would not have been out of place on the pages of a fashion magazine. 'Ciao, Isabella. Giuliano, why didn't you introduce us earlier?' he asked, with just a hint of annoyance in his tone. The conversation had not got beyond the first sentence and suddenly Michael wasn't looking forward quite so much to going home. He recoils at the corny description of 'love at first sight' but readily accepts that of 'mighty interested at first sight'. And he had got it all wrong about Giuliano's intentions. 'Dad had been telling me for months what a nice, young man he thought Michael was,' recalls Isabella. '"You should go and talk to him," he kept saying, "because not only is he shy but he does not speak much Italian."'

A plane trip to Australia was just twenty-four hours away and there wasn't much time to waste. Lynagh invited Isabella to the after-match party in a nearby restaurant. With three hundred people all wanting a piece of him it wasn't the ideal scenario for a get-to-know-you first date. It was two in the morning when Isabella made her farewells. 'Goodnight Michael, it was nice to meet you. May I have your autograph?' Lynagh wasn't going to die wondering. He seized his chance. 'The guys are having a send-off barbecue for me tomorrow afternoon. Will you come along?' 'Sure, I will.'

She got her autograph. He got his wish. By the time he stepped on Qantas Flight 052 bound for Brisbane, he knew he would be back. Treviso hadn't seen the last of Michael Lynagh. Nor, he hoped, had Isabella Franchin.

Taking the Queensland captaincy from Michael Lynagh was one thing. Not selecting him in the Test team was something else altogether. The Italian connection had begun to cause minor tremors in Australian rugby circles and Reds coach and Wallaby selector John Connolly made the Richter scale soar when he publicly announced that neither Lynagh nor David Campese should be considered for the home series against Scotland. 'Spaghetti rugby' the critics liked to call the Italian club competition – unworthy preparation for the standard required to wear the Australian jersey. As both had spent the early part of the Australian season in Italy, Connolly argued it was unfair that they slot immediately into the Test team ahead of colleagues who had been playing the tough domestic Super Six provincial championship. At the same time, he considered it quite proper that Lynagh should go straight back into the Reds team for the next match. It was an argument full of holes, and one that didn't enhance the Connolly–Lynagh relationship.

Paul Kahl was the back-up flyhalf in the Queensland team, and Lynagh was sensitive to the insecurity Kahl might feel because of his own comings and goings. 'I always felt for Kahly when I came back and slipped straight back into the team,' says Lynagh, 'but he was really good. He used to tell me not to worry about it and that if I hadn't gone to Italy he wouldn't have played anywhere near the number of games he had, so he certainly made me feel more comfortable about it.' Importantly, there was no animosity from any other team-mates.

That Connolly should want one rule for Australian teams and another for Queensland made no sense to the analyst in Lynagh. He had been to Italy with the full blessing and knowledge of both the Australian Rugby Football Union and the Queensland Rugby Union, and the fact his team had made the final necessitated a late homecoming. He also took offence to the spaghetti rugby reference, arguing that although the lower Italian teams were of an ordinary standard, the top six clubs provided rugby of a high quality. 'In a sense I understood Connolly's argument,' says Lynagh, 'but rugby is a game that allows you to travel overseas and play with foreign clubs. It is part of its attraction. I'd been receiving offers for the best part of a decade and had always refused. As soon as I took one up, there were people all too willing to punish me by not allowing me to play for Australia.'

As it turned out Connolly was outvoted by his fellow selectors, and both Lynagh and Campese were chosen for the first Test, despite their arrival in the country only four days earlier. 'I've mellowed a bit since then in my attitude toward Italy,' says Connolly. 'I just felt it was tough on the blokes who had been slaving their insides out trying to get a gold jersey, to be deprived by two guys who hadn't even been in the country.' There was however, no credit for services rendered. Lynagh feels this attitude wasn't helped by the fact Campese hadn't returned to Australia as soon as his playing commitments were completed. 'Campo's team had got knocked out early but rather than come back and play for Randwick or New South Wales … he went on a holiday. The press and Connolly got on his back about that and I got caught in the backwash, even though I'd been playing right up to the week before the Scotland game. It annoyed me too that everyone was having a crack at the standard of Italian rugby when probably none of them, including Connolly, had ever seen a game there.' Connolly could appreciate the irony when early in the Test, Lynagh, sensing a fast-closing defence, lobbed a chip kick behind the Scottish backline for Campese to gather on the full and score in the corner. Between them, the Italian connection scored twenty-three of Australia's twenty-seven points: Campese, two tries and Lynagh a try and four goals.

Lynagh hadn't turned eight when he went to his first rugby Test. It was in July 1971, and his father Ian made a special journey from their Gold Coast home to take his young son to that controversial second Test between Australia and South Africa at the Brisbane Exhibition Grounds. Wild demonstrations protesting the presence of the Springbok team in Australia had taken place at earlier matches in the southern states, and to ensure the Queensland Test went ahead, Premier Joh Bjelke-Petersen proclaimed a state of emergency. Security could not be guaranteed at the unenclosed surrounds of Ballymore, so the game was transferred to the Exhibition grounds. Placard-waving protesters were everywhere as Ian and Michael walked to the entrance. 'I remember walking down Gregory Terrace,' says Ian, 'and being a bit stunned by the seriousness of the demonstrations. I hadn't expected any of the kerfuffle – I really was pretty naïve. I'd just thought we would go to a game of football. If I think about it now, I should proba-bly have been on the footpath with the protesters. At the time, it was pretty scary.'

It wasn't so much fright as apprehension that gripped Lynagh twenty-one years later when the first Australian team to play South Africa since that 1971 series landed at Jan Smuts Airport, Johannesburg in August 1992. The political scene was brighter but far from settled, and although South Africa was once again part of the international sporting scene, he wasn't convinced the tour should have taken place. His long-held beliefs ensured an uneasiness about their presence in this still-unequal society, while for rugby reasons alone he felt the tour was ill-advised. As world champions and Bledisloe Cup holders courtesy of a two-one series win over the All Blacks just a month before, he could see no advantage in going to South Africa.

'We had everything to lose and nothing to gain by going there. As the recognised top side in the world, we were putting everything on the line in a one-off Test. It all seemed too premature. I am not against title defences but South Africa hadn't earned the right to have a shot at it so soon and under conditions that had everything in the Springboks' favour.'

His mood wasn't helped by the attitude of a large number of the Springbok supporters. The Afrikaaner population is not renowned for its love of outsiders and although as rugby fanatics the vast majority was delighted to once again witness international competition, no one would have guessed it by their demeanour towards the visitors. The tone was set before the opening match against Western Transvaal at Potchefstroom when, aiming at no one in particular, one supporter yelled at some passing Wallabies, 'Hey, man! You might think you're world champions but you wait until you're at the bottom of a South African ruck. We'll find out who's boss then!'

After the famine, South African rugby was gorging itself. Not only were the Wallabies in the country but the All Blacks as well. Three days before the New Zealand–Springbok Test at Ellis Park, the three teams gathered for an official reception. It took place half a kilometre underground in a disused gold mine at Gold Reef City. If you were an autograph hunter, this was the place to be. Naas Botha, Grant Fox and Michael Lynagh – three of the greatest points-scorers in the history of the game – were there but the honour roll wasn't confined to rugby. President F. W. de Klerk, Zulu leader Chief Buthulezi and African National Congress representative Steve Tshwete added considerable clout to the gathering. And hovering on the outskirts, to complete the picture, there was a group of can-can dancers who every now and then would grab the attention of the lads with a quick routine.

'I found it all quite eerie,' says Lynagh. 'It was a unique experience. There I was, half a kilometre underground, having a barbecue and a drink with some of the finest rugby players in the world, chatting to F. W. de Klerk about the vagaries of our respective golf swings and at the same time being entertained by a bunch of can-can dancers.'

The unauthorised playing of the Afrikaaner anthem 'Die Stem' at the All Black match, during what was supposed to be a minute's silence for the victims of the recent Boipatong massacre, threw a cloak of uncertainty over the Wallabies' remaining games. Understandably, the ANC was incensed and contemplated withdrawing its support for the Australian tour. An early-morning phone call from team manager John Breen alerted Lynagh to the drama that was unfolding. 'We were told we may have to abort the tour and fly to Mauritius and spend some time there. After our first week in Pretoria, it was news plenty of us were pleased to hear. We were getting fed up with the rudeness of the Springbok supporters.' The tensions eased though, as the week progressed. The Wallabies moved camp to the far more relaxed, almost convivial atmosphere of Port Elizabeth. Late-night meetings between rugby officials and ANC representatives resulted in the tour going ahead, while the people of Port Elizabeth made the Wallabies feel welcome. For the first time Lynagh began to look forward to Saturday's Test in Cape Town and his first sighting of a South African jersey since the match at the exhibition grounds a generation ago.

It was a significant occasion in rugby history in more ways than one. The main headline certainly was that a bridge between the two countries had been rebuilt, but while one new era was unfolding another one was about to end. It was the forty-seventh and final time that Michael Lynagh and Nick Farr-Jones would join forces as halfback and flyhalf in international rugby. With their union had come the most successful period in Australia's rugby history – no one viewed that as coincidental. They had a rapport in everything they did. They were different personalities undoubtedly, but with similar characteristics and similar goals. 'I really enjoyed Nick's company. He was good fun to be around and although he is a more garrulous kind of person than me, we share plenty of interests,' says Lynagh. 'I think the captain–vice-captain combination worked well, he would do a lot of talking to the big group while I was more likely to sit down and have a quiet yarn with an individual. On the field, he was fantastic. He was physically very strong, but at the same time one of the most naturally gifted athletes I've seen. If you needed big tackles, he'd make them. If the wind was blowing a gale at Wellington he'd be the one to probe the short side, but if I needed the ball I'd always get it quickly and right where I wanted it. He looked after what was happening in front of him and he trusted me to look after what was going on behind. His greatest feature though, was his ability to give everything for the team. The team was always the most important thing.'

Australia were World Cup and Bledisloe Cup holders, but there remained that lingering uncertainty about South Africa. Perhaps it was one of the reasons the arrogant Afrikaaners had annoyed them so much. As Lynagh and Farr-Jones had done on each of the previous forty-six occasions there was little more than a handshake, a wink and a quick, here we go again, between the two. It was the ultimate way to end the partnership. In atrocious conditions, the Wallabies showed the chasm that existed between the two sides. South Africa might have a plethora of strong provincial teams, but when it came to the big time, they were still back in the 1970s. The Australian forwards were dominant – one thunderous Willie Ofahengaue tackle of the rampaging Springbok hooker Uli Schmidt sent a message to the locals this was not a team that could be intimidated. 'Willie made that tackle right in front of me,' recalls Lynagh. 'It was one of those hits that really lift your spirits and tends to deflate the opposition. I was pleased on selfish grounds as well, because I was right behind Willie and if he'd missed, I'd have had the dubious honour of trying to stop the runaway tank!' The match featured David Campese's fiftieth Test try, and a double to

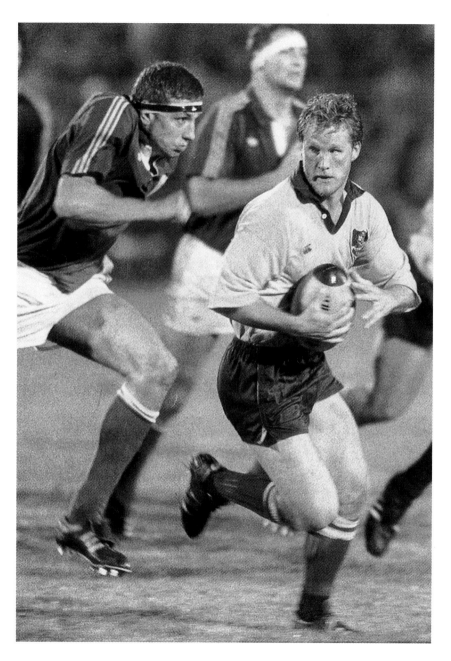

Paris, 1989. *Au revoir* – Lynagh sends the
French defenders in the wrong direction.

(far left, top)
Putting All Blacks on the back foot. The New Zealand tour, 1990. (Reuter)

(far left, bottom)
Saitama, 1991. This formal Japanese photo gives no clue to the free-for-all lunch that followed. (Lynagh collection)

(above)
The great Queensland and Australian midfield trio of Michael Lynagh, Tim Horan and Jason Little, Ballymore, 1991. (Garry Taylor)

(left)
Two of Queensland's greatest players. Paul McLean and Lynagh prior to Lynagh passing McLean's points-scoring record, 1991. (Queensland Newspapers Pty Ltd)

(above)
The cold beer that got him into hot water.
The controversial Power's commercial
with Australian rugby league captain,
Wally Lewis. (Power's Company)

(right)
The World Cup, 1991. The concentration
begins. (Presse Sports, L'Equipe)

(far left)
The World Cup, 1991. On his way to a try against Wales at Cardiff Arms in his fiftieth test. (Presse Sports, L'Equipe)

(above)
The day before the 1991 World Cup final. Marie and Michael get the feel of Twickenham. (Lynagh collection)

(left)
Ian and Marie celebrate the World Cup win in the stands at Twickenham with Michael's friend and business colleague, Ian Crichton. (Lynagh collection)

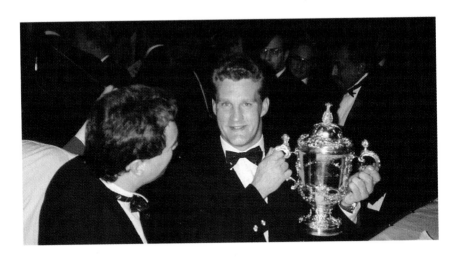

(top)
You've had your turn Foxy – it's ours now.
Lynagh keeps the William Webb Ellis
Trophy away from New Zealand's Grant
Fox at the World Cup dinner in London
on 2 November 1991. (Lynagh collection)

(above)
Here it is. At Sydney airport, arriving
home with the World Cup in 1991.
(Patrick Hamilton, *The Australian*, News
Ltd)

(left)
To the victor, the spoils. Vice-captain and captain show the Sydney crowds the World Cup booty in November 1991. (Wayne Venables, Illawarra Newspapers Holdings Pty Ltd)

(below)
Treviso, 1992. Lynagh interprets the advice of former French player and Italian club coach, Pierre Villepreux. (Bernard Garcia)

(top)
A Benetton dinner in 1992. Luciano
Benetton is on Lynagh's left, good friend
and Italian representative Guido Rossi is
on his right. (Lynagh collection)

(above)
Quickly the hero. Lynagh in the Treviso
dressing-rooms in 1992. (Lynagh
collection)

(top)
A day trip to London from Italy in 1992.
Benetton club members at Heathrow,
about to return to Treviso on Luciano
Benetton's private jet after watching
England play Wales at Twickenham. All
Black John Kirwan is on the far left,
Lynagh is second from right. (Lynagh
collection)

(above)
'Advance Australia Fair'. Australia versus
Scotland, Ballymore, 1992. (Garry Taylor)

(far top left)
South Africa, 1992. A special day, one
kilometre beneath Johannesburg. F. W.
de Klerk, Lynagh and Nick Farr-Jones.
(Lynagh collection)

(far bottom left)
Queensland Sports Star Award, 1992.
(Queensland Newspapers Pty Ltd)

(above)
Where did he go? A Treviso club match,
1993. (Lynagh collection)

(left)
Jamming in Italy in 1993 with former All
Black saxophonist, John Kirwan. (Lynagh
collection)

(top)
Ian Lynagh and Isabella Franchin in the
Piazza San Marco, Venice, 1993. (Lynagh
collection)

(bottom)
The World Sevens final, Edinburgh, 1993.
Despite this Lynagh try, England won the
tournament.

(left)
Considering another query from the press,
1993. (Queensland Newspapers Pty Ltd)

(below)
What the fans think. (Lynagh collection)

Michael Lynagh and Isabella Franchin at
Noosa Heads, 1994. (Mike Larder)

Lynagh's good mate and surfing buddy, Paul Carozza. The final tally was 26–3 to Australia. The Wallabies weren't just World Cup holders – they were the world champions. There could be no dispute.

'Hello, Andrew. It's Michael Lynagh speaking. Sorry to ring you at home.'

'No problem Noddy,' I replied.

But I thought, you don't have to apologise for ringing me at home. We're old friends, remember? We've been on a million tours, experienced plenty of highs and a few lows together. Okay, we haven't seen a lot of each other over the past couple of years but, hell, you don't have to apologise for ringing. I realised this was just the formal, perhaps slightly nervous Noddy taking over.

A few days earlier he had been chosen as captain of the Wallaby party to tour Ireland and Wales. Farr-Jones was gone. Lynagh was in charge.

'Congratulations Nod. You must be delighted.'

'Yeah, thanks, I am. That's actually what I wanted to talk about. I wonder if we could go for a bite to eat and chat about the role.'

I was touched by the approach and indicated my willingness to help in any way possible. We met for lunch and he didn't hide his misgivings. Although as flyhalf and playmaker he had made a lot of the decisions for the team over the past seven years, this was the first time he was the one with the ultimate responsibility. He had no fears about the on-field role, but was honest enough to realise he would have to make adjustments if he was to grasp all the facets of captaincy. I knew he wasn't the table-thumping type, but I'd heard enough from him during team-meetings in the past to know that when he spoke, it made sense. It surprised me then, when he admitted how nervous he was about addressing the team as first-choice captain. He didn't possess the gift of the gab, like his immediate predecessor, but he was friends with most of the team and had, over a long period, earned and kept their respect.

There was, however, a hint of insecurity as he stepped into his new role.

When Bob Dwyer selected Lynagh as the new skipper, he knew he was a long way from a Farr-Jones replica. 'I wanted the team to get used to someone quite different from Nick. It was important we didn't fall into the trap of being dependent on the memory of Nick's leadership. I think it is good for the team to have to adjust to different personalities ...'

David Nucifora, the Wallabies reserve hooker and long-time friend of Lynagh, saw how desperate he was to make the role work. 'When they gave him the captaincy, they were basically asking Noddy to come out of himself a bit more. He realised himself that he had to be more open, and he made a hell of an effort to do just that. Noddy's a smart bloke and he realised his limitations – he knew he wasn't the world's most outgoing person, so to that end he used Vice-captain Phil Kearns really well.'

Although he had the (c) beside his name, Lynagh still maintained his old role of the less outspoken voice of authority, while he ensured Kearns took over some of Farr-Jones' duties. 'Noddy knows himself pretty well,' agrees Kearns. 'From day one he said to me that he wasn't the type of person to carry on too much in the dressing room. He told me he wanted me to help him get the boys in the right frame of mind.' A bit of strong motivation was necessary from time to time. Lynagh realised that, and he understood it would be more effective coming from Kearns. It was sensible delegation. 'I made a real effort to be more accessible and a little more talkative,' recalls Lynagh, 'but at the same time, I wanted other people to play their roles as well.'

Nervous or not, Lynagh quickly made a good impression on his team-mates in Ireland. Centre Anthony Herbert saw the effort he was making. 'He knew what he had to do and I reckon the blokes also understood him pretty well. They didn't force Noddy to be someone he wasn't. There was enormous respect for him and if he asked for something from the team, he would get it.'

The Powers episode, his decision to play in Italy and, perhaps, the
mere fact he was one of the code's best-known players gave the disci-
ples of the tall-poppy syndrome ammunition to accuse Lynagh of selfishness. Such critics, according to Herbert, were well wide of the mark.
'He is pretty singleminded, but there was no way he would do anything
to hurt any individual. Had you given some players Michael Lynagh's
profile, you can be sure they'd have got very wrapped up in their own
importance. Noddy is one of the best players in the world – others are
only self-proclaimed. He has earned his stripes. They weren't mailed
to him in the post.'

The tour progressed well. As usual Lynagh loved Ireland, the team
seemed to be responding to his leadership and he was getting pretty
damn efficient at 'Guinness Golf'. Sitting in the clubhouse at
Portmarnock, after a taxing day on the course, Lynagh, Herbert and
several of their team-mates were involved in a typical post-round
shout. Guinness was ordered all round, and the discussion then centred
on how long it takes to down a pint of the good stuff. 'Yep, she's a real
par five,' volunteered prop Ewen McKenzie. Within ten minutes,
Herbert and Co. had turned that comment into a drinking game. Each
pint was nominated as a par three, four or five. With six players in the
shout, it became a six-hole competition, wherein each new shout
became a new hole. A par five meant you had five gulps in which to
reach the bottom of the glass. Should it take only three, you were two
under and in good shape. Commentary was a necessary part of the
game. As glasses were raised, there would be reminders of the importance of getting off the tee well. One gulp was followed by analysis.
'Yes Noddy, you've struck it beautifully. That's 250 down the middle.
Sorry Herbie, you topped it mate. You'll need a good second from
there.' The game became more sophisticated each time they played.
Chalk marks were drawn on glasses to indicate water hazards. Stop at
the mark and you dropped a shot.

Despite being a long way short of a hardened drinker, Lynagh
performed creditably. 'We played nine holes one night,' recalls

Herbert. 'Nine pints of Guinness is a fair amount and Noddy went well. I think he was three under. It wasn't often he'd sit at a bar and drink nine pints of anything. But this was a game – there was a bit of competition involved and he was with his mates, so he loved it.'

Crunch. Lynagh wouldn't be raising a glass for a while now. Late in the first half of the Test against Ireland at Lansdowne Road, he made a covering tackle on an Irish player. A supporting Irishman then grabbed the ball and tried to leap over the Wallaby captain. In attempting to make his second tackle in three seconds, Lynagh's arm was dragged over his head, in the process dislocating his shoulder. He knew at that instant his tour was finished. It was a painful evening, both mentally and physically. Team doctor Cameron Osborne and physiotherapist Greg Craig presented two options. Let the injury repair itself and run a 75 per cent risk of it recurring, or undergo surgery and drastically lessen the chances of this. Lynagh chose the latter course, immediately returning to Brisbane and in the care of orthopaedic surgeon Peter Myers, underwent the operation.

When an injured player is sent home from a tour, that usually signals the end of his participation. The union, which pays for accommodation and other expenses, is less than anxious to continue payments for the injured player as well as for his replacement. Injured players themselves often prefer to go home rather than hang around the team. In Lynagh's case, he felt very much that he could still contribute to the success of the 1992 Wallabies and, due to the wishes of the team management and the generosity of the ARFU, he went back to Britain for the Welsh leg of the tour immediately following his operation.

On his return Lynagh temporarily lost his nickname of Noddy. He was christened 'Neale Fraser'. 'The blokes concluded the Davis Cup squad and the Wallabies were the the only teams with non-playing captains,' recalls Lynagh. 'They even asked me if they could provide an armchair by the sideline for the remaining matches!' He declined the

offer, ending his first season as Australian captain sitting in the grandstand with his arm in a sling.

13
ISABELLA AND ONWARDS

After the initial uncertainty, Lynagh's first Italian season hadn't been too bad. Partly through his own efforts and partly because of the unconditional friendship shown by the Treviso community, he started to feel more at home. The people and the culture had taken effect. Even so, there was another, more important reason he made the decision to return for a second season at the end of 1992. Her name was Isabella. He wasn't sure if he was following his head or his heart but after that brief meeting with her six months earlier, he knew he had to return. 'I went back to Italy because of that last day, after I'd met Isabella,' recalls Lynagh with no hint of embarrassment. 'I felt there was something special there.'

Isabella herself was not yet so sure. As a teenager who played junior international tennis for many years and who was once ranked in the top ten in Italy, she admired sporting champions. A naturally inquisitive person, she was anxious to find what made this rugby champion tick, but her curiosity wasn't based on any romantic notions. Knowing the trouble Lynagh had experienced adapting to the Italian way of life when he'd first arrived, Isabella was impressed by the way he'd stuck it out. 'When he came back in December, I wasn't sure I liked his personality. I couldn't understand him. One day he was really nice and the next day a little bit moody. But I think he did a good job at being persistent.'

In many ways it was a case of opposites attracting – Lynagh the measured introvert, Isabella an extrovert who enjoys a crowd and relaxes easily within the larger group. 'I'm Italian and therefore I'm basically outgoing and happy. I love laughing and I get along with people like me.' Lynagh likes a laugh too, but Isabella quickly realised he wasn't a type she was used to. 'When he first came to Treviso I think everybody expected him to be arrogant because he was a superstar and had just won the World Cup but he was very different from that. He was humble, very responsible, thoughtful and sensitive – over-sensitive actually!'

By March 1993, the platonic relationship they'd enjoyed had turned into something far more serious. 'I was always pretty nervous around girls,' says Lynagh. 'I certainly was uncomfortable with any signs of public affection. With Isabella, I don't care. I'm no longer afraid people might laugh or point fingers. My attitude with Isabella is that this is us, and others can take us or leave us for what we are.' Damien Frawley, his old friend, noticed the change. 'I've never before seen him as a relaxed person when women are around. I think he may have mellowed a bit over the years too, but there's no doubt Isabella has had a profound influence on him. It's as if he doesn't worry now what the world thinks, and that hasn't always been the case.'

However, it has always been the case that a player of Lynagh's class has a considerable appeal to sportswear manufacturers like Adidas, Puma or Asics. Footwear companies vie for the chance to get their boot on a revered foot and there are few more revered than his. If Lynagh ever doubted the commercial value of providing free footwear to top footballers he was convinced during his second season with Benetton. After experiencing some problems with a particular type of boot given by team supplier Lotto, he wore a new model to training one Tuesday evening. Nothing was said by his team-mates, but he noticed on the next Thursday that three of his colleagues were wearing the same style. By the end of the following week, the entire team trotted out in what became known as 'Lynagh's Lottos'. (Lynagh wasn't the only trendsetter. When David Campese played for Milan he was asked to stop taping his wrists before each game because everyone in the team started doing it and it was costing the club a fortune.)

Star treatment also has its upside. In March 1993, on one of Benetton's free weekends, England was playing Wales at Twickenham in a match that would decide the Five Nations Championship. There was no better way to spend the day than slip across to London on Luciano Benetton's fourteen-seat Lear jet with Luciano himself and some selected guests. Lynagh and John Kirwan had used their contacts to secure tickets for the game in exchange for a couple of pre-match chats to corporate groups. The party arrived at Heathrow where a waiting limousine couriered them to Twickenham. They watched the match, then enjoyed a few post-game drinks with Luciano's business acquaintances before returning to Treviso by eleven o'clock that night, in time for Lynagh to meet up with his friends in the piazza and share the day's events with them.

The piazza is a central part of Treviso social life. Most nights after training, Lynagh can be found at the team's second clubhouse – Bar Enoteca. There copious quantities of pasta are provided by proprietress Tilla, whose love for the team and the game is demonstrated by the rugby memorabilia that decorate the walls. After games there are no specific arrangements to meet at anyone's home for a drink as might be the case in Australia. If you are socialising, which most people are almost all the time, you just arrive at the piazza around ten o'clock to be assured of finding some action. It's a far cry from the heavy rugby atmosphere that can pervade post-match activities in Australia. Lynagh catches up with team-mates or friends like Vic Tesser. Vic, who spent twenty-seven years in Sydney as a wine merchant, befriended Lynagh when he first arrived and was a comforting presence in those difficult early months. Vic had been a rugby league follower during his time in Sydney, but once he met Lynagh he soon became a Benetton fanatic. So much so in fact, that when the 1992 championship was won he delivered an early-season promise by opening a sixty-three-year-old bottle of port worth $1500, and sharing it with team-members so that the success could be toasted in style.

By the end of the 1992–93 Italian season Lynagh had no doubts as to where his heart and perhaps his future lay. He approached Benetton and suggested a three-year agreement – an arrangement he believed would be mutually beneficial. The company had never previously committed itself to anything like this, but when he argued that he had surely proved both his worth and his loyalty, Benetton could but agree. Lynagh likes to plan, to know where he's heading, to be in control. The agreement allowed that. It also guaranteed he will be wearing the united colours of Benetton until at least 1996.

Although unhappy to be leaving Isabella behind in Treviso, if only temporarily, he arrived back in Brisbane anxious to resume the Australian captaincy for the 1993 season's main bill – a three-Test series against the touring South Africans. His first priority though, was a spell in hospital. During the World Cup Sevens tournament in Edinburgh in March he'd experienced some discomfort at what was initially diagnosed as a groin strain. In Brisbane the real problem was discovered – he had a double hernia. During the operation the surgeon became concerned at the appearance of an enlarged lymph node in Lynagh's left side. He removed it and, to everyone's relief, confirmed it was harmless and not as he had feared, a sign of something more sinister. Lynagh missed a month of rugby but was back on the field in time to lead the Wallabies to a win over Tonga at Ballymore. It was a one-sided affair but it marked yet another world first for Lynagh, as he became the only player to be involved in Test matches against sixteen different countries.

The following Saturday he made one of his by now very rare appearances with club team University, and there was no sign that he was in anything but the top of his form and at the peak of fitness. 'He was absolutely fantastic,' remembers Bob Templeton. 'Just because he was playing, a huge crowd attended the match and they saw him exert an enormous influence on his young team-mates. He never told them how they should play. He just took over.' As was usually the case when Lynagh played, University won – the only dampener was the few stitches in the back of the head he received after encountering an errant boot.

The next morning he was back in the air travelling to Sydney for a Wallaby camp to prepare for a one-off Test against New Zealand in Dunedin. He felt a little off-colour but attributed this to the knock on the head the day before. By the time he was at the Australian team meeting, he began to feel worse and mentioned to Tim Gavin that it was bad timing to be coming down with the 'flu. Within half an hour he was suffering severe stomach cramps. So bad was the pain, he struggled to reach the phone to ring team doctor Cam Osborne. Osborne rushed to Lynagh's room but had to be let in by a maid as the patient lay writhing on the bed unable to get to the door. He administered morphine to ease the pain before taking him to the neighbouring Prince Alfred Hospital.

Just a few weeks before there had been a very public drama in England involving Test cricketer Craig McDermott. He had also undergone a double hernia operation earlier in the year, but after a seemingly full recovery was struck down with significant abdominal pains in the middle of a Test. It was discovered one of the staples used in the hernia operation had wrapped around his bowel causing severe pain and necessitating emergency surgery. Lynagh seemed to be heading in the same direction until tests confirmed peritonitis – a stomach infection, which is a potentially fatal condition. It had developed after the removal of the lymph node in the initial hernia operation.

As his mates continued to train for the Bledisloe Cup match, he was in hospital with a temperature of forty degrees and tubes draining his stomach. 'He was a very, very sick boy,' says Osborne, 'and he needed lots of reassurance.' By the end of the week, he had shed twelve kilo-grams and any thoughts of further rugby in Australia in 1993 had disappeared.

His medical condition was at an all-time low, and so too was his rela-tionship with the press. He believed the Brisbane media had taken a dim view of his decision to play in Italy and had treated him warily ever since. 'As soon as I stepped outside the comfort of Queensland I was looked at in a different light. I'd left the family and that wasn't deemed to be a good thing,' claims Lynagh. An article in the *Sunday-Mail* on 25 July 1993, written tongue in cheek, suggesting that his hernia had happened as a result of 'falling off his wallet (or picking it up)' – a crack at his estimated earnings in Italy – was not taken in the spirit it may have been intended. 'Admittedly something like that could, in certain circumstances, have been humorous,' says Lynagh. 'It was hard to see it though when I was not only the butt of the joke, but at the same time ill in hospital.'

Once more he was measuring others according to the benchmark he sets himself. He refuses to take short cuts in achieving results on the football field and he gets annoyed if he feels a journalist has failed to get the full story. He detests errors, particularly those that arise from sloppiness, lack of attention to detail or laziness. 'I like being correct and it annoys me when others aren't, and that happened regularly when I was sick. Some journalists didn't even bother to find out what the problem was. They just took guesses,' he says. 'Often people will write about me but not bother to check or hear my side of the story. They prefer to make comments for themselves that are wrong and that annoys me. If you asked representative players if they like what the press writes, the answer would largely be no. Because I've said so, when other players have preferred to keep quiet, means I'm over-sensitive or a whinger ...'

If a statistician were to assess the hundreds of thousands of words written about Lynagh during his career, it would be certain that the far greater percentage of comment would be favourable. According to Lynagh, that does not excuse the incorrect and unresearched criticism that has been levelled at him. 'Much of the press has been pretty fair and I would count rugby writers like Peter Jenkins, Greg Growden and Frank O'Callaghan as respected,' he says. 'But if something is wrong, it should be pointed out. If we win five games and then get beaten we'll be criticised. That's okay. You're only as good as your last game. But journalists should be subjected to the same rules. They're only as good as their last article and if it's not properly researched, and consequently incorrect, the writer should be open to criticism.'

By the time the Wallabies set off for France at the end of 1993 Lynagh had recovered fully and was back in charge. Although his absence allowed Phil Kearns to lead Australia to a series win over South Africa, Lynagh was restored to the captaincy as soon as he was fit and available. Playing in matches in the United States and Canada on the way to France, his readiness for the rigours of international rugby were quickly put to the test. At half-time in the match against an American selection in Los Angeles spectators enjoyed the bizarre sight of Wallaby players standing on the field in front of two huge fans specially set up to help ease the effects of the stifling conditions. Lynagh made his return to the playing field in forty-degree heat at airless Riverview Park, and then found himself three days later lining up against Canada B in Calgary with the temperature a chilly minus five. Surviving this forty-five degree turnaround in temperature within seventy-two hours convinced him that his body was back in shape.

A lacklustre display by the Australians in the first Test at Bordeaux wrecked the aspirations of winning the Test series in France. For both Coach Dwyer and Captain Lynagh it was their third French tour and their third failed attempt to attain that much sought-after prize. A lapse in defence allowed French halfback Aubin Heuber to score a vital try, and while Peter Slattery, his opposite number, was blamed (incorrectly) by some sections of the media, it was the skipper for whom Dwyer saved most of his vitriol.

From a scrum close to the Australian tryline the French enjoyed a wide blindside in which to manoeuvre. The various roles played by flankers, fullbacks, flyhalves, halfbacks and number eights in blindside defence is practised *ad nauseum* by representative teams at training. There is every expectation it will not fail. On this occasion however, the Australians presented a passage to the French as wide as the Champs-Elysées. Dwyer's recollection is that teenage fullback Matthew Burke called to Lynagh to stay on the open side, thus giving the French one less cover defender to avoid. Throughout his rugby career Lynagh has rarely been chastised by a coach. For most it would have seemed counter-productive. And as captain, Lynagh had certainly not been on the receiving end until then. 'How can you alter the defensive pattern in the middle of the game on the suggestion of a nineteen-year-old kid who's never played at this level before?' screamed Dwyer. 'I don't care what he says. Tell him to get out of it and play the pattern we've been practising for a month.' Lynagh took it on the chin. 'He just pulled in,' recalls Dwyer. 'He admitted he was in strife and off he went. He doesn't give you the impression he's an easy person to direct and because he gives you that impression, he isn't an easy person to direct! But if you're definite and positive and aggressive he's fine.' Although Lynagh says he has no problems with reprimands when in error, he has no recollection of Dwyer becoming upset with him over that particular match.

Between the coach and the captain the decision was made that Lynagh would relinquish the goalkicking for the second Test at Parc des Princes in Paris. Dwyer ran the suggestion past back-up goalkicker Marty Roebuck. 'Marty, we might give Noddy a rest from the kicks on Saturday and let you have a go. How do you reckon you're kicking?' 'Mate, I feel as if I couldn't miss,' replied Roebuck. 'Good,' said Dwyer. 'That's exactly what we had in mind.' As well as giving Lynagh a rest from the pressures of kicking, the Wallaby brains trust also felt he was the man to exploit a possible weakness in the French defensive pattern. So much attention was being paid to the potent attacking prowess of the Wallaby three-quarter line, which included Tim Horan, Jason Little and David Campese, that there might be some gaps close to the scrum. As the French backrow was extremely physical but not so mobile, it was decided Lynagh should run with the ball himself more than was normal, so that he might find a few holes as the opposition zeroed in on Horan and company. The plan worked to perfection and Lynagh produced arguably his finest individual performance in a Wallaby jersey. Ironically it was only the second time in his sixty-seven Test matches in which he had failed to contribute directly to the score. Roebuck had done his job admirably, notching twenty of the twenty-four points.

'Hey mate, haven't I seen you some place before?' The breath reeked of rum and Coke and hit Lynagh like a slap in the face. Friends Kim Weller, Tim Vallance and Mick Hellen had arranged a traditional Brisbane welcome-home for Lynagh early in 1994, following his third Italian season with Benetton. They went off to the Breakfast Creek hotel, where the steaks have become the stuff of legend, for a quick beer in the public bar before sitting out in the garden restaurant for lunch. While Lynagh ordered the beers, a worse-for-wear regular took his chance to accost the celebrity. Lynagh's mates disappeared. 'They all knew how much I hate being in the situation where some bloke I've never laid eyes on suddenly wants to chew my ear off because he's had too many beers and thinks he's seen me on television ...' Welcome home, Noddy.

Unfortunately for Lynagh, such recognition has become part of his life. Friend, rugby writer and QRU media director Michael Blucher believes he is the most recognisable player in the game. 'He's got a distinctive face, those deepset eyes and blond hair, and when people see him in person I think they are quite surprised at how small he is. When I go out with him people always come up to him and chat. Usually a few drinks have given them the confidence to take a bold step but as long as they aren't too drunk and just being smart alecs he is very good at responding. He doesn't give them the time of day though if they've had too much to drink and are showing-off.'

David Nucifora agrees he is the most visible face in rugby, but adds it is not only in Brisbane and Sydney that his fame attracts Joe Public. 'Everywhere you go with him, even in the most obscure countries, someone will jump out from behind a lamp-post and want his autograph. It's difficult for a guy who's naturally shy but he's adjusted pretty well.'

The famous feet weren't in Brisbane for too long before stepping onto another international flight. In Lynagh's absence, the Queensland Reds had secured a place in the final of the provincial Super Ten competition against Natal in Durban. It was of considerable significance for Lynagh that he and his team-mates were able to share in a piece of world history. The Reds arrived on 10 May, the day of Nelson Mandela's inauguration as president of South Africa. After a quick meal and a surf to get the jet lag out of his system Lynagh retreated to his room to watch the Cape Town proceedings on television. After the unenjoyable Wallaby tour of South Africa two years earlier, he found this trip totally different. 'Away from Pretoria and the more conservative types, we found the people in Natal far different,' says Lynagh. 'They couldn't help us enough and there were no comments about what they were going to do to us on the field.' The Reds were staying in the beachside Elangeni Hotel, he was rooming with good friend David Wilson and plenty of time was spent in the surf with fellow enthusiasts Paul Carozza and Peter Slattery, all of which enhanced his enjoyment. A round of golf with Errol Stewart, the South African cricketer and Natal rugby player, and John Murray, a former Natal squash player, helped the relaxation process even more and by the time the Reds ran on to the magnificent Kings Park on Saturday afternoon Lynagh was ready to run the show.

In an astonishing match all four centres were forced to leave the field with injury early in the second half. The Reds' backline was in disarray, winger Damian Smith and reserve Anthony Herbert made up a makeshift midfield after severe knee injuries had been sustained by both Tim Horan and Jason Little. Lynagh took over. Watching the match live on television back in Sydney, Australian coach Bob Dwyer wore a big smile. 'He had such a commanding presence on the field,' Dwyer recalls. 'It was so obvious that it almost came through the television set. Even before Jason and Tim went off, I looked at him and said to myself, gee I know who's running this game.' Lynagh executed a beautiful chip kick for Queensland winger Barry Lea to score and, with the pressure mounting with each minute in the second half, calmly slotted a field goal and a penalty to secure the Reds the Super Ten trophy. Because of his injuries and Italian commitments, Lynagh's Queensland performances in recent seasons had been rare. He made sure this would be one to remember.

A fortnight later, Lynagh was back on the more familiar territory of Ballymore. Queensland played the touring Irish side, and a try two minutes from full-time by talented hooker Keith Wood seemed to ensure a 26-all draw – a pleasing result for the tourists who had been annihilated by New South Wales the week before. However, after an infringement from the final kick-off Queensland was awarded a penalty, and as Lynagh prepared to take the kick the full-time hooter sounded. No other player's actions could now influence the result of the match. Of the thirty players on the field there was only one who did not appear fazed by the tension. The man in the red jersey with number ten on the back glided rhythmically into the ball, struck the forty-metre attempt flush and, while the Ballymore patrons rose as one, the ball never deviated from its intended course of flight. Ireland were beaten and the final act seemed unquestionable proof that in any Irish rugby player's nightmare, Michael Lynagh would figure large. Greg Growden's match report in the *Sydney Morning Herald* on 30 May ran:

> Michael Lynagh is the ultimate Irish party-pooper. Luck of the
> Irish ... well now that's become the luck of Lynagh ... For the

third consecutive time, the Australian captain and Queensland flyhalf has taken special delight in deceiving the Irish into believing victory was theirs, before delivering the final destructive stroke to douse a shindig.

He then elaborated on previous deadly acts Lynagh had perpetrated, in the World Cup quarter-final in Dublin and in the World Cup Sevens semi-final, where his last minute try spelled doom to Irish hopes.

Lynagh led Australia to a two-nil series-defeat of Ireland and then captained the Wallabies against the Italians in the first-ever night Test at Ballymore. That game was to be his swan song for 1994 – a strained thigh muscle forced him from the field early in the second half. 'It was the first time I'd strained a muscle in my life,' says Lynagh. 'It might have been fatigue from all the training we'd been doing coupled with the stop-start nature of the match. It could have been the effects of the cold night or it may simply have been the first signs of age creeping up on me.' Whatever it was, it caused some soul-searching. Despite his match-winning efforts for Queensland, he maintained an arms-length relationship with the local press and this, added to the illness and injuries he had suffered over the previous twelve months meant he began to question whether the rewards were adequate for the effort expended. That Isabella was 15 000 kilometres away added to his doubts. He decided to retire.

There was only one prize left for him to win in rugby. He'd played ninety-nine games for Queensland and the match against Western Samoa in July would see him register a century of games for the state. He figured this occasion would be an appropriate finale and wrote to Isabella to tell her of his plans. She took three hours to pen her response. 'My letter basically told him that there were many, many people who enjoyed watching him play,' says Isabella. 'I exlained that even in Treviso there were kids who'd love to be what he was. I'd always wanted to be a sporting champion. Michael was there and yet wanted to give it all away even though his performances were as good as ever. He'd done a lot for rugby and it had done a lot for him but I felt he was withdrawing because of the constant pressure and because of the media and to me they were the wrong reasons. It wasn't the game, it was other things surrounding it and I argued that he shouldn't let them interfere. I believed he should get on and do his job and not care what others might say or think. I also told him that I would dearly love to see him captain Australia in the 1995 World Cup.'

Isabella arrived in Australia a fortnight later – her presence and support helped him to shelve his plans. 'I had told Bob Templeton I was giving it away. I was very, very serious but Isa's letter helped me change my thinking and having her close made me a lot happier. I guess I felt less vulnerable and the enthusiasm she had about me playing made me think it was not the right time.'

He was afforded a tumultuous reception from the Ballymore faithful as he ran on to the field for the Western Samoan game. Some of the diehards would not have missed any of his home appearances since his debut against Wairarapa-Bush in April 1982 and they were there for the hundredth game in July 1994. It wasn't quite the fairytale occasion all had hoped for, the thigh muscle that had been troubling him again cut short his contribution. As he walked from the oval that had been the scene of so many of his triumphs, he waved to the crowd in an expression of gratitude for the support they had provided over such a long period. In turn they responded; many of them realised they were probably seeing Michael Lynagh in a Queensland jersey for the last time.

It was in 1993, at a lunch with a group of friends and Wallaby team-mates at Doyle's restaurant in Sydney, that Lynagh was informed by David Campese of a new ARFU ruling on overseas playing commitments. As the 1995 World Cup was scheduled to start in South Africa in May, Australian officials were keen to ensure they could keep a check on the progress of World Cup squad members during the off-season. They decided this would be best achieved by running a series of camps throughout the Australian summer, which necessitated the presence in the country of all the squad members. There were to be no off-season stints in Italy, France or anywhere else. World Cup aspirations meant staying put. The news Campese bore gave the incumbent Wallaby captain indigestion. Lynagh had gone to Benetton on his own initiative to secure a three-year agreement to play in Treviso and, much to his delight, the company had come to the party. How would he look now if he went back and called off the deal? More worrying though, was the prospect of being forced to spend six months away from Isabella. He failed to see how that could help him prepare properly for rugby's biggest event.

He immediately informed Benetton of impending problems and pursued the matter with the ARFU to find a suitable resolution. It was easier to tackle a flying French three-quarter than pin down an administrator prepared to take responsibility for the issue and discuss it with him. Eventually one put his hand up. Dick McGruther, who'd gained Lynagh's respect over his handling of the Powers issue, was again in the hot seat. He was chairman of the Mission Repeat committee, a group formed to ensure the best possible preparation for the World Cup. McGruther suggested to Lynagh he write a letter outlining the reasons he should be given a dispensation. He did so, explaining that he understood the reasons for the ruling but also arguing his special circumstances. He had checked with Benetton and was able to promise he would return to Australia for every camp, while Benetton coach, former All Black Wayne Smith, would monitor his progress. Lynagh maintained that the training facilities were at least the equal of those in Australia and, from a personal point of view, he would be far more relaxed and happy with Isabella than if they were forced to be separated. A sub-committee comprising Australian officials Paul McLean, Ian Ferrier and Bob Dwyer studied Lynaghs' letter, then applied some conditions. He had to return for every camp, he was to play no more than five games before January and he had to have six weeks' rest between the last game in Australia in 1994 and his first in Italy. Lynagh readily accepted those provisos and the full committee unanimously voted he should be allowed to return to Treviso.

Jason Little, Tim Gavin, David Campese and Warwick Waugh were among several of Lynagh's Wallaby colleagues who had also enjoyed recent Italian seasons. Lynagh realised they might perhaps be annoyed if they perceived the captain was getting special treatment. He tried to address the problem. 'I spoke to a few of them and explained my situation and suggested if they felt they had special circumstances they too should go and speak to the officials. I also asked the committee to communicate with any players contemplating overseas stints, and although I was told this would be done, it obviously wasn't and that led to problems.'

Lynagh heaved a sigh of resignation when he picked up the *Australian* newspaper on 30 July 1994 and saw the headline: 'Lovesick Lynagh Beats Ban'. In the article that followed, Peter Jenkins hinted at dissatisfaction among the players.

> ... But there have been rumblings among other Wallabies, not
> directed at Lynagh, but against the ARU for imposing the ban
> in the first place and then watering it down. Wallaby coach Bob
> Dwyer said Lynagh had put forward a case based on personal
> grounds. 'We figured people have other lives apart from rugby,'
> he said. 'And Michael's personal life is pertinent. His fiancée
> can't leave uni and come out here and he wants to spend time
> with her.' Wallaby winger David Campese said the introduction
> of the ban was a dangerous step in an amateur game where play-
> ers were not under contract to the ARU and should be free to
> play where and when they want.

Campese incensed Lynagh by continuing to throw fuel on the fire '... Suddenly Campo started saying he wanted to go to Japan, and complaining that there was one rule for me and another for the rest of the players. I was annoyed because he hadn't given the full story, and because the press hadn't come back to me and asked me to respond to him.' At a major corporate lunch for the Wallabies in Sydney, Channel Ten's Gordon Bray interviewed Campese. 'Well, Campo, tell us. Are you going to Japan or are you staying in Australia?' There were a few moments of silence, to enhance the theatre of the occasion, before 'Yes, I'm staying,' announced Campese, amid wild applause and cheering from the assembled throng of admirers. Lynagh was seething. 'I sat there wondering to myself what he was going on about. He created all this self-promotion and good-guy stuff, which made me look like a villain. I'd done everything the correct way. I'd gone to the ARU, I'd gone to Benetton, and when the committee gave me the nod I asked for a press statement to be released citing the reasons. No clear statement was forthcoming and Campo suddenly became the white knight ...'

Lynagh let his frustrations with Campese simmer inside before deciding to meet with Bob Dwyer and Peter Falk, the Wallaby team management. The last thing they wanted was any major blowup between their two star players. The consensus of the meeting was that Campo was Campo, and nothing and no one would change his capacity sometimes to talk first, think later. 'Campo can basically say whatever he likes and people will believe him because he plays the game so well,' says Lynagh. 'If you criticise him, you run the risk of being accused of jealousy.' Although recognising the downside, Lynagh was annoyed enough to disregard management advice and, after the meeting with Dwyer and Falk, he confronted Campese at a Wallaby training session.

'Campo, I think we'd better have a chat.'

'G'day Noddy, how are you?'

'I'd be better if you hadn't given the press that false impression concerning the overseas issue.'

'Mate, I wasn't having a go at you, just the ARU. I couldn't care if you went or not.'

'David. Why didn't you say that?'

'Oh, you know me mate.'

Yes indeed, he knew him.

He knew him well enough not to be surprised when, some months after that episode, Campese publicly supported Lynagh when Italian commitments necessitated a delayed arrival at one of the camps. They may be quite different characters, but Wallabies management is relieved that on the eve of the World Cup defence, the on-field relationship between the two stars is in top order.

Lynagh went back to Treviso in the 1994–95 northern winter, faithfully returning to Australia for the three camps he was required to attend. Isabella accompanied him to the first one at the Hyatt Coolum resort on Queensland's Sunshine Coast in November and there was no doubt that here was a man whose focus and fitness was enhanced by a relaxed frame of mind. One evening he amazed several long-time team-mates by getting on the dance floor with Isabella and boogieing the night away. This was something they'd never witnessed before. This was a first. Under the influence of a favourable atmosphere he had been known in the past to grab a broom and stick a cigar in his mouth in his best rock-star impersonation, but this was Michael Lynagh being Michael Lynagh and not caring what the world might think. As ever he was in control.

And what of the future? Michael Lynagh and Isabella Franchin plan to marry in late 1995 – when Isabella has completed her economics degree and Michael might hopefully have led Australia to a World Cup triumph in South Africa. Beyond that there is some uncertainty. Isabella has had interviews with banks in Australia while Michael has maintained his interests in the commercial property field, as well as taking up consultancy roles recently with Corrs, Chambers and Westgarth and Jones Lang Wootton. Whether they settle in Australia or Italy has not been decided. The future Mrs Lynagh is unperturbed.

'Michael likes to plan, but I am exactly the opposite. That's our biggest difference. He gets pretty nervous if he doesn't have everything under control. For me, I find planning ahead a difficult task, but everything appears to be falling into place.'

Lynagh now considers both Brisbane and Treviso as home and feels equally comfortable in each. 'The idea of living six months in Italy and six months in Australia is exciting and romantic but the reality of planning our future once my Benetton career is over is a little nerve-racking.

Italy, or Australia: a decision will have to be made. When that time arrives, doubtless Michael will recall those words of Brother Buckley from so long ago. 'Michael, a decision has been made. Now all you have to do is make it work.'

PERSONAL STATISTICS
(as at 29 April 1995)

Legend	Y	Year		C	Conversions
	M	Matches		P	Points
	T	Tries		W	Wins
	PG	Penalty goals		L	Losses
	FG	Field goals		D	Draws

Annual statistics: Test matches

Y	M	T	PG	FG	C	P	W	L	D
1984	5	2	10	1	5	51	5	–	–
1985	3	–	6	1	11	43	2	1	–
1986	7	–	24	2	14	106	6	1	–
1987	8	1	16	2	23	104	4	3	1
1988	7	2	13	–	17	81	4	3	–
1989	6	–	16	1	10	71	2	4	–
1990	7	2	20	2	17	108	4	3	–
1991	10	4	21	–	23	125	9	1	–
1992	7	1	19	–	5	71	6	1	–
1993	4	–	5	–	4	23	3	1	–
1994	3	1*	9	–	3	38	3	–	–
Total	**67**	**13**	**159**	**9**	**132**	**821**	**48**	**18**	**1**

Lynagh's only five-point try was scored in the first Test against Ireland at Ballymore in 1994.

Against individual countries

	M	T	PG	FG	C	P	W	L	D
New Zealand	16	–	35	2	11	133	7	9	–
France	9	–	29	3	15	126	5	4	–
England	7	2	19	–	13	91	6	1	–
Ireland	6	2	12	1	8	64	6	–	–
Argentina	5	1	15	–	11	71	3	1	1
Wales	4	4	5	1	12	58	3	1	–
Scotland	4	1	15	–	8	65	4	–	–
Canada	3	–	8	1	12	51	3	–	–
Italy	3	1	4	–	15	46	3	–	–
British Lions	3	–	7	1	6	36	1	2	–
USA	2	2	1	–	14	39	2	–	–
Fiji	1	–	3	–	–	9	1	–	–
Japan	1	–	–	–	5	10	1	–	–
Western Samoa	1	–	3	–	–	9	1	–	–
South Africa	1	–	3	–	1	11	1	–	–
Tonga	1	–	–	–	1	2	1	–	–
Total	67	13	159	9	132	821	48	18	1

Record for Australia including Test matches and tour games

M	T	PG	FG	C	P
103	19	222	10	211	1157

Queensland record

M	T	PG	FG	C	P
100	24	205	23	193	1166

INDEX